P9-CDU-037

SCHOOL ADMINISTRATOR'S PUBLIC SPEAKING PORTFOLIO:

With Model Speeches and Anecdotes

Also by the authors:

Educator's Lifetime Library of Stories, Quotes, Anecdotes, Wit and Humor

Encyclopedia of School Letters

The New Psychology of Classroom Discipline and Control

101 Pupil/Parent/Teacher/Situations and How to Handle Them

School Administrator's Encyclopedia

SCHOOL ADMINISTRATOR'S PUBLIC SPEAKING PORTFOLIO:

With Model Speeches and Anecdotes

P. Susan Mamchak

and

Steven R. Mamchak

PARKER PUBLISHING COMPANY, INC.

West Nyack, New York

10   9

Library of Congress Cataloging in Publication Data

Mamchak, P. Susan.
  School administrator's public speaking portfolio.

  Includes index.
  1. Speeches, addresses, etc.   2. School
administrators.   I. Mamchak, Steven R.   II. Title.
PN4305.04M35   815'.01'0892371   82-22588
ISBN 0-13-792556-5

DEDICATION

...for Danny Vespa
who was always there to help...

About the Authors

P. SUSAN MAMCHAK conducts workshops in education, lectures, is a past member of Toastmistress International, and has held positions throughout the educational spectrum from substitute teacher to school disciplinarian. While currently serving as president of her own research company, she still finds time to do extensive public speaking.

STEVEN R. MAMCHAK has been involved in public education for over twenty-two years. In that time he has done comprehensive public relations work for schools, hosted a weekly radio program on education, and lectured extensively before both educators and community members.

THE MAMCHAKS are vitally involved with education and are the authors of seven books aimed at educational excellence.

HOW ADMINISTRATORS MAY
EFFECTIVELY USE THIS BOOK

School administrators are faced with never-ending demands upon their time and energy. Few of us can disagree with that statement. Indeed, we know only too well that an administrator's day begins too early, ends too late, and is a continuous succession of matters that require here-and-now attention.

It is an evident fact that the school administrator is in demand. This is true not only of school-time hours and problems, but for other areas as well. Administrators are constantly being pressed to serve on committees, to aid in community projects, and to express opinions on a variety of subjects and in a variety of situations.

Indeed, within our professional lives, we are often asked to act as hosts on a myriad of formal and semi-formal occasions, to actively participate in honors for educational colleagues, to deliver our own or district points of view on educational matters to various groups of laymen and professionals, to address students or staff on rules, policy or programs, to act as spokesperson for the school or district, to inform, to congratulate, to appease, to educate.

In each of these and similar situations, our tool is speech and our problem is time. We are, after all, educational leaders, and that must remain our number-one priority. Often, however, the demands of that priority are so exacting that there is little time left to effectively prepare those speeches, addresses, and commentaries that are required of us. Yet, we must meet these needs and meet them well as an essential part of our educational and professional responsibilities as well as our duty to the community and our fellow educators.

Tonight an auditorium filled with parents will await your greeting and your comments about the special activity in which they are about to participate. Tomorrow evening you will speak at a dinner to honor a teacher who is retiring after having served the community for thirty years. Next week you are expected to present an address to a professional association of administrators to which you belong. Then there is the upcoming faculty meeting where you will have to explain that new board policy. There is so much for which to prepare.

Where do you find the time? Budget requests are coming in from all departments. Monthly reports are due. There are meetings of curriculum and planning committees. Department coordinators want to meet with you to discuss a new instructional program. The PTA Executive Committee is due to arrive at any moment.

You'll be lucky to find time for lunch, let alone the time to research, write, and revise a dynamic and effective speech for each occasion.

It is precisely at times like these that we have all dreamed of a magic source to which we could go and in which we could find models of the exact speeches we required. Moreover, they would be models that we could readily adapt, perhaps with little more than the change of a name, to our particular circumstances. And, as long as we are dreaming, they would be speeches that were dignified, intelligent, and appropriate not only to the situation and the topic but to our positions as professional educators.

It was exactly this sort of dream that led to the creation of this book. *SCHOOL ADMINISTRATOR'S PUBLIC SPEAKING PORTFOLIO: With Model Speeches and Anecdotes* isn't magic, but it will provide that source of model speeches that will save you hours, perhaps days, of tedious preparation time. Here is a volume that is crammed with speeches specifically tailored to the school administrator and written for those occasions most frequently encountered by the eduational executive— speeches that may be used as is or adapted by the change of a few words to meet the school administrator's most exacting requirements; speeches that are perfected and polished and professional; speeches that will express exactly what you want to say in the exact way you want to say it.

If you're looking for the perfect way to greet those parents, you'll find a variety of models in Section Four (speeches for laymen) and Section Nine (speeches for special events). Section Seven (speeches for retirements and testimonials) will provide you with the exact speech for that retirement dinner no matter what the status of the retiring educator. If you look in Section Five (speeches for educators) you'll find a number of dynamic speeches that would be perfect for your appearance before the professional association. You'll explain that new policy or program to the faculty in a professional and inspirational manner using one of the many models in Section Six (speeches that inspire).

In addition, you'll find models of icebreakers that will set everyone at ease; you'll find models of introductions for all occasions; you'll find the perfect speech for opening or closing any activity; you'll find dignified eulogies and memorial speeches; and, you'll find special speeches for every holiday occasion in the school year.

After every model speech you'll find a SPECIAL DATA section that details specifics about the speech such as the time of delivery, the precise circumstances under which the speech is most effectively used, and other audience-tested hints that will ensure the best possible delivery.

Finally, for those exceptional occasions when you must spend time preparing a speech, there is a step-by-step guide derived from years of experience that will make the task easier and ensure a superior product. There is even a section that will tell you the secrets of dealing successfully with those problems that pop up occasionally in public speaking. Add to this a special LOCATOMATIC INDEX which allows the administrator to find the topic or subject area he or she desires in mere seconds, and you have a volume worthy of attention!

All in all, this is a book that you will use often. The special nature of the model speeches that are geared to the needs of the school administrator, the ease with which these speeches may be adapted to all occasions, the data and specifics on each speech, and the wide variety and number of speeches from which to choose make this a reference source that you will use again and again to save time and energy in developing and delivering quality speeches. For the active and involved school administrator, this portfolio of model speeches is a reference source that will occupy a prominent space on the professional bookshelf—a book that will be used for successful public speaking throughout the school year.

P. Susan Mamchak
Steven R. Mamchak

CONTENTS

SECTION TWO: An Administrator's Guide to Introductions, Transitions, and Benedictions   57

SECTION THREE: A Complete Collection of Opening and Closing Speeches   93

SECTION FOUR: Administrator's Speeches for Laymen   125

SECTION FIVE: Administrator's Speeches for Educators   157

SECTION SIX: A Variety of Speeches That Inspire   185

SECTION NINE: Special Speeches for Special Events 271

SECTION TEN: Holiday Speeches Throughout the School Year 295

**PART TWO:
AN ADMINISTRATOR'S BLUEPRINT FOR
PREPARING AND DELIVERING A SPEECH 321**

**SECTION ELEVEN: A Step-By-Step Guide for Preparing and Delivering a
Speech 325**

SCHOOL ADMINISTRATOR'S PUBLIC SPEAKING PORTFOLIO:

With Model Speeches and Anecdotes

part one

effective model speeches for all occasions

Part One of this book contains model speeches and anecdotes specially crafted for the school administrator. Here, you should find the right speech for the occasion YOU have in mind.

This part is divided into ten sections covering general areas of speaking that affect the school administrator. Check the one appropriate to your wants, then look in the Table of Contents for more exact listings. Finally, check the LOCATOMA-TIC INDEX for convenient listings by topic.

May these speeches serve you as well as they have us.

SECTION ONE

A Collection of Usable Icebreakers for School Administrators

Nothing has a greater impact on an audience than the use of appropriate humor in a speech. When people laugh, they are almost immediately put at ease. For the speaker, this is a secret that has been used to advantage on innumerable occasions. "Laugh and the world laughs with you," or so the saying goes. Well, speakers know that this is only part of it. The audience that laughs with you is also more apt to be well-disposed to your ideas, and, generally, they come away with a feeling of friendship for you.

While humor may be used anywhere in a speech, it is usually most effective when used at the beginning and end of a speech. Obviously, any serious matter you have to present should be taken seriously and be presented without interruption. Asking an audience to shift moods quickly or frequently can be confusing. A speech that begins with humor, eases into serious matter, and ends on an upbeat that leaves a smile on everyone's lips, is one that is likely to be remembered and appreciated by an audience.

Remember that merely getting up before an audience and "telling jokes" will not do. The anecdotes or "icebreakers" that you use should be appropriately suited to your audience and your speech. They should have meaning within the context of what you are saying, and they should not be offensive to any member of the audience.

Within the following pages, you will find a number of icebreakers on a variety of subjects appropriate for any audience. Use them to get your audience on your side, to prove or exemplify a point, or to set the audience at ease. Try to personalize them by changing the names or places to those with which the audience is familiar.

One final suggestion: Don't forget to laugh along with your audience. If you enjoy yourself, the audience will enjoy you.

1

TOPIC: **Communications; misunderstanding.**

AUDIENCE: **Appropriate for all audiences.**

When I was working my way through college, I got a job one summer as a delivery man. I had a small pick-up truck, and if anyone had an item they wanted delivered, I did it.

One day, I had a very unusual delivery. I was to pick up six penguins and deliver them to the local zoo before closing time.

I loaded the penguins into the truck and I was doing fine until I developed a flat tire on a major highway. I pulled over and surveyed the damage. I knew that I could fix the flat, but it was getting late, and I doubted that I could get my cargo to the zoo before it closed.

I was just wondering what it would be like to spend the night with six penguins when I saw a friend of mine driving down the highway in his own truck. I flagged him down and explained the situation to him.

"Look," I told him, "I have to get these penguins to the zoo before it closes. I'm going to be at least a half-hour fixing this flat, so I wonder if you'll do me a favor. I'll give you ten dollars. Will you take them to the zoo?"

My friend said that he would, so we transferred the birds to his truck, and he took off down the highway.

By the time I had fixed the flat tire, it was rather late. I drove into town and decided that what I needed was a cup of coffee. I parked my truck and went into the local diner.

I was sipping my coffee and gazing absent-mindedly out the front window of the diner, when all at once, my eyes went wide. There, coming down the main street of the town was my friend—followed by the six penguins, all in a row, looking like a procession of head waiters.

I rushed out of the diner and ran up to my friend.

"What is this?" I shouted. "I thought I gave you ten dollars to take them to the zoo!"

My friend was puzzled.

."I did take them to the zoo," he answered, "and they enjoyed it very much, but that only cost four dollars, so I figured that with what was left I'd take them to the movies."

SPECIAL DATA: *Time of anecdote: two and a half to three minutes. The point of this anecdote is the value of exact communications to prevent misunderstandings. It might be used to advantage in a speech about the necessity of keeping open the lines of communication in a school system, between parents and educators, etc.*

2

TOPIC: **The difficulty of a particular profession or job.**

AUDIENCE: **Adults; particularly members of the profession mentioned.**

I was in New York recently, and I got a chance to watch a skyscraper being built.

I was fascinated by everything, but I was particularly interested in one worker. He was on what they call the "high steel," the steel beams and girders that provide the skeleton of the building. This man, and he was no youngster, either, was unbelievable. There he was, thirty stories above the street, hopping from beam to beam with nothing under him; walking these beams with as much confidence as if he were on the ground; swinging out into nothing on those loose and wobbly girders. I tell you, he was fearless. I grew dizzy just watching him.

Suddenly a whistle blew, and it was quitting time, so I waited for him. I just had to tell him how much I admired his courage.

When he passed by, I stopped him and told him how entranced I had been by what I had seen.

He thanked me, and I went on to remark that he looked to be about my age.

"I'll bet you've been doing this all your life," I said.

"On the contrary," he answered. "I've only been doing this for the last two weeks. You see, I used to be a high school principal, but I had to quit—I just lost my nerve!"

SPECIAL DATA: *Time of anecdote: about one minute. This is a particularly adaptable anecdote. "New York" could be changed to any large city, and the "high school principal" could be any profession you happen to be addressing. This anecdote has never failed to get a large round of applause. We all know the difficulties of our profession. Letting the audience know you recognize how hard they work is always appreciated.*

3

TOPIC: **Simple solutions; wisdom in the innocence of children.**

AUDIENCE: **Adults; fellow educators or parents.**

When I was appointed vice-principal, I wasn't prepared for the amount of work that would be facing me. I was literally overwhelmed—there was just so much to do.

I really wanted to do a good job, however, so I took a deep breath and waded into the work. Soon, I found myself staying later and later at school. I would leave my house at seven in the morning, and often would not return until seven or eight in the evening—later than that if I had a meeting.

My son, who was seven at the time, couldn't understand why Daddy was never home any more. It really must have bothered him, because one day he came to me and asked me point-blank why I wasn't home; why I had to stay away so much.

I sat him down and tried to explain the situation.

"Son," I told him, "you know that Daddy has a new job now. It's like you going into a new grade at school. Well, the work is very hard, and it takes Daddy longer to finish the work that it did before, so I have to stay later after school."

"Is that all?" my son said, his face exploding into a smile. "Daddy, that's real simple. If you can't do the work, just go to the principal and tell him to put you into a slower group!"

SPECIAL DATA: *Time of anecdote: approximately one and a half minutes. Telling jokes on yourself is always an excellent practice. Not only does it set the audience at ease, but it makes them well-disposed to you as well. This might lead into a speech concerning the need to ask for help when we need it, how the school or administration stands ready to provide that help, etc.*

4

TOPIC: **How children view things.**
AUDIENCE: **Adults; parents or educators.**

I hadn't been superintendent very long before I began visiting the schools in our district. I wanted to get acquainted, and I wanted to see firsthand what was happening in the schools. One of the first schools on my agenda was this one. I called the principal, Mrs. Rowland, and informed her that I would be dropping by the next day. Mrs. Rowland told me that I would always be welcome, and graciously said she would be looking forward to my visit. We also arranged a time for the next day.

As chance would have it, however, that following day I was swamped with unexpected work. When I finally looked up from my desk, I found that I was over half an hour late for my appointment with Mrs. Rowland. I grabbed my jacket and literally ran for the door.

Meanwhile, not knowing what had happened to me, Mrs. Rowland was getting justifiably upset. She had been on the lookout for me for quite some time, and she had to get back to work. Therefore, she sent for a fourth-grade lad and stationed him at the entrance to the school with instructions that when the superintendent arrived, he was to send the man directly to the main office and see that he got there.

When I finally got to the school—somewhat out of breath, I might add—I burst into the entranceway and came face to face with the fourth-grader.

"Are you the superintendent guy?" he asked.

"Yes, son, I am," I answered. "You see, I'm a little late, and...."

"Never mind tellin' me," the boy interrupted. "Mrs. Rowland says that she's sending you to the office, and I have to go with you to make sure you don't run away. I don't know what you did, but, boy, are you in trouble! If I was you, I'd hide!"

SPECIAL DATA: *Time of story: two minutes. This might lead to a discussion of how children, especially elementary-school children, might view things differently; the need for explaining clearly and in terms the child understands; etc. Be certain to adapt this story by mentioning a local elementary school and its principal.*

5

TOPIC: **Experts; specialization of knowledge.**

AUDIENCE: **Adults, particularly teachers and fellow administrators.**

I was at a party recently, and our hostess introduced me to another guest. She told us that this gentleman was the world's outstanding expert on raising guppies.

We must have spoken with this man for over an hour. Well, I'll have to correct that statement—he talked and we listened. He told us everything we ever wanted to know about guppies. He explained their breeding habits, how to care for them, the varieties within the species, how to handle illnesses among guppies, and more than we could ever remember or want to remember.

I'll say this: He was truly an expert on guppies. Finally, he remarked that the best food for young guppies was the larvae of male mosquitos.

I was somewhat taken aback by that, and I asked him, "I understand that, but how would you be able to tell male mosquito larvae from female larvae?"

He looked at me as if I had just uttered some unforgivable blasphemy.

"Now, how would I know that?" he said. "I'm an expert on guppies—not mosquitos!"

SPECIAL DATA: *Time of anecdote: one minute. This anecdote might be used to exemplify the need for a complete and rounded education. You might also use it to point out that we cannot afford to see only one side of a problem.*

6

TOPIC: **Perceptions of education, parents, students.**

AUDIENCE: **Adults, especially parents.**

I suppose it all depends on point of view.

THE COLLEGE PROFESSOR SAYS, "What are they doing in the high schools of this nation? This student can't even think!"

THE HIGH SCHOOL TEACHER SAYS, "What can you expect? Those junior high school teachers just aren't doing their job!"

THE JUNIOR HIGH SCHOOL TEACHER SAYS, "Good grief! Those elementary school teachers didn't teach this child anything!"

THE ELEMENTARY SCHOOL TEACHER SAYS, "What did that kindergarten teacher do? This child isn't prepared for school!"

THE KINDERGARTEN TEACHER SAYS, "This child is impossible! What must his parents be like?"

AND MOTHER SAYS, "Don't blame me—have you seen his father's side of the family?"

SPECIAL DATA: *Time of anecdote: less than a minute. This is a very good anecdote for use in a speech before parents. That last line never fails to get a good laugh. We originally used it to end a speech before a PTA group, and it is a good ending, for it leaves the audience smiling. End the anecdote, wait about three seconds for the laughter to start to die down and, before it ends, say, "Good night and thank you!" and leave. The applause will invariably follow.*

7

TOPIC: **An adult's perception of youth; the problems with young people.**

AUDIENCE: **Adults; parents and teachers.**

Let's face it—we all get fed up with our kids sometime. Oh, of course we love them, but there are often times when they will try our patience to the limit.

In fact, just the other day, I was reading an article by a famous author, and I'd like to read you part of it:

"The children of today are too much in love with luxury. They have execrable manners, flaunt authority, and have no respect for their elders. They no longer rise when their parents or teachers enter the room. I can only fear what kind of awful creatures they will be when they grow up."

Of course the only trouble with that statement is the fact that it was written by Socrates, and he wrote it in 399 B.C.

SPECIAL DATA: *Time of anecdote: one minute. The quote used in this anecdote is absolutely accurate. You can use it to show that the generations were in conflict over two thousand years ago as well as today. Use it also to point out that exact perceptions of what constitutes a problem may change from person to person.*

8

TOPIC: **Discipline; ingenuity.**

AUDIENCE: **Adults; parents or teachers.**

One day, a young man appeared before me seeking a teaching position in our schools. He was extremely young, just out of college, and thin as the proverbial rail. I mean, he was really a lightweight, standing about six feet tall and weighing about 120 pounds, if that.

"Son," I told him, "the only position that's open at this time is in a class of all but incorrigible youngsters. You know, they can be pretty rough on a teacher, and, frankly, I think you're a little light for the job. However, if you want it, it's yours."

Despite my warning and my misgivings, the young man accepted the job and left. Several months went by, and I had heard nothing from him. I was anxious to see how he was getting on, so one day I summoned him to my office.

When the young man appeared, he was smiling happily, and he had put on considerable weight.

"Good grief!" I exclaimed, "you must have put on fifty or sixty pounds since I last saw you. I can't believe it. Your job must be agreeing with you."

"It certainly is," the young man answered, "and I don't have any of those discipline problems you anticipated, either."

"That's tremendous," I remarked. "If you don't mind my asking, how do you control your class?"

"It's easy," the teacher replied. "I found out that the only thing they really like to do is eat, so when one of the kids gets out of hand, I just eat his lunch!"

SPECIAL DATA: *Time of ancecdote: two minutes. This story is good when speaking before teachers. Of course they realize that this is an unacceptable* *method of discipline, but it always gets a laugh. Parents, also, seem to appreciate this story.*

9

TOPIC: **Gifted children.**

AUDIENCE: **Adults; parents and teachers.**

I'd like to set a situation for you: Two individuals are sitting under a tree and talking.

"Come now," says one, "do you seriously believe that William Shakespeare didn't plagiarize everyone from Plutarch to Bacon to Marlowe? He should be considered exemplary for his purloining abilities alone!"

"That may be true," answers the other, "but new research turned up by the British Museum and interpreted by Professor Bartlett of Oxford University would seem to indicate...."

"Shhh!" interrupts the first individual. "The playground teacher is coming back, and we're supposed to be playing hopscotch!"

(Wait for laughter to die down.)

Congratulations, you've just been introduced to the gifted child. Yes, they do exist, and they can be spotted. Parents know and so do teachers. For the parent, it happens when Mom leaves a note for Junior and comes home to find the message corrected for punctuation, spelling and grammar....

(Wait for laughter to die down.)

...and for the teacher, it happens when the first-grade teacher holds up a card, asks who can tell what letter it represents, and has some kid remark, "Would it shake you up too much if I asked whether you meant the Phoenician or Celtic alphabet?"

SPECIAL DATA: *Time of anecdotes: one and a half to two minutes. This is the opening of a speech on gifted and talented children given before a group composed predominantly of parents of the gifted with some educators also in attendance. Notice that it is a combination of three anecdotes, one "topping" the other. Make certain that you wait if the audience laughs. They can't hear what you are saying if they are still laughing.*

10

TOPIC: **Point of view.**

AUDIENCE: **Adults; parents and educators.**

Just down the block from our school, there are two houses. In the front yard of one there is a little tot who is always screaming and pounding on the gate to get out. In the front yard of the other house, however, there is an equally young child who always seems to be content, happily playing with his toys.

Well, I had to pass this scene every day on my way to and from school, and one afternoon, I stopped at the house of the screamer and asked his mother the reason for the continual upset.

"Oh," she told me, "I just told him that I locked the gate so he couldn't get out, and that upset him, so he carries on like that."

As soon as I left there, I went to the other house and asked the parent the reason for her son's gentle and calm behavior.

"It's simple," said the lad's mother. "I told him that the gate was locked to keep the other children out!"

SPECIAL DATA: *Time of anecdote: one and a half minutes. You may use this story to advantage in speaking about people's perception of education. Various individuals may see what happens in the school as an attempt to keep them out, whereas the reality is that the schools stand ready to welcome parents and concerned citizens.*

11

TOPIC: **Getting organized.**

AUDIENCE: **Appropriate to all audiences.**

During my freshman year of college, I was walking on the campus with a friend of mine, another freshman, when he stumbled and stubbed his toe. It didn't look to be serious, but I suggested, for safety's sake, that my friend go to the college infirmary and see a doctor.

We arrived at the building and went in the front door. Immediately, we found ourselves faced with two doors, side by side. One was labeled

SERIOUS and the other NOT SERIOUS. Well, a stubbed toe was hardly life-threatening, so we went through the NOT SERIOUS door.

We went down a hallway, at the end of which we were faced by two more doors, this time marked ILLNESS and TRAUMA. A stubbed toe was certainly a trauma, so we went through that door.

Again, we were faced with a hallway and two more doors, this time marked as BLEEDING and NOT BLEEDING. My friend's toe was rather bruised, but the skin had not been broken, so we opened the NOT BLEEDING door and went through.

And we found ourselves back out on the campus. That last door had led directly out of the building.

"Well," I said to my friend, "we didn't get to see the doctor after all."

"No, we didn't," he answered, "but I'll tell you one thing: Man, are they ever organized!"

SPECIAL DATA: *Time of anecdote: one and a half minutes. This could be followed by a talk on the need for proper organization. Unlike the infirmary in the story, however, explain how we need organization in order to better serve the needs of our students and the community.*

12

TOPIC: **Pride.**

AUDIENCE: **Appropriate for all audiences, high school students to adults.**

An American industrial arts teacher I know drove to Kennedy Airport to meet his Russian counterpart. You see, as part of a cultural exchange program, the American teacher was to show the Russian industrial arts instructor around the city of New York.

As they drove past one huge office building, the Russian asked, "How long it take to put up that building?"

"About eight months," answered the American.

"In Russia, we do in four months!" commented the visitor.

A while later, they were driving past a multi-story apartment building when the Russian teacher again asked, "And how long that take to go up?"

"I think it took six months," the American teacher replied.

"In Russia, it take three months!"

At that moment, they passed the World Trade Center.

"That's odd," remarked the American teacher, "That wasn't there when I drove past this morning."

SPECIAL DATA: *Time of anecdote: slightly over one minute. It's amazing how we all develop pride when faced with an outside force who is being negative. We should all take justifiable pride in our schools, our students, and our work with them. This anecdote could be used to advantage in a speech along those lines.*

13

TOPIC: **Leadership, seeking for answers, confronting the unknown.**

AUDIENCE: **Adults; teachers and parents.**

When I visited one of our elementary schools recently, I was watching the children at play during recess. I particularly noticed one first-grade boy who swaggered around the playground. This tough little boy went up to one of his first-grade classmates, grabbed him by the shirt and snarled, "Who's the toughest kid in the first grade?"

"Y-y-you are," stammered the victim.

Again the little tough sought out another first grader and confronted him with the same question.

"It's you!" came the frightened answer.

Finally, he came up to one youngster and, shoving his fist in the boy's face, demanded, "Who's the toughest boy in the first grade?"

With this, the would-be victim retaliated, sweeping away the offending fist and knocking the attacker to the ground with one well-placed punch.

"Hey!" sobbed the ex-bully from the ground, "you don't have to get sore about it just because you don't know the right answer!"

SPECIAL DATA: *Time of anecdote: approximately one minute. This could be effectively used in talks about the need for strong leadership in the face of troublesome times, continuing education, and not assuming that we automatically know all the answers, or expecting to come up against hardships when we venture into new fields of learning or new programs.*

14

TOPIC: **New approaches, new programs, seeking for answers.**

AUDIENCE: **Adults; particularly educators faced with a new program or situation.**

One of my professors once told me that he had been troubled by a recurrent dream. Each night he would dream that he was being given the secrets of the universe; the secrets of life. When he awoke, however, he could never remember what those secrets were. This bothered him so much that he went to a colleague and told him about it.

"If I were you," said the friend, "I would keep pencil and paper beside my bed, and try to force myself into waking from the dream and writing down those 'secrets of life' while they were still fresh in my mind."

The professor decided to try it. That night he did his best to concentrate on awakening as soon as he began to dream.

To his amazement, it worked. In his dream, he was given the secrets of life and the universe, and after he had read them, he forced himself to awaken. Feverishly, he scribbled on the pad beside his bed. When he had finished, the effort proved so much for him that he dropped the pencil and fell into a deep and exhausted sleep.

The next morning he awoke and immediately reached for the paper. There, he knew, would be the secret of the universe and the secret of life. With trembling hands, he held up the paper and read what he had written.

It said, "THINK IN OTHER TERMS."

SPECIAL DATA: *Time of anecdote: about two minutes. Unlike the previous anecdotes, this has no humor in it. It is, however, an extremely powerful anecdote for pointing out that we must never allow our thinking to become stagnant; that we must welcome and investigate new ideas; and that we must view education as a viable and ever-changing process where we continually must "think in other terms."*

15

TOPIC: **Misunderstanding.**
AUDIENCE: **Adults; parents and educators.**

Some time ago, my eight-year-old daughter came home with some information from her school. Over supper one evening, she told us that her teacher was going to be married during the winter break. We sent the teacher a note of congratulations and then generally forgot about it.

On the first day of school after the winter break, my daughter came home from school and announced, "I don't think our teacher is ever going to go on another vacation with her new husband after the terrible time they must have had on their honeymoon."

I asked her, "What makes you say that?"

"Well," my daughter answered, "our teacher said it was fun, but I could tell it wasn't. They went all the way to Hawaii, but she doesn't talk about what they did, and she didn't even get a suntan!"

SPECIAL DATA: *Time of anecdote: about one minute. This anecdote always gets a laugh from every audience. Use it to point out that misunderstandings can easily occur unless we are certain of our facts.*

16

TOPIC: **Teaching.**
AUDIENCE: **Adults; educators.**

As a teacher, I have taught a thief, a schizophrenic, an evangelist, and a murderer.

The thief was a tall boy who hid in the shadows and whom the other children avoided. The schizophrenic rarely spoke but gazed at me with tiny eyes filled with terror. The evangelist was class president and the most popular boy in school. The murderer sat and stared out the window, occasionally letting out a shriek that would shiver the glass.

The thief stands looking through the bars of his prison cell. In the state mental hospital, the schizophrenic is restrained from beating his head on the floor. The evangelist sleeps in the church yard, victim of a disease contacted during his missionary work. The police no longer search for the murderer since he was, himself, killed in a barroom brawl.

And all of them sat in my classroom and listened as I taught.

I must have been a great help to them. After all, I taught them the difference between a noun and a verb and how to diagram a sentence.

SPECIAL DATA: *Time of anecdote: less than a minute. We heard this anecdote from another speaker, and we couldn't get over the effect it had on us and the audience. It is a graphic and extremely dramatic reminder that we do not only teach subject matter—we teach students. We must be interested in the development of the child's whole being, not just his marks on the report card. This is a powerful piece that will make its point with your audience.*

17

TOPIC: **Advice, following instructions too literally.**

AUDIENCE: **Adults; parents or educators.**

I remember when I once hired an extremely energetic young man as a vice-principal for one of our schools. I was told that this man really wanted to fire up the faculty, so he spent the first few days on the job putting signs all over the school. These signs read, "Do It Now!" and "Don't put off until tomorrow what you can do today!" and "Don't Hesitate—Do It!" and other exhortations to be vital and act decisively.

About a month into the school year, I chanced to be visiting the school and I met with the vice-principal. Naturally, I asked him how his poster campaign was going.

"It's too early to tell for sure," he told me, "but so far, the drop-out rate has increased, four teachers have asked for maternity leave, and the football coach just ran off with my secretary!"

SPECIAL DATA: *Time of anecdote: forty-five seconds. The point, of course, is that educators must be judicious in giving advice. If you are speaking to a group of teachers from a particular school or district, you might want to use the name (with permission, of course) of a principal or vice-principal known to them. You would, naturally, adapt the story accordingly.*

18

TOPIC: **How children can misinterpret what happens in school.**
AUDIENCE: **Adults; teachers and parents.**

When I was principal at Harvey Elementary School, one of the teachers on the staff told me that she was teaching her third-grade class how to observe using all their senses. She specifically requested that I observe the class, and, of course, I agreed.

It was a wonderful class. The teacher placed an object on her desk, and various children attempted, by smell or touch, to identify it. Finally, the teacher turned to me and asked if I would like to test the class.

I agreed, and, turning to the class, I said, "All right, boys and girls, close your eyes."

When their eyes were closed, I took a piece of chocolate, which was one of the objects the teacher had used in the lesson, and I ate it, making loud smacking noises with my lips as I did, so they could all hear me.

"Now, open your eyes," I said when I was finished. "What did I do while your eyes were closed?"

One little girl jumped to her feet.

"I know!" she exclaimed. "You kissed the teacher!"

SPECIAL DATA: *Time of anecdote: slightly over one minute. The point to be made here is that children often relate what happens in school, and often, what they tell is what they have interpreted rather than the facts of the matter. When speaking before parents, you can add that if they hear something from their child that might be upsetting, they should feel free to call the school and find out the facts.*

19

TOPIC: **The difficulty of the job.**
AUDIENCE: **Adults; educators.**

> A man knocked on the heavenly gate,
> His face was scarred and old.
> He stood before the Man of Fate
> For admission to the fold.

"What have you done," St. Peter asked,
    "To gain admission here?"
"I've been a teacher, Sir," he said,
    "For many and many a year."
The Pearly Gates swung open wide;
    St. Peter rang the bell.
"Come in and choose your harp," he said,
    "You've served your time in hell!"

SPECIAL DATA: *Time of poem: less than a minute. This poem goes over very well with groups of teachers. It is adapted with ease to any group you might be addressing by merely changing the word "teacher" to the profesison you are working with. We've even heard the word "parent" substituted when talking to that group.*

20

TOPIC: **Universality in education, effective teaching.**

AUDIENCE: **Adults; particularly educators.**

A teacher told me once that during the course of one school day, her class had spent most of the morning on their science reports.

One little girl, not overly scientifically-oriented, approached the teacher's desk.

"Ma'am," she asked, "when are we going to have reading today?"

"Why, Abby," the teacher replied, "we've had reading, penmanship, science, and spelling all morning long as you did your reports."

"Wow!" exclaimed the student, "You really fooled us. You were teaching us, and we didn't even know it!"

SPECIAL DATA: *Time of anecdote: less than a minute. There is an object lesson in this anecdote. The skills we teach in one subject are not isolated, but they transcend and permeate all the educative process. Moreover, when children can learn "without even knowing it" then we have some fine education going on. Use this anecdote before a group of teachers—they are quick to grasp the point.*

21

TOPIC: **Advice, the difficulties of being an administrator.**
AUDIENCE: **Adults; teachers and particularly administrators.**

When I was a new principal, the first thing I did in my new school was to clean out the old principal's desk. As I was doing this, I found three sealed letters, each bearing the legend, "To the New Principal." The first envelope stated, "Open During Your First Crisis," the next stated, "Open During Your Second Crisis," and the final one stated, "Open During Your Third Crisis."

Well, I wasn't principal for very long before a crisis arose, so I went to the desk and opened the first leter.

In it was a single sheet of paper with two words written on it: "Plead ignorance!"

Following this advice, I stated that I was unfamiliar with the case, had just been appointed, etc., and sure enough, the crisis passed.

Presently, a second crisis arose. Again, I opened the appropriate envelope, and this time I read: "Ask for more time!"

Finally, there arose a crisis from which I could see no escape. You can imagine how eagerly, therefore, I ran to my office and extracted the last envelope from the desk, tore it open, and spread the paper before me.

The letter began, "First, write three letters...."

SPECIAL DATA: *Time of anecdote: about two minutes. School administrators generally appreciate this anecdote. School administration often consists of handling one crisis after another, and this anecdote cleverly acknowledges that fact.*

22

TOPIC: **Achievement, education.**
AUDIENCE: **Adults, all audiences.**

There was a janitor who had been working at our school for some time, when a member of the board of education discovered that the man could neither read nor write.

"I'm sorry," said the board member, "but we're going to have to let you go. We can't have someone as a janitor who can't read or write."

The janitor left and invested his savings in a small business of his own. He worked at it diligently, and soon it grew and grew. It was not too many years before the man had amassed a small fortune.

One day, his chauffeur-driven limousine passed through the neighborhood of the school where he had begun. On an impulse, he stopped and went in.

As he entered the office, he was just in time to hear the board member who had once fired him telling the principal that there would be no new gym equipment due to lack of funds.

The ex-janitor snapped his fingers. "Write out a check for fifty thousand dollars," he told the chauffeur. "Sign my name to it and then give it to me so I can put an X on it."

"I remember you," said the school board member. "You still can't read or write, but you've become very rich. Just imagine what you would be doing if you had had an education!"

"Yes," said the ex-janitor, "I'd still be sweeping your hallways!"

SPECIAL DATA: *Time of anecdote: two minutes. We heard this anecdote used to point out the fact that mere knowledge is not enough—a person must also apply himself and work at what he does in order to succeed. Whatever purpose it may serve for you, rest assured that it always gets a chuckle.*

23

TOPIC: **The humorous answers of students on tests.**

AUDIENCE: **Older students and adults; particularly parents.**

(SPECIAL NOTE: The following fifteen definitions are taken from answers on tests given to children of various grade levels. For suggestions on their use in speeches, see the SPECIAL DATA section.)

"An Octopus is a person who hopes for the best!"

★ ★ ★

"Letters printed in sloping type are said to be in hysterics."

★ ★ ★

"A corps is a dead gentleman, and a corpse is a dead lady."

★ ★ ★

"The smallest veins in your body are called caterpillars."

★ ★ ★

"The chief cause of divorce in the United States is marriage."

★ ★ ★

"In Christianity, a man can only have one wife. This is called monotony."

★ ★ ★

"A bibliomaniac is a person who reads the Bible from cover to cover."

★ ★ ★

"The Bourbons were a French family who used to make whiskey."

★ ★ ★

"The U.S. Constitution was adopted in order to secure the domestic hostility."

★ ★ ★

"A polygon with seven sides is called a hooligan."

★ ★ ★

"Algebraic symbols are used when you don't know what you are talking about."

★ ★ ★

"The difference between exports and imports is that exports are ports that used to be and imports are new ones that ain't yet."

★ ★ ★

"The difference between a king and a president is that a king is the son of his father, but a president isn't."

★ ★ ★

"The Magna Carta provided that no free man should be hanged twice for the same offense."

★ ★ ★

"A census taker is a man who goes from house to house increasing the population."

SPECIAL DATA: *Time of various definitions: a few seconds. Numerous individuals have, over the years, been kind enough to supply us with these* *definitions from student test papers. We have used them many times in speeches, and they always provide a light moment. Parents seem to enjoy them most of all. In a speech, they may be used in various ways to introduce or "get into" a topic. Here's an example from a speech we gave: "... You know, I once gave a test where I asked for definitions. One child wrote, "An octopus is a person who hopes for the best." Well, while I can't boast of having eight arms, I can't help seeing bright and hopeful futures for our students...."*

24

TOPIC: **Budget, money, money-related problems.**

AUDIENCE: **Adults; parents, the general public, educators.**

The other day my daughter came to us and asked, "Mommy and Daddy, how much am I worth to you?"

"Honey," we replied, "why you're worth a million dollars to us."

"In that case," she stated, "would you mind advancing me fifty cents?"

I think there's a moral in that story: Everybody is concerned with money because, in today's world, everybody has to be concerned.

As we all know, money is not easy to come by. A second-grade teacher told me that a while back she had her class writing letters. One child addressed his letter, "To God." The teacher read it, and it stated, "Dear God, please send me one hundred dollars, love, Timmy."

The teacher was struck with the innocence and sincerity of the note, and she showed it to her minister who, in turn, sent it to our local congressman. He, in turn, sent it to the president, knowing that the president would enjoy it.

The president chuckled over it, and, on an impulse, took five dollars from his pocket, placed it in a White House envelope, and sent it off to Timmy.

It happened that the teacher again held a letter-writing class shortly after Timmy had received his letter from Washington.

Again, Timmy wrote a letter, "To God," and, again, the teacher read it.

This time, Timmy had written, "Dear God, thank you for the one hundred dollars. I see you sent it through Washington, and they deducted their usual ninety-five percent!"

Yes, between inflation and taxes, there isn't much left, is there? In fact, just the other day, there was a robbery in a nearby school district. An armed gunman entered the salary office, pointed a gun at the secretary, and demanded, "Never mind the salaries, just give me the dues, tax, and pension deductions!"

SPECIAL DATA: *Time of anecdotes: two and a half to three minutes. Let us tell you how this was used. It was the opening of a speech on a school budget being delivered to a group of concerned citizens. The speaker talked along the lines that, while everyone agrees that money is tight, he knew the citizens would agree that the budget would show that the school system had made judicious use of what they had. This opening got the audience well-disposed to listen to what would come later.*

25

TOPIC: **Poise, quick thinking.**
AUDIENCE: **Adults; educators primarily.**

I am told that in a nearby school district, at the local high school, the chairman of the Science Department, the school principal, and the district superintendent of schools are good friends who, for many years, have enjoyed a Friday night poker game.

One Friday, however, an overzealous rookie policeman spotted them through an open living room window and arrested them for gambling. They were taken down to headquarters and almost immediately found themselves brought before the night court judge.

"Mr. Jones!" exclaimed the judge, "why, you have my son in your class. Don't tell me you were playing cards for money?"

Thinking of the shame and difficulties that might follow were he convicted, the teacher took a deep breath and lied, "No, sir, I was not."

"And you, Mr. Smith," the judge continued. "You are the principal of the high school; a leader of youth. Were you playing cards for money?"

With a furtive glance toward heaven, Mr. Smith sighed, "No, Your Honor, I was not."

Finally, the judge glared at the superintendent.

"And, Dr. Baker, were *you* playing cards for money?"

The superintendent looked at him, spread his hands palms upward, and asked, "With whom?"

SPECIAL DATA: *Time of anecdote: one and a half minutes. This might be used to introduce the fact that difficult situations often require quick thinking or that, as educators, we must always keep control and have poise in trying times. You might, with their permission, substitute the names of local educators for those used in the anecdote, as the audience generally understands that this is a fictional anecdote.*

26

TOPIC: **Discipline.**

AUDIENCE: **Adults; parents, but especially educators.**

Recently, my little son did something that required I take some stern action.

"Son," I told him, "you know that what you did was wrong, and I'm going to have to punish you for it."

"OK," he answered, "I'll take my punishment, but can I ask you a question?"

"Certainly," I said.

"Dad," he asked, "did Granddad spank you when you were little?"

"Yes, son, he did."

"And did Granddad's father spank him?"

"He certainly did," I answered.

"And did Great Granddad's father spank him, too?"

"Yes, he did."

"Well, Dad," my son said, "don't you think it's about time we put an end to this inherited brutality?"

SPECIAL DATA: *Time of anecdote: less than a minute. This is an effective anecdote to use when introducing a new discipline policy. It can also be used as a lead-in to any speech or discussion on discipline problems in a school or system and effective methods of handling them.*

27

TOPIC: **Leadership; independent thinking.**
AUDIENCE: **Adults; educators.**

I remember observing a class once where the teacher got up and addressed the class.

"Today," he said, "we are going to begin a series of lessons that are specifically designed to increase your leadership potential by developing your initiative, your creativity, and your individuality. Now, put a clean sheet of paper on your desk at a forty-five degree angle, and take down precisely what I dictate to you."

SPECIAL DATA: *Time of anecdote: less than a minute. You do not sponsor initiative and creativity and learning by doing everything for your students. You must let them make their mistakes and learn. This is the point of this anecdote, and it can be used in a speech along that line or in any discussion of teaching techniques.*

28

TOPIC: **PTA.**
AUDIENCE: **Adults, PTA group.**

When my sister gave birth to her fourth child, I called her at the hospital to congratulate her. I had no sooner begun to talk when she began to sob into the phone.

"What is it?" I shouted. "Is something wrong with the baby?"

"Oh, no," she whimpered. "The baby's fine. It's just that when you called, I remembered that you were a school principal, and then it suddenly occurred to me with frightening clarity that I'm *never* going to get out of the PTA!"

Now, don't get me wrong. I think the PTA is great. In fact, being a parent as well as an educator, I belong to two PTA groups. It's just that, considering my son's behavior, when I go to the PTA at his school, I go under an assumed name.

In fact, the other day, my son came home and said, "Guess what, Dad? You're invited to a PTA meeting that is going to be an intimate gathering."

"What do you mean, 'intimate gathering?'" I asked.

"Well, Dad," he answered, "so far it's just you, the principal, the English teacher, and me."

SPECIAL DATA: *Time of anecdote: about one minute. This was used as the opening of a speech to a PTA group during a "Back-To-School Night" activity. It helped to break the ice and get the evening off to a positive start. It could also be used with positive effect in any speech before a PTA group.*

29

TOPIC: **Sports and sports activities.**

AUDIENCE: **Adults and older students; mixed gathering at a "sports night" activity.**

Personally, I love sports. As many of you know, I'm an avid golfer. In fact, come the spring, I'm afraid that my wife is often a "golf widow."

I remember one Saturday morning when the weather was perfect for golf, but my wife had other ideas.

We were having breakfast, and she really laid down the law.

"There are lots of repairs to be done," she told me, "so don't think you're going to run off and play golf and leave me here with all the work."

"Golf is the furthest thing from my mind," I assured her. "Now, will you please pass me the putter."

SPECIAL DATA: *Time of anecdote: forty-five seconds. This could be used as part of a welcome or a formal speech at any activity that involves sports. Since there are many such gatherings during a school year, it is best to be prepared with several "sports stories."*

30

TOPIC: **Remarks to make when you have blundered during a speech.**
AUDIENCE: **Any audience at any time.**

(SPECIAL NOTE: Mistakes happen. They happen to everyone, whether he or she is an experienced speaker or only a beginner. When these blunders happen during the course of a speech, it can often be embarrassing to the speaker and the audience, particularly if the speaker becomes flustered. Therefore, we'd like to give you four lines that we use when we have stumbled over a word, mispronounced something, or blundered in some other way.)

"Bear with me, ladies and gentlemen, and we will assuredly grow old together."

★ ★ ★

"You must understand. It's not that I'm absent-minded; it's just that I have difficulty taking a shower because I keep forgetting in which pocket I left the soap."

★ ★ ★

"You know, folks, as I grow older, I find that I have trouble remembering three things: the first is names, the second is telephone numbers, and the third ... the third ... er ... the third...."

★ ★ ★

"Well, as George Bernard Shaw said, even the youngest of us may be wrong sometimes."

SPECIAL DATA: *Time of remarks: a few seconds. We suggest that you memorize these lines. Then, when speaking, if you do make a blunder, they will be ready for your use. Remember, the audience wants you to succeed. If you make a mistake and then, rather than becoming uncomfortable yourself, you rise above it by using one of the lines above, you will surely get a laugh from the audience. They may even applaud your ingenuity and quick thinking.*

31

TOPIC: **Teamwork, an illustrated anecdote.**

AUDIENCE: **Adults; particularly educators.**

(SPECIAL NOTE: What follows is an illustrated anecdote about teamwork. Whenever we have done it, we have used a white square of posterboard and a black magic marker with a wide felt tip. The drawing is progressive, ending in the final surprise. It is very simple, but we suggest that you practice on a sheet of paper first. Just remember that you should be speaking the text as you draw the appropriate figures.)

What to Say   **What to Draw**

Let me show you just what I mean about teamwork. Let's, for the moment, assume that this white paper is our school system. (*Hold up blank, white posterboard, as seen in Figure 1-1.*)

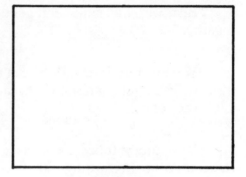

(Figure 1-1)

Within that school system there are basically three groups of individuals. There is administration, there are students, and there are teachers. (*As you mention each group, draw a small oval until you have the configuration seen in Figure 1-2.*)

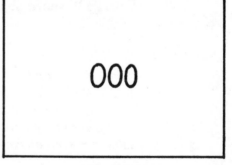

(Figure 1-2)

Quite often, when the administration works on its side, and the teachers work on their side, all without communication and teamwork, the students are left in the middle. *(As you mention the administration, place a large dot in the center of the left-hand oval; as you mention the teachers, place a large dot in the center of the right-hand oval; as you mention the students, merely point to the center oval. You should end up with the configuration shown in Figure 1-3.)*

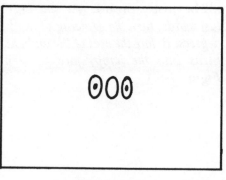

(Figure 1-3)

When this happens, when there is no teamwork or communication between these two sides, the whole school system can get to looking pretty unhappy. *(As you say, "... when there is no teamwork ..." draw the curved line above the three ovals as seen in the figure. Then, as you say, "the whole school system can get ..." draw the curved line under the three ovals. The configuration should now resemble the sad face shown in Figure 1-4.)*

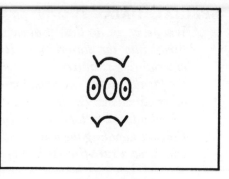

(Figure 1-4)

But, let's add teamwork. Let's get everyone working together to make the school system into one, unified, cooperating entity.... *(As you mention working together, draw a large, encompassing oval around the sad face so that it looks like Figure 1-5.)*

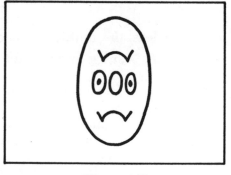

(Figure 1-5)

... then, thanks to the teamwork that exists between these two groups, we will have a happy and functioning school system of which we may all be justly proud. *(As you utter the last words, turn the drawing around 180 degrees. Before the eyes of the audience, it turns into the happy face as seen in Figure 1-6.)*

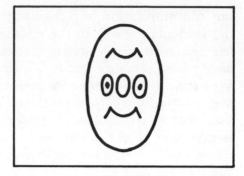

(Figure 1-6)

SPECIAL DATA: *Time of presentation: slightly more than one minute. Whenever we do this, it always draws a round of applause as the sad face turns into the happy one. It gets its point across in a dramatic and entertaining manner. Of course, while we have used the administration and the faculty in this example, there is no reason why it could not be adapted to other situations. For instance, it could be used to point out that parents and school administrators need to cooperate for the ultimate good of the students. Practice handling the board and marker until you can do it smoothly, and you will have a sure-fire method of commanding attention.*

32

TOPIC: **Ideas, the development of new ideas.**

AUDIENCE: **Adults; suitable for all.**

> I had an idea just the other night;
>   A fantastic idea it was, too.
> Magnificent, wonderful, clear and concise,
>   Ingeniously smart through and through.
> It was just unforgettable, wondrously bright,
>   Immortal and eternal, too.
> And once I remember it, then I just might
>   Be able to share it with you.

SPECIAL DATA: *Time of poem: 45 seconds. We used this poem in a speech about creative thinking. It draws a chuckle at the end, but the point to be made* *is that while many people have good ideas for solutions to problems, they sometimes fail to share those ideas or act upon them. Consequently, what might have been an ideal solution is lost. The rest of the speech exhorted the audience to share their ideas with each other in the hope of growth of all involved.*

33

TOPIC: **Two poems on humor and the value of laughter.**
AUDIENCE: **Appropriate for all audiences.**

> The value, the worth, and the power of mirth
> Can help each of us to get through
> When the going is rough and incredibly tough,
> And even the sunshine looks blue.
> For once you give in to a chuckle or grin,
> Your spirits just natur'ly lift,
> And life is worthwhile each time that you smile,
> For a laugh is a God-given gift!

★ ★ ★

> Laugh, and the world laughs with you;
> Weep, and you weep alone;
>   For the sad old earth
>   Must borrow its mirth,
> But has trouble enough of its own.
>
> —Ella Wheeler Wilcox

SPECIAL DATA: *Time of first poem: 45 seconds. Time of second poem: 30 seconds. It seems especially appropriate to end this first section with these two poems. Professionals have long known that humor is an essential element in education. It can enliven a class or a faculty meeting; it can make a point in such a way that the listener just has to agree; it can make the most insurmountable of problems and the most trying of times a bit easier to get through. Humor has a place in our speeches, just as much as it has in our daily lives.*

AFTERTHOUGHTS

While we have been exhorting you throughout this section to use humor in your speeches, also remember that we are professional educators and not stand-up comedians. Indeed, while humor is a tasty dish, remember that it is a garnish and not the main course. We could think of no worse mistake for an educator than to give a speech consisting solely of one humorous anecdote after another. If we are going to speak, our very positions as educators demand that we give speeches of sum and substance.

Of course we should use humor when appropriate. At the beginning of a speech to set the tone, relax the audience or lead into your topic, it is a fine device. During your speech, to occasionally make a point or as an example, it is outstanding. At the conclusion of your speech in order to leave your audience in a favorable mood to accept what you have said, it can't be beaten. Combine these techniques with a speech in whose body rests workable, practical, and sincere ideas, observations, and suggestions, and you will have a speech that your audience will long remember.

SECTION TWO

An Administrator's Guide to Introductions, Transitions, and Benedictions

Not all the public speaking you will do as a school administrator will be in the form of full-length speeches. You will have your share of invitations to speak formally before many types of gatherings, but there will also be those occasions where your main speaking task will be to "fill in." We speak, here, of those times when you are acting as a Master of Ceremonies and must introduce other speakers or activities; when you must announce a transition from one activity to another or one part of a program to another part; or, when you are called upon to pronounce a benediction of some sort over an activity, meal, or event.

As a general rule, introductions should be kept short. After all, it is the speaker who is the main attraction. Nevertheless, introductions cannot be sloughed off. They must be precise, and they must prepare the audience for the speaker or event that is to follow. Humor may be used in introductions when appropriate (for example, when the audience realizes that you and the speaker are close friends), but it should not be overdone.

Transitions are perhaps the most difficult of the "informal" speaking tasks to handle. Moving an audience from one hall to another, for example, can be disastrous unless done properly. Here, preciseness of language, a good sense of humor, and a sense of leadership and command are the keys to the effective handling of the situation.

Benedictions can also be tricky. We live in a pluralistic society, and numerous religious viewpoints may be represented in any audience. Care must be taken to phrase benedictions in such a manner that no individual in the audience feels offended or left out.

Within this section, you will find short but effective introductions for a variety of individuals; practical transitions for a wide range of situations in which the school administrator may find himself; and, dignified but nonsectarian benedictions and blessings for many occasions. We are certain that you will find what you are looking for.

Introductions

34

TOPIC: **Introduction of a newly-appointed superintendent.**

AUDIENCE: **Adults; educators and concerned citizens.**

Ladies and gentlemen ... before I introduce you to our new superintendent of schools, I think you should know a little bit about him.

When Jim Harvey graduated from college, he taught science at the junior high school level for three years. Following that, he taught high school science for two years. By that time, he had earned his master's degree and was appointed guidance counselor, a position in which he served for three more years. At that time, he left to take a position as the vice-principal of a high school, a position he held for five years before taking over as principal for the next four years. He left that position to become an assistant superintendent in our district six years ago, and, now, he has just been appointed as our new superintendent of schools.

And, you know, considering the fact that he has trouble holding down a steady job, he's a darn nice fellow.

Ladies and gentlemen, I give you our new superintendent, Dr. Jim Harvey....

SPECIAL DATA: *Time of introduction: about one minute. This is a rather standard introduction with a twist of humor added. Outlining the accomplishments or career of the speaker is always a good tactic, for it adds to the speaker's credibility. The slight bit of humor draws a small laugh and is appreciated.*

35

TOPIC: **Introduction of a superintendent of schools.**
AUDIENCE: **Adults; educators and parents.**

What is a superintendent?

A superintendent is a person who occupies the office where the buck stops; the place where the responsibility piles up.

A superintendent is a person who must plan for the future of education, keeping a delicate balance between the best of the new while not forgetting the excellence of the past.

A superintendent is a person who must be a diplomat, a confessor, a sounding board, an innovator, a protector of values, a consummate business person, a dedicated educator, and a general—all at the same time.

To hold that position requires knowledge, tact, leadership, foresight, daring, and compassion.

It is indeed rare to find these qualities in a single individual, and that is why it gives me the greatest of pleasure to introduce to you a person who exemplifies all of those values and more; a person whose record as superintendent of schools speaks for itself in terms of accomplishments for students, staff, and community; a person I am proud to call my friend.

Ladies and gentlemen, I give you Superintendent of Schools, Dr. Myra Handberg.

SPECIAL DATA: *Time of introduction: about one and one half minutes. Defining the position of the speaker and then telling how the person to be introduced measures up to that position is another excellent technique for an introduction.*

36

TOPIC: **Introduction of a principal.**
AUDIENCE: **Adults; educators and parents.**

Picture a city composed, as most cities are, of a variety of groups, all with different interests. Think of the complexity of caring for the welfare of each citizen within each group. Think of the difficulty of directing each day's activities in order that the whole functions smoothly and efficiently, without forgetting the individual's need for recognition and growth.

Now, take this "city" and place it within a single building. In charge, place an individual who truly knows the meaning of the phrase, "The buck stops here!" Make that individual responsible for our "city"; make him mayor, police chief, traffic controller, head of the planning board, and chief financial officer.

It is overwhelming, and we would all agree that the person in charge would have to be rather special, indeed.

Well, when we look at the modern high school, we cannot help but see our "city." Here is a place filled with human beings living out their lives, striving, learning, growing. The principal of that high school, that "city," has all the responsibilities we have mentioned plus the fact that he must be an educational leader, setting the pace and tone of the learning situations within that school.

We are pleased to have with us, tonight, just such an individual, an educator who has accepted the heavy responsibility that goes with the title, "principal." For more than seven years, now, he has been principal of one of our largest high schools. During that time, his accomplishments have spoken more loudly than any praise I could hope to give here. He is a man of foresight, integrity, and knowledge, who takes daily responsibility for the learning of his students.

Ladies and gentlemen, it gives me great pleasure to introduce the principal of North Central High School, Dr. Edward McCabe.

SPECIAL DATA: *Time of introduction: two and a half to three minutes. Of course, you would change the specific data in the speech to match the principal you would be introducing. Also, if there were any specific accomplishments of which the principal was particularly proud or which you felt were significant, you would mention those as well.*

37

TOPIC: **Introduction of a vice-principal.**

AUDIENCE: **Adults; educators and general public.**

If we want to talk about "unsung heroes," let's talk about the vice-principal. As a principal, I can assure you that my job could not be done effectively without the aid and support of the vice-principals on the staff.

A vice-principal is a person "on the move." From before the first school bell of the day until long after the last student reaches home, the vice-principal is busy handling a variety of educational tasks, all designed to help us, as principals, function to the best of our abilities.

It isn't often that these people get the credit and recognition they deserve. Perhaps it is representative of their dedication and abilities that, despite that lack of recognition, they continue to function as vital and dynamic educators within the system.

This is why I am delighted to have the opportunity to introduce a vice-principal who exemplifies the best of the best; a person who is as dedicated as she is efficient; as knowledgeable as she is practical.

Ladies and gentlemen, I am overjoyed to have the opportunity of presenting to you a top-notch vice-principal and an outstanding human being, Mrs. Patricia Granelli.

SPECIAL DATA: *Time of introduction; about two minutes. Notice that this introduction uses the position of the speaker to lend authority to the status of the speaker about to be introduced. This is an acceptable technique that can be used to advantage from time to time.*

38

TOPIC: **Introduction of a guidance counselor.**

AUDIENCE: **Adults; parents and educators.**

When I was in high school, I went to our guidance counselor for advice on what career to pursue. I took a battery of tests for aptitude and ability, and finally, the counselor called me into his office.

"Son," he said, "the results of your tests are back, and I'd seriously like you to consider some job in a field where your father is the boss!"

Guidance counselors have changed a great deal since then, and today's counselor needs to know a great deal more than how to administer a test. With the complexities and pressures of today's society, a counselor's role in the school becomes one that requires a diversity of qualities, not the least of which are tact, understanding, compassion and expertise.

Our guest tonight is just such an individual. She has been a guidance counselor for over fourteen years, seven of those years at our own Park High School. I, personally, cannot help but think of the thousands of youngsters who have come into contact with her and be grateful, for them, that she was there to care.

I am happy to present to you tonight the Head Guidance Counselor of Park High School, Mrs. Alicia Perry.

SPECIAL DATA: *Time of introduction: about two minutes. Notice that this introduction begins with a humorous anecdote. Notice, also, that the "joke" is on the person doing the introducing, and not on the speaker. If you use humor in an introduction, it should never be aimed at the person you are introducing.*

39

TOPIC: **Introduction of a department chairperson.**
AUDIENCE: **Adults; educators and the general public.**

Take a handful of twenty multicolored marbles in one hand, try to sort them into neat piles by color, weight, and size, do it all with one hand and make certain you don't drop any, and you will have some idea of the difficulty facing the department chairperson in today's high school.

Whether it be coordinating and preparing budgets, getting requisitions for books and materials ready, planning curriculum, supervising instruction, or any one of hundreds of tasks that they face during the school day, the department chairperson is a busy individual.

Obviously, it takes a particular type of individual to handle this arduous position; a person with special knowledge, special compassion and feeling for the job, and special proficiencies—indeed, a very special person.

And just such a person is with us tonight, a person who for the past five years has been chairperson of the English Department, handling that position with efficiency and creativity.

I am pleased to present to you, the Chairperson of the English Department at North Central High School, Mrs. Edna Carroll.

SPECIAL DATA: *Time of introduction: about two minutes. Here, again, the position and accomplishments of the speaker are generally detailed for the audience. Of course, if you have specifics regarding an accomplishment of particular merit on the part of the speaker, you would be wise to use this as well.*

40

TOPIC: **Introduction of a teacher.**
AUDIENCE: **Adults; suitable for all audiences.**

The great educator, John Mason Brown, once wrote, "The good and the great teachers are that way because what they are as men is always a vital part of what they know as scholars. Theirs is the reason to realize that knowledge is no end in itself but desirable only as a means to enjoyment and life. If they teach well (in other words, if they are able to make the hard process of learning seem pleasant, exciting, and important to others) it is because they have so lived a subject that they can incite others to feel the need of adding it to their own living."

Surely, we can all agree with that. Each of us, in his own life, can remember a teacher who made the subject "come alive"; who broke into our minds and fired us with an enthusiasm for the subject and for all learning.

Indeed, ladies and gentlemen, we have just such a person with us tonight. As a teacher with more than twenty-five years of experience, he has fired countless students with the love of learning that he has carried in his personal life. Talk to his students, and they will describe a man who teaches passionately, with a love for his subject, for his students, and for teaching itself.

Ask a member of the faculty of Park High School, and they will tell you of a person who is as willing and able to help his fellow educators as his students; a man whose advice is sought out and respected by all.

Ask the administration of the school system, and they will unhesitatingly tell you of a man whom they are proud to have as a member of the teaching team; a man whom they respect for his wisdom, insight, and understanding.

I feel very privileged to be able to introduce to you a superlative human being and an outstanding teacher, Mr. George Farley.

SPECIAL DATA: *Time of introduction: about two and one half minutes. This introduction was for a highly respected and veteran teacher in a township. The technique used of viewing the person from the points of view of the students, faculty, and administration is an effective one that may be used in many types of speaking situations.*

41

TOPIC: **Introduction of a speaker who is a recognized expert.**

AUDIENCE: **Adults; a mixed audience of educators, parents, and the general public.**

I will admit to you quite freely that when I was asked to introduce our chief speaker tonight, I was both excited and worried. I was excited because of the admiration and respect which I hold for him and which I gained through reading his many books and articles. I was worried, because what do you say about someone of the stature of our guest tonight?

Others have spoken far more eloquently than I of his contributions in the field of education. Let it suffice to say that education today is all the better because of his contributions.

Anyone who has read his books knows of the wit, the insight, the concern for excellence, and the humanity that flows from his pages. We can only be grateful and honored that he has consented to speak to us tonight.

Therefore, it is with pride and a great deal of admiration that I introduce our speaker for this evening, Dr. Henry Kalner.

SPECIAL DATA: *Time of introduction: less than a minute. Don't worry if you never heard of Dr. Henry Kalner. That name, like all the names used in this book, is fictional. The introduction, however, was actually used to introduce a* *noted expert in education. It is purposely short, as the audience at such an occasion is eager to hear the speaker.*

42

TOPIC: **Introduction of a local politician.**

AUDIENCE: **Adults; educators, parents, and the general public.**

We all know how beautiful a well-made clock can be. When each gear is functioning properly, it works as a viable unit, ticking away the hours with a proud precision.

And our country, our government, is rather like that clock. Composed of many parts, our country runs on the functioning of the myriad of units of which it is composed. Like the clock, when all the units are working well, it is a joy to behold.

It is the job of public officials to look after the gears of our clock, if you will, and to see the functioning of the unit. We, in education, do our part to add to the working whole. When politicians understand this; when they understand our problems and frustrations; when they do all in their power to aid our unit, our gear in the clockwork of society, then the society as a whole must ultimately benefit.

We are pleased to have with us today just such a politician. He is a man who has a proven record as a friend to education in our system. His countless actions in behalf of our schools and his dedication to excellence speak for themselves. We are extremely pleased that he could be with us today.

Ladies and gentlemen, I am pleased to present the Honorable James R. Matthews.

SPECIAL DATA: *Time of introduction: slightly over a minute. We believe that the analogy works well in this context. If the politician has done something outstanding relative to education, be certain to mention that in your introduction as well. This would come after the analogy and before the final introduction.*

43

TOPIC: **Introduction of a member of the board of education.**
AUDIENCE: **Adults; suitable for all adult audiences.**

A board of education has been defined as a group of citizens who are concerned with the proper functioning of the school system.

To me, the operative word in that definition is *"concerned."* A person who runs for a board of education knows that the job entails long hours, frustration, and little recognition. Indeed, in a pluralistic society, the concern of many groups often manifests itself in outcries against policies and programs proposed by board members. At such times, sitting on the board can be a frustrating and thankless experience.

It follows, therefore, that only someone who feels a deep and abiding concern for education; only someone who is dedicated to excellence and progress; only someone who has a need to give of himself for the good of others—only such a person would seek and be elected to a board of education.

Our guest tonight has served on the board for over fifteen years. For the past three years, he has served as president of that body. He is respected by educators and the general public for his concern, his sagacity, and his dedication.

I know that you, as I, take pleasure in welcoming our guest this evening, Mr. Harold Bailey.

SPECIAL DATA: *Time of introduction: about two minutes. Local school boards often come in for a great deal of criticism in most systems. Perhaps this is a natural occurrence due to the diversity of interests present in any community. This introduction acknowledges this possible conflict while reflecting beneficially on the board member to be introduced.*

44

TOPIC: **Introduction of an old friend.**
AUDIENCE: **Adults; suitable for all adult audiences.**

Our guest tonight and I grew up together. In those days, our concerns centered first around marbles, baseball, and the frogs we used to catch. As we grew older, our interests turned from polliwogs to girls, and soon we were off to college.

Those were fantastic days, and I would not change them for anything. In those days, and especially through high school, we would joke with one another, double date, and do all the things expected of us as teenagers.

There was one thing, however, that we never did. We never told each other the depth of what our friendship meant. Perhaps we couldn't as adolescents, unsure of ourselves and seeking for what we were.

Indeed, it is only now that I can tell him how much his being there meant to me; how much I came to admire and rely on his kindness, his wit, his support, his quiet strength, his intelligence; how I knew him as a person of honesty, dignity, tact, and diligence who could be relied on to come to your aid at any time.

And, today, I can verify that the years have only sharpened those qualities.

It is with pride, therefore, that I have the honor of introducing my friend, Tom Seeley.

SPECIAL DATA: *Time of introduction; about one and one half minutes. This is an introduction that is carried off by its sincerity. If you can say this and mean it, it is an excellent introduction for an old friend as well as an honor for him. The only thing you might want to add would be any career accomplishments your friend might have.*

45

TOPIC: **Introduction of a PTA president.**

AUDIENCE: **Adults; suitable for all adult audiences.**

Let's face it. If it weren't for parents, there would be no teachers and no school.

While this seems to be a very simplistic statement, it carries behind it some weighty philosophy. We have schools in order to educate our youth, because our founding fathers as well as all people of foresight and knowledge knew the value of education. Yet when a child enters school, he enters a new environment, but he remains part of the family from which he came. Throughout the school years, that family continues to be the child's base, the nourishing source that will help to shape the adult.

The school and the home—two mighty and powerful forces that have in the past, are now, and will in the future be the shaping forces for our students. When the two are working together, the student cannot help but benefit and grow and learn in an atmosphere that tells him constantly that he is cared for, appreciated, and loved.

Our next guest lives by that philosophy. As president of our PTA, she is respected by the parents and faculty of our school, and this respect comes from the knowledge that she works untiringly for the good of our students and the betterment of our school. She is a leader, an innovator, and a friend.

With great pleasure, I introduce this year's PTA president, Mrs. Hilda Greene.

SPECIAL DATA: *Time of introduction: slightly less than two minutes. Parents can play a very special role in any school system, and it is well to acknowledge their contributions. This introduction was originally given at a school function for all parents of the school.*

46

TOPIC: **Humorous line for acknowledging an introduction of yourself.**
AUDIENCE: **Suitable for all audiences.**

> *(SPECIAL NOTE: This is our favorite line for use when we have been introduced, particularly if the introduction has been generous or flowery.)*

Ladies and gentlemen, I'd like to thank George Townsend for that fine introduction. All I can say is that now I know how the toast feels after the butter and the jam....

SPECIAL DATA: *Time of remark: a few seconds. This remark never fails to get a laugh and break the ice, particularly if the introduction has been highly complimentary, as they usually are. Try it the next time you are introduced, and see if it doesn't get very positive results.*

AFTERTHOUGHTS

In ending this part on introductions, let us bring your attention to the fact that, in all the introductions, the name of the speaker is reserved for the very end. This is a very good technique, as it ends your introduction positively. Your voice should rise a bit toward the end, and the name of the speaker should be loud and clear. It is also wise if you, as the person doing the introducing, lead the applause for the speaker. Say the person's name and begin applauding. The audience will join you. Turn toward the speaker, acknowledge him with a slight nod, and back away from the podium. Never turn your back on the speaker.

Transitions

47

TOPIC: **Moving an audience of adults to a new location.**
AUDIENCE: **Adults; parents and educators.**

... and that brings to a close this section of tonight's program. In a few moments, I'm going to ask for your cooperation, but first, I'd like to ask you a very important question.

How many people here believe that using logic and reason is better than ranting and raving?

(You will find that all hands will go up. In a group such as this, no one is going to say that he or she is emotional. Review the sea of hands for a moment.)

Well, this is really something! It looks to me as if everyone here believes in reason. That's just fine.

Why did I ask you that question? Well, the next part of the program is going to require that this entire audience get up, move out the two exits to my right *(hold up your right hand)* and take seats in the auditorium down the hall.

Considering the size of this audience and the size of our hallways, if we all try to do this at once, there is going to be a lot of that ranting and raving I spoke about a moment ago and which you just told me you don't like.

But, you do like reason, or so you said, so I'm going to ask you to be reasonable—and do it my way! *(Smile)*

Therefore, what I'd really like is for everyone on the right side of the center aisle *(hold up your right hand again)* to leave slowly by Exit A, which is right over here *(indicate Exit A)*, turn left, and enter the auditorium through the doors you will find that say "AUDITORIUM." *(Smile)* At the same time, I'd like everyone on the left side of the center aisle *(hold up your left hand)* to leave slowly through Exit B, which is that door in the back of the hall *(indicate Exit B)*, turn right, and enter the auditorium through the same door as the other half of the audience.

All right, now I have another question. Would someone in this audience be kind enough to give me five hundred thousand dollars? No? Well, would any person who has that half-million dollars to give me please stay seated, and all the rest of you please rise.

(Smile as you say this. You may have to encourage the audience by repeating that last line. When they are all standing, smile broadly, and keep smiling as you say ...)

Well, since nobody wants to give me money, and since you're all on your feet anyway, let's leave here as was just described and assemble in the auditorium, all right?

Oh, and one more thing, thanks for the cooperation, I really appreciate it.

I'll see you inside....

SPECIAL DATA: *Time of transition: three to four minutes. This is a case where you are dealing with a large group of adults and must move them to another location. Notice that nowhere was the audience "ordered" to do anything. Rather, through the use of humor, they were gently guided into the move. Naturally, the logistics of your auditorium will differ from the one used above, but if the move is well-planned in advance, and the entire speech is delivered with a smile on the lips and the proverbial "twinkle in the eye," the audience will not only go along with it, they will admire your cleverness. Be certain to follow the directions in the speech, as you must make certain that the audience knows exactly where to go and how to proceed.*

48

TOPIC: **Transition from a program to a social hour.**
AUDIENCE: **Adults; mainly parents, but some educators as well.**

Ladies and gentlemen, I'd like to add my thanks to those of your PTA president. I think that this has been a fantastic evening, and I'd like to thank Mrs. Harris, Mrs. Bell, Mr. Hartly, and all the people who made this evening enjoyable.

We've all learned a great deal tonight, and perhaps that learning is the first step to a fuller understanding of ourselves, our schools, and our students.

I don't mean to imply that because you were present tonight, all the problems of the world will disappear, but I remember my grandmother had a favorite saying that ran, "There is no problem that can't be helped by good conversation and a cup of tea."

We've had the conversation, and I am happy to report that the cup of tea, or coffee if you prefer, is waiting for you now in the cafeteria.

You are all cordially invited to join us there for that cup and the other refreshments which look great (I can tell you that, because I peeked).

So, I hope you can join us. Thank you for coming tonight. Thank you for participating in our program, and I'll see you in the cafeteria!

Good night!

SPECIAL DATA: *Time of transition: slightly over a minute. This transition acknowledges the efforts of the people who put on the program, the people who planned the evening and refreshments, and the audience who attended. It is also an injunction to continue the dialogue in an informal setting. Transitions to a social hour should always sound like an invitation from a close friend.*

49

TOPIC: **Transition from social hour to program.**
AUDIENCE: **Adults; mainly parents.**

Ladies and gentlemen, I should be very upset. The reason is that I am positive that this past hour has added at least three inches to my waistline.

I don't know who to blame for that. Perhaps it's Mrs. Powell, who coordinated this whole affair. Or should I blame Mrs. Jennings, Mrs. Smith, and Mrs. Carter, who served us this evening and made the whole thing so pleasant that I was forced to eat and eat and eat. Of course, if I really wanted to place blame, I could point to all those who were generous enough to prepare and bring the delicacies in which we have indulged. All of them must share the blame for fattening us up and providing us with a most enjoyable evening. I know you'll want to join me in telling them how we feel. *(Begin to applaud, and the audience will join in.)*

And now that we have fed our bodies on this delicious fare, we had best not neglect our minds. Toward that end, the committee has prepared an equally delicious menu of topics for the rest of the evening.

If you will please stay seated exactly where you are, I know that the program which is to follow will entertain and enlighten you.

Therefore, I am delighted to present your Mistress of Ceremonies for this evening's program, the President of our PTA, Mrs. Helen Randall. *(Lead the applause as you step down.)*

SPECIAL DATA: *Time of transition: one and one-half minutes. Quite often, a planned evening begins with socialization and then moves into a program. In such a case, your objective, as the transitional speaker, is to get the audience quieted and prepare them to accept the program that is to come. Like the last transition, this also manages to acknowledge the efforts of the people who have contributed to the evening's program.*

50

TOPIC: **Transition into a new school year for teachers.**
AUDIENCE: **Adults; teachers and staff members.**

Good morning, ladies and gentlemen.

Wow! Did I have a fantastic summer! I really did. During my vacation I slept late every morning, I played tennis, I got a chance to just sit down and read for pleasure, my wife and I went sailing, we went to the theater—it was wonderful.

I had the opportunity earlier this morning to talk to some of you, and from what I've heard, the summer was equally kind to you.

Vacations are beautiful things. They allow us to rest, to replenish our energies, and they give us a new perspective on our lives. I know that happened to me, and I'll wager it happened to you as well.

When we are relaxing and doing all the activities that give us pleasure, we realize just how hard we all work during the rest of the year. If we think about it, however, we realize that while that work is difficult and demanding, it is also a part, and a very vital part, of our lives as human beings.

We all chose education for our careers, because we all believed. We believed in the future, and we knew that we could take a hand in that future by helping to educate our nation's youth. We are professional educators, and we are proud of that fact, because we are making a real contribution to society, and that gives purpose and meaning to our lives.

It is natural, therefore, that we look back with fondness on the lazy, easy days of summer, but it is also natural for us to look forward with equal anticipation and fondness at the days to come during this school year.

Yes, there will be troubles; yes, there will be setbacks; yes, there will be long hours. But, yes, there will the joy of opening up new vistas for young minds; yes, there will be the child who discovers something new and never realizes that you led him to it; yes, there will be accomplishments and growth and learning, and we will be a part of it.

I was in the past and am now, extremely proud of this faculty, and it is a pleasure to welcome you back to Park High School; may this school year be our best ever.

SPECIAL DATA: *Time of transition: slightly over two minutes. Getting back into "the swing of things" is a problem for everyone after the summer hiatus. This speech, delivered at the first faculty meeting of the school year, acknowledges that fact. It also gives direction to the faculty, clarifies the philosophies of the school, and offers a smooth transition into the new year.*

51

TOPIC: **Transition into a new school year for students.**
AUDIENCE: **Students; teenagers.**

Good morning.

First, let me tell you that I understand perfectly well that you would rather be anywhere but here. *(This invariably brings a loud response from the students. Wait for a moment until it dies down, then continue.)*

That is only natural, believe me. All of us, myself included, like to have time to ourselves with nothing to do. It's fun to relax; to enjoy ourselves.

Sometimes we regret the year that is to come, because we feel that it will require work and long hours, and most of all, a lot of planning and thought.

That's all true, of course. But, I want to suggest to you that you be thankful for that work, thankful for those long hours, and thankful for the chance to think.

If you have ever seen a stream in the mountains, you know that it bubbles along over rocks and sometimes over rapids. There are waterfalls and whirlpools, and it can often be rough and violent. Yet, that water is clear; it sparkles in the sun; it's pure.

Take that same stream and place a dam in its way so that it stays in the same place, never flowing, never changing, and it becomes a stagnant pool, the water dull and unfit to drink.

Well, our lives are like that. We all like to stay in one spot, to avoid the rocks of work and the rapids of life. But, if we do, we become as stagnant and uninteresting as that pool.

When we let ourselves get into life, however, then our lives pick up speed and flow like the river. Sure, there are troubles and work, and sure, we get tired and weary, but we also grow, and we learn, and we come alive as we work to be the best we can be.

So, in the name of the entire faculty, I welcome you back to Park High School, and I wish each and every one of you the success you deserve during this coming school year.

SPECIAL DATA: *Time of transition: slightly over three minutes. This is a speech given to high school students on the first day of the new school year. Like the previous transition, it acknowledges the reluctance on the part of the students to start the new year. It also presents a short, understandable analogy which gives the students something to think about.*

52

TOPIC: **Transition to a new policy or program.**

AUDIENCE: **Adults; teachers or parents.**

Ladies and gentlemen, have you ever wondered about how much things have changed over the years? I have. I know that we can all remember those days when we were in school, and we also remember how differently things were done then as opposed to nowadays.

If you listen to some people, those were the best days. Then, they claim, there were no pressures of society, no inflated prices, no problems with juvenile delinquency.

Well, I tend to think that those people have developed selective memories. They remember carefree days and forget the sweatshops and twelve hour workdays and child labor. They remember the prices of food and forget that wages were pennies an hour and starvation was not an uncommon method of death. They remember highly mannered children and forget the children in coal mines and the shame of the dunce cap and the sting of the hickory stick.

Indeed, when closely examined, some of the practices of the past are unthinkable by today's standards. At one time, mentally ill people were paraded before visitors on Sundays in order to provide entertainment for the guests who laughed uproariously at their "antics." Today, that thought turns our stomachs, as well it should.

And if we can project a bit; if we can look ahead, we can only wonder what the practices of today will seem like to citizens a hundred years from now. What will they say of us? How will they assess what we have done?

Perhaps the best we can hope for is that they will look at us and say, "They tried. They tried their best to examine what they had, determine what was needed, and seek new ways of accomplishing their goals."

Perhaps they will say this, and perhaps they will say, "They had the courage to try new ideas."

In a few moments, I'm going to be turning this meeting over to Mr. Halvorsen, who will be explaining the new discipline program that will soon become policy at our school. I know you will give him your attention, and I hope that you will appreciate what he has to say. I hope you will understand the philosophy behind this change and how it was designed to deal with our problems in the hope of making things better for everyone. I hope that, like our speculative future generation, you will end up saying, "They had the courage to try!"

SPECIAL DATA: *Time of speech: about three and one-half minutes. This speech enlists the audience's cooperation and open-mindedness in listening to the new policy or program that is to come. This particular speech was about a new discipline program, but there is no reason why it could not be adapted to any new program or policy that must be presented to faculty or parents.*

53

TOPIC: **Transition from school year to summer hiatus.**
AUDIENCE: **Students; teenagers.**

Good afternoon.

I wanted to speak to you today, because tomorrow you begin your final exam schedules, and when that is completed, you will be leaving for the summer.

I am aware that while you may not be looking forward to the exams, you certainly don't mind the summer that will follow.

We have been together now for almost ten months, and over that time we have grown to know each other a little better. Throughout this past year, we have grown in knowledge, faced problems, solved problems, had our share of tears and laughter, and here we stand—we have come through.

Now, the summer is calling us with its promises of warm and lazy days. We all look forward to that, because we can all use the rest. Let none of us forget, however, that what we have learned and experienced during this past school year has become a part of us forever. When you start that summer vacation, the knowledge and experiences you have gained here will go with you. It is, I am sure, a rich heritage that will add to your lives.

So, study now for those final exams and then enjoy the summer. The entire faculty and I wish you health and happiness during the days that are to come. Enjoy yourselves, and we'll see you in the fall, rested and ready for another year as great as the one we have just had.

Good luck on your exams, and have a happy summer!

SPECIAL DATA: *Time of speech: under two minutes. This might be used to advantage in the type of assembly program held in most schools prior to the close of the school year. Usually, these programs present awards to students, and many parents are often present. Consequently, it doesn't hurt public relations to deliver a transitional speech of this nature.*

54

TOPIC: **Transition from school year to summer hiatus for teachers.**
AUDIENCE: **Adults; faculty and staff of a school.**

Ladies and gentlemen, it has been said that there is no better place to "meet one's maker" than at a faculty meeting, because there is no other place on earth where the transition between life and death would seem so natural or go more unnoticed. *(Pause for laughter.)*

Therefore, I'm certain you'll be happy to know that this is the last faculty meeting of the year, and my talk to you will be extremely short.

In fact, my speech consists of two words — Thank You!

Thank you for this year that now draws to an end. Throughout these months I have come to know you as true professionals—capable, knowledgeable, dedicated, and cooperative.

Thank you for sharing. We've had problems, some of them seemingly insurmountable, but we have come through them, because we have worked together, because we have shared our frustrations and worked out solutions—together.

Thank you for caring. Every day of this past year, I could walk down a hallway and feel—yes, feel—the care and concern that eminated from every classroom. I could feel the dedication to knowledge and the commitment on your part to provide the best education to every student.

And, now, we are ready to "pack it in" for this school year and take that rest to which we are all entitled. I know in my heart that you have earned it every day of the school year, and I sincerely hope that this summer brings to each and every one of you the happiness and health you deserve.

Stay well, enjoy yourselves, and rest up, because I will have the honor of welcoming you back in the fall when, I know, we will enter another school year filled with knowledge and dedication and growth.

With a faculty such as the one before me, we can do no less.

Thank you, and have a wonderful summer!

SPECIAL DATA: *Time of speech: slightly over two minutes. Not only is this a transition from school year to the summer, but it is thanks and praise for the faculty. Everyone, even adults, needs encouragement and praise, and everyone needs to be told that he or she is doing a good job. A speech such as* *this can only have a very positive carryover effect for the school administrator as well as sending the faculty off to the summer well-disposed to coming back and working during the year that will come.*

AFTERTHOUGHTS

In any speech where a transition is involved—between one place and another, between one time and another, between one situation and another—the key elements should be threefold. First, there should be recognition of the past. That is, the speaker should acknowledge what has been done previously—the program just completed, the summer just past, the year just completed, etc.

Next, there should be recognition of the feelings of the audience. That feeling may be positive, as in the feeling of contentment at the program just completed, or it may be negative, as in the reluctance to return to work after a vacation or the reluctance to change existing programs. Whatever it is, the speaker must acknowledge that it exists. Tell your audience you understand that they are sorry to have to give up the pace of summer or that there may be those who do not want to enter the new program, etc. This lets the audience know that you understand their feelings.

Finally, there must be a "looking forward" and a rationalization of the new phase to come. This can be as simple as explaining the procedures for moving from one place to another or as complex as providing the rationale for a new policy, but it must be done in order that the audience understand the next move in the scheme of things.

Put together in this manner, the audience will understand and appreciate the transition that is to come. They may not like or approve of it, but they will understand the necessity for it and be better disposed to cooperate.

Benedictions

55

TOPIC: **Benediction for a dinner.**
AUDIENCE: **Suitable for all audiences.**

Ladies and gentlemen ...
We have come together tonight in peace and in fellowship. We share this time together and we share a part of our lives as, soon, we shall share this dinner.

May the food of which we partake be blessed by the love we share for each other. May that food nourish our bodies as the time we spend together nourishes our minds and hearts.

And, as we share the same meal, may we continue to share our thought, our insights, and our understanding in order that our spirits may grow ever closer.

SPECIAL DATA: *Time of benediction: 30 seconds. Blessings before meals should be kept short and to the point. This is adaptable to all audiences from a student dinner or breakfast to a mixed affair of students and parents to an entirely adult audience. It is completely nonsectarian, and may be used upon any occasion at which you may be asked to provide such a blessing.*

56

TOPIC: **Benediction for a dinner.**
AUDIENCE: **Suitable for most audiences.**

Dear Lord,
We ask your blessing on this gathering here tonight.
We have come together to learn, to grow in spirit, and to share this evening in our lives.

Bless this food which we are about to share. As we partake of it, may it nourish our bodies as our fellowship tonight has enriched our souls.

We thank You for Your bounty as we thank You for each other. May we prove worthy of both blessings.

SPECIAL DATA: *Time of benediction: less than 30 seconds. You will notice some similarity between this benediction and the previous one, the chief difference being that this benediction invokes the blessing of the Supreme Being. It is nonsectarian in that there is nothing in it that may offend any religion, but it does mention God. You would have to analyze your audience to ascertain whether or not this may be used. We will say, however, that we have used it on several occasions, and no one has objected yet.*

57

TOPIC: **Benediction for the closing of a program.**
AUDIENCE: **Suitable to all audiences, but basically for adults.**

We have joined together to share this time.

The knowledge and opinions that we have shared this evening have enriched our lives, and this is no small blessing. We have grown together in understanding, and we shall all be the better for this.

We are thankful for the knowledge that enriches our lives, as we are thankful for the fellowship which makes all of life bearable.

May we continue to grow together, ever closer, in order that we may share our problems and our triumphs and add to each other's lives.

SPECIAL DATA: *Time of benediction: less than 30 seconds. This may easily be adapted to all programs. It is a fitting ending for an evening's activities involving parents and faculty or even parents, faculty and students. We have even heard this used as a benediction for a program composed entirely of educators. It works well.*

58

TOPIC: **Benediction for the opening of a program.**
AUDIENCE: **Suitable to all audiences.**

There is so much in this life for which we may be thankful.

We are thankful for our lives, for our minds, and for our health. We are also thankful for our fellow human beings with whom we share burdens, work for goals, and grow in understanding.

It is, therefore, fitting and proper that we be thankful for evenings such as this; evenings in which we will all learn and share and understand.

May the activities that follow enrich us all, and may we grow ever closer as we act together for our common good.

May this evening be one of growth and progress for all.

SPECIAL DATA: *Time of benediction: about 30 seconds. As with the first benediction in this section, this is completely nonsectarian and may be used at any time. We have heard it used and used it ourselves to start PTA meetings, special student-faculty-parent programs, and programs of an informational nature, as with a guest speaker/expert. It is generally well-received by any audience.*

59

TOPIC: **Benediction for the opening of a program.**
AUDIENCE: **Suitable for most audiences.**

Dear Lord ...

We seek for understanding as we seek to do Your will. There are problems in this life with which we all contend. We strive toward their solution mindful that we are human beings and imperfect, but also mindful that with Your help, all things are possible.

We gather together tonight to seek for knowledge and for understanding. In peace and in fellowship, we seek to learn, to know, to exchange ideas in the hope of growing ever closer.

Humbly, we ask Your blessing on this evening's activity and on our quest for truth and enlightenment. Under Your guidance, may we grow ever closer.

SPECIAL DATA: *Time of benediction: slightly over 30 seconds. Again, this benediction has more religious overtones than the preceding one. It is, however, acceptable by all religions. The final decision as to which type to use, the one which mentions God or the one that does not, will have to be yours, based on a knowledge of your district and your audience.*

60

TOPIC: **Benediction for a sports or athletic activity.**
AUDIENCE: **Mixed audience; students and adults.**

Dear Lord ...
In a few moments, these fine young people will engage in a contest of their skill, their knowledge, and their physical ability.

We ask Your blessing on their actions. We ask that they may play well, striving on the playing field as they will strive in life; striving for excellence, using the knowledge they have gained, doing their best at all times, even when things seem hopeless. And, most importantly of all, playing as they will live, with honor, fairness, sportsmanship, and an appreciation of others.

We ask You to look after their well-being and to protect them on the field.

We ask You to bless this endeavor. Whatever the outcome, may we have given our best and take consolation in the fact that, win or lose, we have given what we had.

We thank You for this opportunity as we thank You for each other. May we continue to grow ever closer.

SPECIAL DATA: *Time of benediction: less than one minute. If you are ever asked to give an invocation or blessing before a game, whatever you say, don't ask God to let your team win. We know of one administrator who got into fantastic troubles when he gave an invocation in which he asked God to defeat the opposing team. You can well imagine what the local press did to him, not to mention the alumni association of the opposing school. The purpose of the* *activity is the playing of the game, not the winning or losing. This should be reflected in whatever type of benediction you give.*

61

TOPIC: **Benediction for a patriotic activity.**
AUDIENCE: **Suitable for all audiences.**

"... One nation, under God, indivisible...."

Let us take those words to heart and learn to live by them, for they are more, so much more, than mere words. They are a belief, a creed if you will, that has shaped the course of our nation as it has shaped the course of our lives.

For we are one nation. We are united in our belief in the quality of life. We, who are concerned with the education of our youth, strive always with that ideal in mind, providing to each and every child the best education of which he or she is capable.

And we are "under God," for we know that with the help of the Almighty, we will continue to grow as a nation, continue to offer the best we have, continue to grow closer into one people with the common goal of achieving the best possible society that will nourish and support each and every citizen.

And, we also know that "under God" we are truly indivisible. Working together, with God's blessing, our nation will become a solid force for peace and democracy in the world—a stronghold of freedom of which we may all be justly proud.

So, we ask God's blessing on this activity in which we are about to engage, and we ask that our efforts here today may bind us together as Americans, as one people—now and forever more!

SPECIAL DATA: *Time of benediction: close to one minute. There was a time several years back, when "patriotism" was a "dirty word" in some segments of our society. Fortunately, that time seems to have passed. There is nothing wrong with being proud of one's country, and we have much of which we may be proud.*

62

TOPIC: **Benediction for a graduation.**

AUDIENCE: **Suitable for the audience who would attend any graduation.**

We are of one mind.

We have worked; we have striven for the best we could be; we have labored for knowledge; we have opened our minds to new ideas. We have done all of this, and we have succeeded—we have come through.

Yet, even as we realize this, we realize that this evening is not an ending, but a transition from one phase of our lives to another—it is but the breaking of the shell; the hatching of the egg; the step that leads to new and different pathways.

There is love and fondness for what we have done, and there is anticipation and joy for what yet will come.

We pray that this night will be the start of lives that are productive and satisfying. We pray that we may always use the knowledge we have gleaned in our school for the betterment of our lives and those of our fellow human beings. We pray that the days we have spent here may be but the prologue for happy and fulfilling days yet to come.

And, we pray that the graduates here present may know lives that are filled with challenges which allow them to grow, knowledge which allows them to succeed, and peace, which makes every thing worthwhile.

SPECIAL DATA: *Time of benediction: about one minute. This speech combines a benediction with the transitional type of speech found earlier in this section. We have found it to be generally well-received by graduates and their parents.*

63

TOPIC: **Benediction for a class reunion.**

AUDIENCE: **Adults; alumni and their spouses.**

Dear Lord ...

As children, we were brought together to learn and grow. This we did, and in the process we formed bonds that drew us closer and closer.

Now, as adults, busy with our lives in the adult world, we are together once more. We have found that those bonds have not diminished, not weakened under the sword of time. Rather, they have strengthened, and we are, as of old, one body again.

We ask Your blessing on this gathering. We ask that, in Your mercy, You care for our absent classmates until such time as we will join them in Your love and understanding.

As once we worked and learned together, grant that tonight we may share a similar closeness; a closeness that will bind us together ever stronger through the years; let us come to an even greater appreciation for one another.

We pray that You may bless us now and throughout the years, that what we do with our lives may be fulfilling for us and pleasing in Your sight.

And, finally, we thank You. We thank You for our education. We thank You for our teachers. We thank You for each other. We thank You for this opportunity to say that we are here, and it is satisfying and good, and our lives are truly worthwhile.

SPECIAL DATA: *Time of benediction: about one minute. Administrators are frequently asked to officiate at class reunions. The alumni of a school can be a powerful force for beneficial public relations. It is well, therefore, for an administrator to be prepared for all alumni functions.*

64

TOPIC: **Benediction for the dedication of a new school.**

AUDIENCE: **Mixed audience of adults and students, containing educators, students, parents, and the general public.**

We are gathered today to dedicate this school, and we ask Your blessing, dear Lord, upon our endeavor.

We are mindful that this building is nothing more than brick and steel and paint and plaster. As such, it is nothing more than a shell. With today's dedication, however, it becomes a school, a place where our young people will come in order to learn and grow in understanding of themselves and the world around them.

We pray that they may find happiness in this building as well as knowledge. We pray that they may learn respect and understanding along with their academic subjects. We pray that they may be prepared in this building to meet with the challenge of life and be better human beings because of those challenges.

Bless this building, oh Lord, and grant that it may be a place where everyone—students, teachers, parents, and all concerned with the schools—may come to find answers, to discuss and share problems, to work together for the ultimate goal of a thorough education for every child.

We pray that this goal may lie within our reach, and that, through work and understanding, we may achieve it together.

We pray that today may be the beginning of many tomorrows filled with laughter and learning, with work and recreation, and, most importantly of all, with dedication and resolve that all who enter its doors may leave having achieved the best of which they are capable.

Bless this school, dear Lord, and may it be always used in accordance with Your divine will.

SPECIAL DATA: *Time of benediction: about two minutes. A speech such as this at a dedication ceremony can often set the tone for what is to come, particularly if delivered by the administrator who will be in charge. It also allows the public to know the administrator's philosophies concerning education. It is important, therefore, that the administrator's speech be well-planned and well-delivered upon such an occasion.*

AFTERTHOUGHTS

It is a strange thing about benedictions or blessings or whatever you may wish to call them. The separation of church and state mandates that prayer of any kind not be allowed in public schools, yet the general public often requests benedictions at any number of activities that are related to school. Many times, a visiting or local clergyman will be asked to do the honors, but it has been our experience that, just as often, it will fall to the administrator.

When that happens, some general rules should be followed. For example, blessings or benedictions should always be kept short. It is far preferable to say one or two lines than to ramble on at great length and "lose" your audience.

Then, it must always be remembered that, as we said at the start of this section, in our pluralistic society it should be the speaker's goal to see to it that no one in the audience is slighted, offended, or made to feel inferior or left out because of the content of what is said. Therefore, extreme care must be taken to see to it that the benediction is either one which mentions no particular religious references or is of such a nature that no person in the audience of any religious faith would feel slighted.

The benedictions in the last part of this section are specially tailored to meet just those requirements. Even the ones that invoke God's blessings directly are written in a way that no religious group could possibly object.

Remember also that a benediction is no place for humor of any kind. Rather, it is the sincerity, honesty, and forthrightness of the speaker that will inevitably carry it off.

SECTION THREE

A Complete Collection
of Opening and Closing Speeches

Part and parcel of every administrator's life are the various programs held within a school or school district during each school year. It seems that hardly a week goes by without some program, usually held in the evening, to which the parents or citizens within the district are invited. Add to this the programs of a strictly professional nature which an administrator is expected to attend or at which he is expected to officiate, and there is a hefty schedule with which to contend.

Frequently, especially when the program consists of a number of speakers or a single expert who will speak at length or a panel discussion of some sort, the administrator is asked to open or close the program with a speech. This is not a task that can be taken lightly.

The speaker who opens a program sets the tone or theme of the evening. The speech is not expected to be overly long, but it is lengthier than an introduction. Such a speech generally gives an overview of the subject to which the speakers to follow will address their remarks. It should focus the attention of the audience on the evening's subject matter and make them anticipate what is to come.

When a speaker closes a program, generally he or she is expected to summarize what has been done over the course of the program. The audience has gone through the entire program, and, now, the closing speaker should clarify the totality of the program for the audience. If he can also enjoin the audience to a greater understanding of what has been said, so much the better.

There is an old saying among speakers, "Tell them that you are going to tell them; tell them; tell them that you've told them." Your job as opening or closing speaker lies at both ends of that maxim. You tell the audience what is coming and set the tone, the program is performed, and you tell the audience what has been learned over the course of the evening or activity.

The first half of this section contains opening speeches on a wide variety of topics that are usual subjects for programs. The second half contains closing speeches on the same topics. In this way, you can see exactly what is required for each occasion.

Opening Speeches

TOPIC: **Opening speech for a program on drug abuse.**
AUDIENCE: **Adults; parents and educators.**

Ladies and gentlemen ...

If I were to stand up here and happen to see one of you strike a match, I would be a fool if I concluded from that that the school building was on fire. However, if I were to look out from this same position and notice smoke pouring from every doorway and see a trail of flame creeping up the far wall, then I would be equally foolish if I continued to stand here, choosing to believe that nothing was wrong; that it would probably go away by itself.

I know that we can all agree with this. Indeed, it speaks for itself. As the lyrics of a folk song of some years ago told us, "You don't have to be a weatherman to know which way the wind is blowing."

There was a time when the problem of drug abuse among the young was not considered to be a problem. If one or two juvenile delinquents used drugs, that was regrettable, but hardly something to get upset about. After all, that happened only in the slums of the city or in terrible homes where parents didn't care. Certainly, it could never be a cause for concern for us, the people who maintained good homes, who gave our children the best educational opportunities, who loved our children and cared about their welfare.

Sadly, we know today that drug abuse among the young touches every segment of society. It is not a problem reserved for the city or the poor or the broken home or the ghetto school. In the best of our nation's schools, in the finest and most nurturing of families, in the most affluent of homes, in the loveliest of suburbs, drug abuse is present. Not only is it present, but it is a major problem of such proportions that there is no strata, no segment of society which is unaffected by it.

Indeed, the smoke is pouring in the doorway, and the fire is creeping up the wall.

We cannot afford to pretend that it isn't there or to sit back and hope that it will go away. Rather, to continue our analogy, we must yell "fire" and try to do something to extinguish the blaze before it engulfs and destroys us all.

The program in which you are about to participate is a first step toward dealing with this epidemic. Tonight we will learn the extent and nature of the problem as well as hearing some solutions that have been offered.

I know we are all going to benefit from what we are about to hear. Some of it may shock you, and, hopefully, most of it will enlighten you. With enlightenment may well come understanding, which is our first step toward dealing with this monster that threatens our very lives.

For the sake of our children, we can do no less.

SPECIAL DATA: *Time of speech: five and a half to six minutes. The subject of drug abuse is quite often a topic that draws a considerable audience of parents and teachers when presented as a school-sponsored program. The analogy used in this speech is one which is, at once, vivid and understandable by everyone. Note how the tone of the program is set rapidly and firmly.*

66

TOPIC: **Opening speech for a "Back-to-School Night" program.**
AUDIENCE: **Adults; almost entirely parents.**

Good evening ladies and gentlemen and welcome to Rock Township High School's fifteenth annual back-to-school night.

I recognize the faces of several old veterans of this affair. They've been through this night once or twice or more. You can tell them by the What's-He-Going-to-Say-This-Year expression on their faces. To them I say, "Welcome back."

And, to the new faces in the audience, I say, "Welcome for the first time, and may your experiences tonight be pleasant ones."

To understand why we hold this activity every year, you really have to go back to your own youth. Remember when you were a kid, and you wanted to do something that you were pretty certain your parents wouldn't let you do? I remember wanting to camp out overnight in the woods near our house. There was no way in which my mother and father were going to let me do that, not at the wise old age of seven.

Therefore, I devised a plan. I went to my mother and said, "Mom, can I camp out overnight in the woods? Dad says it's all right with him if it's all right with you."

I see some of you smiling, and I think you know what's coming, or, maybe you did this yourself.

Anyhow, I then went to my father and stated, "Dad, can I camp out in the woods tonight? I asked Mom, and she says it's all right with her if it's all right with you."

This was really a plan that was devilish in its simplicity. It even has a name—divide and conquer. As long as each side is ignorant of the plans or desires of the other; as long as neither side communicates; as long as each side works only on supposition—the person in the middle has it made!

Looking back now, with the distance of years and with children of my own, I would not have let me camp out in those woods at age seven. And, because my mother and father took the time to check with each other, I didn't get to do it then, either.

That is precisely why a night such as this is invaluable. Tonight, you will be meeting with your child's teachers in the classroom where your sons and daughters spend a considerable amount of each day. You will get to know their teachers and learn what is going on in each class as well as what is expected of the students and what help is available to them. At the same time, the teachers will get to know you. We hope this will lead to the type of communication where parent and teacher *and* administration are not separate entities on whom the game of divide and conquer can be played. Rather, they will become a functioning unit with one single purpose, to help your son or your daughter.

You care about your children. I care about them. As you will learn tonight, the teachers in this school care about them as well. Tonight is a first step toward a unity of those three groups which allows communication and understanding to flow from school to home and from home to school. Because of this, there will be no losers at the game and only one winner—your child.

Before I introduce your PTA president, who will outline the procedures for this evening, may I once again tell you how pleased we all are to have you here tonight. As we have come together perhaps out of curiosity or perhaps out of a feeling of responsibility, may we all leave tonight in a new spirit of understanding, which will lead to better and improved communications that will benefit every child in this school.

Thank you.

SPECIAL DATA: *Time of speech: six to seven minutes. Although it is called by many names, most schools have some sort of program in which parents are invited to come to the school and speak with or listen to their children's teachers. Usually, this is very well-attended. A speech such as this not only welcomes the parents, but sets the tone for the evening on a positive note and gives them something valuable to think about.*

67

TOPIC: **Opening speech for an "Awards" program.**

AUDIENCE: **Mixed audience of adults and students; both parents and teachers may be present as well as the students.**

Recently, my son came home from school, knocked over a lamp on his way to the kitchen, and left a trail of muddy footprints all the way.

"Guess what happened in school today, Dad?" he asked, as he spilled milk on the kitchen floor, managing to get some of it on the cat.

"I have no idea," I said as I rescued the jar of peanut butter he had just nudged off the shelf.

"I got an award today!" he beamed as he proceeded to dribble jelly all over his shirt.

"An award!" I said. "What for?"

He looked up at me with a face covered in what had been a peanut butter and jelly sandwich and said, "Neatness!"

Let's face it, we all like to get awards. When we do, it is a visible proof that somebody has recognized how hard we have tried.

Often, working alone is extremely difficult. Sometimes, we get so tired that we think, "Why bother? Why go through all this study and work and pain? Who cares, anyhow?"

The answer is here, tonight. We care. We, who are gathered here this evening, care about hard and thankless work. We care about perfection. We care about trying.

Tonight, many awards will be given out for effort in a number of areas. Whether for academic achievement, athletic prowess, citizenship, or any other of the awards that you will see presented here, these are awards that have been won—and won fairly—by those who shall receive them.

To you students, I say that when you step up here tonight, know that we understand the work in the classroom, on the playing field, in all aspects of your school life that went into this moment. In a very small way, this is our opportunity to say thank you—thank you for trying; thank you for not giving up; thank you for being you.

This is your night. Enjoy it, and take our wishes that this award may be but one part of a rich and rewarding life for you all.

Thank you.

SPECIAL DATA: *Time of speech: about three minutes. Awards dinners, programs, or assemblies are usually well-attended by parents. This is only right, as it is a happy time when their child wins an award. This speech acknowledges this fact as well as apprising the winners and recipients that their efforts will be recognized. This type of speech usually has an extremely powerful effect upon parents, and it definitely does not hurt public relations.*

68

TOPIC: **Opening speech for an educational in-service program.**
AUDIENCE: **Adults; all educators—teachers and administrators.**

Good morning, ladies and gentlemen, and welcome to the first township-wide in-service session of this school year.

There is a story which tells of a young man who had a fantastic professor when he was in college. This professor was a magnificent teacher who always exhorted his students to think.

The young man deeply admired the professor, tried to emulate him and take his advice, and always tried, as the professor had taught him, to think out every situation.

When the professor died, the young man, a teacher then himself, was heartbroken, but consoled himself with the thought that the professor had finally gone to his well-earned rest.

A number of years passed, and finally, it was the young man's turn to pass on. When he reached heaven, the first thing he did was to go looking for his old professor.

He found the man resting on a cloud, his head in the lap of a vivacious young lady who was busy feeding him grapes.

"Professor," the young man shouted, "how pleased I am to see that you are finally getting your reward!"

"Idiot!" the professor snapped, "haven't you learned anything? She's not my reward—I'm HER punishment!"

Which brings me to the subject of in-service sessions.

How, you ask? Simply that when I was teaching, I sometimes looked upon an in-service day such as this as an imposition upon my time and energies. I would much rather have been back in the classroom, working with my kids, than spending a day sitting in a stuffy auditorium listening to "theory" pour from the stage. If they can't give me the day off, I would think, why can't they at least let me work on my classroom materials—something that would be valuable.

Over the years, however, I began to analyze my feelings toward those sessions, and I think I came to a new understanding of myself and those programs. I never objected to learning something new and useful—after all, learning is my chosen profession—what I objected to was having to engage in an activity that was meaningless to me as a teacher. Like the professor in the story, while the powers that be may have thought of them as a reward, I saw them as my punishment.

With that firmly in mind, I am pleased to tell you that today's in-service contains only those programs which you have requested; there is nothing you will see or hear today that you will not be able to use in your classroom; the committee has gone to great lengths to find those people you have requested to give presentations that will be practical, informative, and from which we will all benefit.

Now, the rest is up to us. Shortly, I will be introducing Mrs. Driscoll, who will be outlining the procedures for today's activities. What we do in those sessions and what we take away from them will help determine how we view this activity. Let us firmly hope that at its conclusion we will look back at it not as a punishment, but as a reward that will manifest itself in easier and more effective methods of teaching for us, and an increased appreciation and love of learning in our students, which is a goal we all share.

Thank you, and enjoy your day!

SPECIAL DATA: *Time of speech: about five minutes. In-service sessions are held throughout the nation's schools. There is often resistence on the part of the faculty to attend these sessions, perhaps for the very reasons mentioned in the speech. A speech of this type followed by a program that is truly meaningful,* *however, will go a long way toward alleviating that reluctance. It acknowledges the possible feelings of the audience, analyzes that feeling, and then tells them why this will be different.*

69

TOPIC: **Opening speech for a student/parent guidance activity.**

AUDIENCE: **Adults and students; an audience composed of the students within a particular area and their parents.**

(SPECIAL NOTE: Although this activity may be called by various names, it is the time when parents of children in the grade just prior to high school are invited into a special program, usually with their children, during which they receive guidance as to what schedule of courses their sons and daughters should be taking in high school. This is the opening speech given at one such activity.)

If you hired a carpenter to build a house for you, you would be anxious that the job was done well. What would you think, however, if the carpenter showed up for the job with nothing but his bare hands? The materials were there, the wood and the nails and the plans, but the carpenter had no hammer to hit those nails; no saw to divide the wood; no square or level to make certain that it was straight and even. What would you think?

If you were anything like me, you'd be thinking that it was time to get another carpenter. This one was obviously not prepared. He simply was not prepared to do the job.

Well, I think we can all see the message behind that story. No one can do a good job if he doesn't have the right tools for it. This applies to the carpenter in the story as it applies to life itself.

Each of us has a job to do, whether that job be in business or in the home. To do that job effectively, we need our tools. What are those tools? I'd like to suggest that they are the knowledges and skills which we learned in school and which stay with us throughout our entire lives.

Reading, for example, is one tool which we must all have, whether it be used to read a recipe or scan a business report. Without it, we are like that carpenter in the story. We have the materials all around us, but we are helpless because we have lost the tools of our trade.

Tonight, you are here to learn about the courses that are offered at Rock Township High School and how the schedules you prepare for next year will affect your future lives. This is an extremely important session for all of us. Your course selection for next year and the subsequent selections for the years following will determine how you acquire the tools with which you will have to face the job called life.

Mr. Hastings, chief guidance counselor at the high school, will speak first and explain the various programs offered. After that, he and the guidance staff will answer all your questions. Finally, you will fill out a tentative course selection schedule which you will have time to think about and discuss before handing in.

I know how important this is for you all, and I would like to offer any assistance I may be able to provide. May you select well, and may tonight be the beginning of a happy, prosperous, and rewarding future for you all.

Thank you.

SPECIAL DATA: *Time of speech: about five minutes. An activity such as this is extremely important for the students and their parents. The anecdote at the beginning makes its point well, and many people have told us that it gave meaning to the whole process. This is never an easy activity for parents or students, and a speech of this nature helps to provide an incentive for serious thought on the subject.*

70

TOPIC: **Opening speech for a program on board of education candidates.**

AUDIENCE: **Adults; parents, educators, and concerned citizens.**

Good evening, ladies and gentlemen, and welcome to this "Meet the Candidates" night.

The schools of this nation exist for you and your children. This is not some idealistic nonsense; it is cold, hard fact. Through your support, the schools of our township have grown into the educational institution they are today. Your support has come in terms of the help you give by volunteering your time and services, the cooperation you exhibit in school-sponsored activities. Your concern is manifested in attending evenings such as this, and in the financial contributions you make in terms of your local taxes.

In absolute truth, you own the schools. They are yours in every respect, and they are for your use to educate your children.

However, just as this nation belongs to each and every one of us but is governed by people representatively elected by us, so, too, the schools of a district are managed and guided by a group of people who are elected for that purpose by you.

The choice is yours, and no easy choice it is, either. The individuals who sit on a local board of education will inevitably be responsible for the direction of education within the school which your children will attend. They will be deciding the hard matters pertinent to education in your district.

This is no simple task, and it requires a special, a very special, type of person to do it.

Tonight, we are privileged to have with us four citizens of our township who are running for the two vacant seats on the board. Each, in his or her own way, is that special person—dedicated, concerned, and unafraid of hard work. In a few short days, you will be asked to decide which two will serve you in that capacity.

As we listen to them tonight, let us be thankful for these honest and exemplary citizens who are willing to give of themselves for the betterment of our children.

Whomever we may vote for, our thanks goes to them all.

SPECIAL DATA: *Time of speech: about three minutes. You will notice that this speech is very clear-cut and comes right to the point. You will also notice that it contains no humor whatsoever. We would suggest that your speech contain no humor, either. We know of one administrator who, at a similar function, said something like, "I hear there will be a meeting of the board later this evening. Well, that's for me, because I'm just as bored as anyone else." He meant it as a joke, but it was met with dead silence, and there were repercussions from it for months afterward.*

71

TOPIC: **Opening speech for a creative parenting conference.**
AUDIENCE: **Adults, primarily parents with some educators.**

(SPECIAL NOTE: "Parenting" has come into its own of late. Courses are offered at local colleges in how to be a creative parent, and many school systems hold programs, usually on a one-time basis, in which they invite an expert in the field to address or hold a conference for the parents of the students. These are usually well-attended.)

Good evening, parents.

No matter what you may do for a living, the difficulty of that job pales in comparison to the difficulty of the other job which we all have in common—being a parent.

One sage even remarked that there was proof that insanity was hereditary—parents get it from their kids. Indeed, I know from personal experience that there are times when raising a child in today's world is something akin to re-fighting World War II with a pea shooter.

Perhaps that is why an activity such as this is so valuable. We are all interested in our children, and we all love them. That goes without saying. But, we also realize that being a parent is more, so much more, than providing food on the table and clothing for their backs. We realize that we are also responsible for the moral as well as the physical growth of our children. We realize that this can be the most demanding and frustrating and rewarding part of being a parent. An activity such as the one in which we are about to participate let's us all know that we are not alone; that there is help available.

We all want what is best for our children, not only in terms of the physical necessities of life, but in terms of the growth and development of the total child; the functioning human being who will one day have to make his or her way in this world; who will become a part of the human family; who will one day marry and raise children of his or her own. This is our concern.

We are interested in quality—the quality of the mental and emotional lives of our children as well as their physical bodies; the quality of the experiences we provide for them from which they may mature and grow; the quality of our performance as parents whose desire is to nurture the child in every way from birth to the ultimate transition into adulthood.

And that is why we are here this evening. We wish to listen, to understand, to appreciate, and most importantly of all, to share. We, who have it in our hearts to raise our children to be the best that they can be, want to share our experiences, our insights, our knowledge that, in most cases, has been gained through endless and loving toil.

The famous mystic philosopher and author Kahlil Gibran once wrote of parents, "You are the bows from which your children as living arrows are sent forth." If this metaphor stands true, then let us share this evening as a method of improving our aim. Let our goal be that these "living arrows" may find the target, and the mark may be a rich, fulfilling and rewarding life for them and, by projection, for all of humanity.

Welcome to this evening's activity, and may we all benefit from it.

SPECIAL DATA: *Time of speech: about four minutes. We feel that every good parent knows the feelings which this speech invokes, but they do not take them out very often to look at them. Also, this lets parents know that they are not alone in their feelings, identifies them as a single unit working together for the good of their children, and enjoins them to work together during the activity that follows. This speech is usually well-received.*

72

TOPIC: **Opening speech for a Sports Night Activity.**
AUDIENCE: **Mixed audience; students, parents, teachers, alumni.**

Good evening, and please forgive me.

Forgive me, because I am about to tell you a joke that I once heard that will undoubtedly offend everyone here. All I ask is that you bear with me, because it does have its point.

The story goes that at a conference-leading college, they had a first-string wide receiver who was renowned for his spectacular catches and equally renowned for his miserable grades. Just before the "big game," the math professor announced that the boy would not be able to play, as he was flunking the subject so badly, he couldn't even pass a basic examination. The coach pleaded with the professor to give the boy a make-up exam, and, after much pleading, the professor agreed.

On the day of the exam, the coach came with the wide receiver to the professor's office.

"All right, young man," the mathematics professor said, "we'll make this an oral exam. For your first question, how much is six plus five?"

The football player frowned and thought and finally looked up and said, "Er...twenty-three?"

"This is impossible!" the professor roared. "That's it; this boy has flunked the course!"

"Aw, come on, Professor," the coach pleaded, "give the kid another chance. After all, he only missed it by one!"

(Despite the way in which you have prepared the audience for this story, there will be laughter. Wait for it to die down, and then continue.)

You did laugh, didn't you? That's because it is funny; it's the type of funny story that has been told about athletes for years and years. The image of the big, looming, and incredibly dumb athlete with his equally simple-minded coach has been giving comedians and writers fuel for decades. There's only one trouble with it—it simply isn't true!

Sports are part and parcel of every school curriculum, because we realize that the ancient goal of a healthy mind in a healthy body is no fantasy but a realistic and attainable goal. The playing fields of today have a place for strength, it is true, but as anyone who has ever taken the time to find out knows and knows well, they have no place for mindless strength. Sports, as they are practiced in our school, require quick, intelligent minds as well as healthy, trained and conditioned bodies.

You here tonight are the living proof of that. Indeed, none of you would be on our teams if you did not carry adequate academic averages. We know that participation in sports requires the type of quick thinking, analysis, and decision making that only someone who has trained his or her mind can accomplish. An athlete who must size up a situation on the field, analyze all possibilities, choose the correct option of play, and act decisively to execute that play, all in a split-second's time, cannot—simply cannot—be the mindless brute who is unable to add six and five and come up with the right answer.

So, perhaps it was fitting that we laughed at that story; laughed at it as an example of a false idea that is dead forever; laughed at it as living proof of its falsity; laughed at it because, in our hearts, we realize that it was intelligence—and a good deal of intelligence—combined with dedication and skill, which has brought us to this very night.

I salute you all—I salute you for your prowess on the playing field as I salute you for your academic status and the work that went into it; I salute you for your bodies—AND YOUR MINDS!

This is truly your night, and it is my sincere wish that you enjoy every minute of it. I cannot think of people who deserve it more!

Thank you.

SPECIAL DATA: *Time of speech: approximately six minutes. Today's athletes are often slighted by the stereotyped "dumb athlete" mentioned. This speech is very well-received by the athletes. It is also appreciated by their parents who are most often in attendance at such affairs. Try it and see the favorable reaction you receive.*

73

TOPIC: **Opening speech for a student activities night.**

AUDIENCE: **Mixed audience; mostly parents, but some students and educators as well.**

Good evening, and welcome to the seventh annual student activities night at Rock Township High School.

For those of you who may be attending this activity for the first time, let me tell you what you are about to observe. This is a night when the stars shine. This is a night when the stars of our school, the students who have spent their time and efforts in various classes and extracurricular activities, have an opportunity to shine forth with what they have accomplished and share that with you, our audience, our parents, and our friends.

Tonight, as you tour our school, you will have the opportunity to see our students exhibit, display, and participate in their accomplishments in a wide range of school-related areas, from the fashioning of furniture in the industrial arts classes to the fashion show put on by the home economics classes; from the presentation of our drama club to the songs of our chorus; from the art works of our students to the experiments of our science classes; all this and more awaits you.

I realize how eager you are to get started, so I will not keep you. I would merely like to remind you of a very important fact.

When you view the accomplishments of our students tonight, view not only the painting or the dress or the piece of wood that has become a chair. Rather, take a look at the time and the work and the effort that has gone into each and every item you will witness tonight. Know that this is the result of hours of thought and study and practice which has been shared by our students and faculty. Know also that none of it would have been possible without the support of you, our parents and our friends, for this has truly been done for you, and without you it is meaningless.

So, let us congratulate our marvelous students and staff who have participated in this evening's activity. I have every confidence that you will enjoy it.

Thank you for coming, and—let's begin!

SPECIAL DATA: *Time of speech: two and a half to three minutes. Activities such as this one are notoriously well-attended. They are excellent public relations vehicles and give students a chance to show how hard they have worked. The speech above will be well-received by the parents, students, and faculty, since it recognizes the achievements of all these groups in the evening's program.*

74

TOPIC: **Introduction to a speech before a legislative body.**

AUDIENCE: **Adults; members of the body you are addressing; press.**

(SPECIAL NOTE: Administrators are frequently called upon to "testify" before legislative bodies "for" or "against" a variety of proposed statutes, rules, etc. related to education. This is an introduction that might be used effectively upon such an occasion.)

Honored members of the State Legislature *(Or, whatever body you happen to be addressing. Check locally for the proper form of address, as this may vary from body to body according to custom.)*.

I welcome the opportunity to address this Legislature, and I wish to thank you for affording me the chance to do so.

As human beings, we sometimes get to feeling a bit superior. We make plans, arrange meetings, conduct business, and go on with our lives with the certain knowledge that we are firmly in control. It's just about that time, however, that a hurricane strikes, a blizzard blows, or a river floods, and we find out how easily our plans, our meetings, our business goes by the boards as we find ourselves chastised by the elements. It is as if we had forgotten the basics, and those basics assert themselves and refuse to be forgotten or ignored.

So, too, when dealing with the important and pressing issues of our times, we tend to forget another basic. We read reports; we write legislation; we calculate budgets, and we tend to forget that we could neither read nor write nor calculate were it not for the educator who taught us these skills. Somewhere along the line, we all sat in a classroom and mastered the complexities of reading, conquered the intricacies of writing, and learned to cope with the enigmas of mathematics. We did not do this on our own, but we accomplished these life skills with the help and patience and insights of an educator in a school run by other educators for the benefit of all the children in our district.

Indeed, it is sometimes difficult to remember a time when print on paper was incomprehensible, when we could not sign our name, or when we could not count the change in our pockets, and this very fact is a living tribute to education.

If we are to solve the problems and meet the challenges of our age, it will be through education that we will succeed. Education is, indeed, the *sine qua non* of life. Without it there is nothing; with it, all things are possible.

I know that this body recognizes that fact, and I am pleased indeed to testify before you.

SPECIAL DATA: *Time of introduction; about ninety seconds. Following this introduction, you would proceed to present your major speech or answer questions as the situation indicated. This introduction, however, gets the audience "back to basics" so to speak and places the responsibility for positive action squarely on their shoulders.*

AFTERTHOUGHTS

As we said at the beginning of this section, opening speeches must set the tone for the program that is to follow. We hope you will agree that all of the preceeding speeches do just that. Moreover, they have been crafted to keep that tone upbeat and positive. For the most part, they give praise and recognition to the groups who will be participating in the activity. All opening speeches should have these qualities if they are to be successful.

The speeches that follow are examples of closing speeches. They are on the exact same type of programs as the opening speeches just presented. This will allow you to have an opening and closing speech for the most common types of programs in which you may be involved as a school administrator.

Closing Speeches

75

TOPIC: **Closing speech for a drug-abuse program.**
AUDIENCE: **Adults; parents and educators.**

Ladies and gentlemen:

I know I speak for us all when I say how impressed I have been by the program we have just witnessed. I also know that I speak for all of us when I deeply thank the fine people who have participated in tonight's activity. We thank you for your knowledge and your insight into the problems of drug abuse, and we thank you for sharing your expertise and your compassion with us. We are truly grateful that you could be with us tonight, and we have all profited from it.

Now, this program draws to a close, but the problem of drug abuse and addiction keeps right on plaguing us. Indeed, like the fire of which I spoke at the beginning of tonight's activity, it continues to burn out of control, and, as we have learned this evening, it is fast becoming a threat to each and every one of us. As we have learned, there is no "holy place," no sanctuary where we may remain immune to this poison that threatens the lifeblood of our society—our children.

But, as we have also learned tonight, the picture is not without hope. There is hope in the fine work done by those people who have devoted their lives to the rehabilitation of drug addicts; there is hope in people such as those who have just spoken to us, who take their time and effort to educate us; there is hope in education itself which keeps our students informed and aware of the dangers, as well as offering an alternative to tuning-out, an alternative cased in the positive achievement that allows our students to "tune-in" to life. Yes, there is—there definitely is—hope.

Most importantly of all, there is hope in you. Yes, ladies and gentlemen, there is hope in you. You have given up a night at home to attend this meeting. You have come here willing and ready to learn. You have listened and shared and participated and asked questions and given of yourself in order that you may appreciate the extent of the problem and the difficult yet real possibilities of solutions. You have come; you have learned; you have given.

Now, you will carry away with you this new knowledge. You will use it and spread it. Hopefully, you will influence others, allowing them to become aware and giving them the incentive you have to work, to work together, for its ultimate solution. It is a first step; it is a beginning; but it is a good beginning, and one in which we must all invest our hope for the day when we will no longer need programs of this type.

Therefore, my final thank you of the evening must be for you. Thank you for coming and participating tonight. Thank you for learning how to help. Thank you, most of all, for caring.

Thank you, have a safe trip home, and good evening.

SPECIAL DATA: *Time of speech: approximately four minutes. Drug abuse programs will undoubtedly continue to be necessary activities for schools for some time to come. Notice that this closing acknowledges all who participated, especially the audience, as well as summing up what had been covered during the program. This is the sum and substance of every closing speech, even one on as serious a topic as this.*

76

TOPIC: **Closing speech for a "Back-to-School Night" activity.**
AUDIENCE: **Adults; almost entirely parents.**

(SPECIAL NOTE: Following are two forms of a closing speech for a "Back-to-School Night" activity. The first, the short form, would be used when parents have gone through the evening's activity, and there is to be no further assembly of the whole group.)

Ladies and gentlemen, may I have your attention please. In a few moments the final bell will ring marking the ending of this year's back-to-school night. It is the wish of everyone here in the office as well as every member of the faculty and on the PTA executive board that you have enjoyed this evening and profited from it. If you come away with a deeper understanding of what we are trying to accomplish here at Rock Township High School as well as a commitment to continue the avenues of communication that we have established tonight, then everyone will be a winner, not the least of which will be our students.

You are welcome to join us for coffee and cake in the cafeteria at this time, but whether you do or not, have a safe trip home, and thank you for joining us.

(SPECIAL NOTE: The speech above would be given over the school's public address system at the conclusion of the program. The next speech would be one given by the administrator if the program called for parents to reassemble in a central location after the conclusion of the actual class visitation. Here, the speaker would be physically addressing the group.)

Well, did you enjoy this evening?

(Wait for applause—it will come.)

I'm overjoyed to hear that, ladies and gentlemen, because it is equally true that we have enjoyed being with you. Tonight, we have given you the opportunity to hear what goes on in our school, and we are happy to do this for a number of reasons. We are proud of what we accomplish at Rock Township High School, and we like to share that with you. Moreover, when there is understanding between parents and teachers, and when that understanding blossoms into a firm avenue of communication between home and school, the students, your sons and daughters, come out the real winners. Finally, we need your support for our schools, and we know of no better way of enlisting it than to let you see for yourselves the work that we are doing.

The very fact that you came here this evening rather than sitting at home before the TV set is an indication of how much you care, and we want you all to know how much we appreciate that concern.

Therefore, our thanks goes to the members of the PTA executive board who planned this affair, our faculty and staff who so generously cooperated in this evening's activities, and, most importantly of all, to you, our parents, without whom none of this would have been possible, and with whom it is all worthwhile.

Thank you for caring and for being here tonight.

See you next year!

SPECIAL DATA: *Time of first speech: about one minute. Time of second speech: one and a half to two minutes. Notice that both speeches incorporate a thanks to the people who have arranged the affair as well as to the parents who have* *attended. Both are friendly and upbeat and end the evening on a very positive note. Whatever the circumstances of your Back-to-School night, one of these will serve very well.*

77

TOPIC: **Closing speech for an "Awards" program.**

AUDIENCE: **Mixed audience of adults and students; both parents and teachers may be present as well as the students.**

I love mystery stories, and I particularly like the part that occurs in almost all of them when the detective gathers all the suspects together in one place and points his accusing finger and says, "You did it!"

At this point, of course, the case is solved, and all that remains is for the detective to tell us how he or she arrived at the guilty party.

Well, I feel that I could be a rather good detective myself this evening. In fact, I can definitely point my finger *(point in the general direction of the audience)* and say, "You did it!" You, the people sitting before me this evening. You did it. You will have to take full responsibility for winning these awards which have been presented this evening. I know that you are guilty of the hard work, the hours of study and practice, the effort and energy that went into receiving these honors. I know that you are guilty and fully deserve what you have gotten.

And how did I arrive at that conclusion? That's simple. As a part of this school, I have had the opportunity to meet with you firsthand. I have come to know you. I have come to appreciate your intelligence, your dedication, your endless and seemingly tireless efforts to achieve something great. I have witnessed the way in which you students have given your all and the way in which you parents have supported and helped at every turn without having to be asked. I have seen the way in which you teachers have snuck in there with advice and extra help and the giving of your time to help.

I have seen all of this, and it has led me to conclude that you are all guilty—guilty of a crime of passion; passion for life; passion for learning; passion for being the best that you are capable of becoming now and tomorrow.

And since you are guilty of this, it is only right that tonight you have received the fruits of your labors. Let me assure each and every one of you that you deserve them and more.

Our thanks go out to the people who have worked to make this evening's program a success. We have all enjoyed it. Most importantly of all, however, our thanks go out to you who have won these awards and to all of you, parents and teachers, who have been a part of them. Without you, it would not be possible.

Take your awards now and cherish them. They say, in a very real way, just how much we cherish you. Think of them not as the end of an effort, but rather as one milestone on a long path, and know that you have made an excellent beginning.

Again, my congratulations to each and every one of you.

Thank you, and good night.

SPECIAL DATA: *Time of speech: three and a half to four minutes. Whatever the awards that were handed out, here is a speech that will be appreciated by everyone in the audience. The analogy to the detective story works well, and we have had positive feedback on it. The audience is quick to realize what you are doing, and it holds their attention at a time when they are anxious to get together with family and friends.*

78

TOPIC: **Closing speech for an educational in-service program.**
AUDIENCE: **Adults; all educators—teachers and administrators.**

Many of us here today play a dual role. Many of us are both educators and parents. We know very well that when our son or daughter comes in from school one afternoon and we ask the time-honored question, "What did you learn in school today?" we will very possibly get the standard and equally time-honored response of, "Nothing."

We can all smile at that, because it has been true of many countless generations of children. Perhaps, if we listen well, we can even hear ourselves when were kids.

As educators, we have learned to interpret children's answers. We have learned to listen to what is meant as well as what is said. We know that the answer "Nothing!" really means, "Nothing that I want to take the time to discuss with you now."

Therefore, you will be overjoyed to know that I am not going to stand up here and ask, "What did you learn in in-service today?"

There are two reasons why I'm not going to ask it. The first is that I would probably get the same response we get from our children, and the second is that I know the answer already.

As to the first, we have all worked hard today, it grows late, and we are anxious to get home to our own families. This is right and good, and to re-hash the day's events would serve little purpose except to burden those who have already labored well.

As to the fact that I already know the answer to the question anyhow, well, that comes from having shared this day with you. I have witnessed your absorption in your profession; I have seen the insight and understanding with which you approached each session; I have come to know your concern for your students and for offering them the best that is available; I have felt the dedication and purpose that makes our school system great.

If, by chance, my child should ask me this evening, "Daddy, what did you learn in school today?" I just might say "Nothing." If I do, that will be because my child would have no way of understanding yet the esteem, honor and respect which I hold for all of you; how thankful I am to the fine people who put together today's in-service; how pleased I was with our fine speakers and group leaders; how honored I feel to be working with each and every one of you.

Enjoy your evening, and thanks again for making today the success that it was.

SPECIAL DATA: *Time of speech: about three and one-half minutes. This is a fitting ending to a day's in-service session. In honoring the educators who attended and participated, you are ending the day on a high note, sending the participants off well-disposed to implement what they have learned, and sponsoring good feelings which may have a carryover effect at the next in-service. Give it a try.*

79

TOPIC: **Closing speech for a student/parent guidance activity.**

AUDIENCE: **Adults and students; an audience composed of the students within a particular school grade and their parents.**

Ladies and gentlemen, let us all join together in thanking the fine people who have given so generously of their time and expertise tonight.

(Lead the applause.)

If there is one thing about which we may all agree this evening, it is that these people have done an excellent job of informing us and enlightening us to all the possibilities.

Now, the rest is up to us. We well know how important our choices will be for our futures, but we also know that we can't let that frighten us into inaction. We know that we must make those choices intelligently and purposefully. We also know that, thanks to this program tonight, we are armed with the one weapon that can surmount all obstacles—knowledge. When we know where we are going, we will also know how to get there.

Now we must take the time to think. All of us, students, parents, teachers, and guidance personnel, are involved in this process. Together we have learned; together we will reflect upon our own lives and needs and hopes and desires; and together we will choose well from the educational offerings with which we have been acquainted tonight.

I wish you all health, happiness, and success in whatever area you decide to enter.

I thank you all for attending tonight. The concern and care you have manifested in your questions and comments can only give me confidence that whatever you choose, it will be the right choice for you and for everyone involved.

Thank you, again. Have a very good night and a brilliant and happy future.

SPECIAL DATA: *Time of speech: three to four minutes. There is a great amount of concern among parents and students when they are asked to select course schedules and the like. Guidance programs such as this are not only appreciated, but they serve a real purpose as well. This speech acknowledges all of that.*

80

TOPIC: **Closing speech for a program on board of education candidates.**

AUDIENCE: **Adults; parents, educators, and concerned citizens.**

Ladies and gentlemen:

To paraphrase a very well-known saying, "We have met the board of education candidates, and they are ours."

Tonight we have had the privilege of listening to four individuals who have indicated their desire to serve you, the citizens of this community. In listening to their views and policies on education and the state of our schools, we have come to know them well. We have come to see them as men and women of honor and purpose, each of whom carries a sincere dedication to excellence in our schools and to the best possible education for all of our students—the true ideals of American education.

They differ, of course, but that difference is merely in approach to the common goal to which they are all so firmly committed. It will be up to you, the electorate, to decide ultimately which approach and which candidate best matches your own ideals and philosophies. You will let your conscience decide, based on the knowledge you have gleaned tonight of these candidates' approaches to the problems at hand. Whatever your choice, we can all take comfort in the knowledge that these fine candidates represent the best that our community has to offer.

As I said before, "We have met the candidates, and they are us!" They are a part of us as they are an active part of our community; they are a part of us as they share our own hopes, desires, and aspirations for our school system; they are a part of us as they are committed to working tirelessly in our behalf and in the behalf of our most precious resource—our children.

At the beginning of this evening's activities, I outlined how tiring and thankless a position a seat on the board of education may be. We found that only someone who cared, really cared, would have the stamina, the will, and the dedication to run for the office. As we said at that time, they must be very, very special people, indeed.

Therefore, I know I speak for everyone in the audience when I thank each and every one of the candidates for taking the time and the trouble to be with us this evening to talk to us and to share their views and opinions.

I also know that I speak for each of them as well when I thank you, this audience, for attending this meeting tonight. It is people like you, an informed and knowledgeable electorate, who will ultimately give all the citizens of this country the kind of government they deserve.

Thank you again for attending, and thanks once more to our candidates for caring.

This concludes this evening's program.

Thank you and good night.

SPECIAL DATA: *Time of speech: four to five minutes. The school administrator must be particularly careful when moderating an activity such as this one. Particularly in a board of education election, you must be careful to avoid* *taking sides or showing partiality. A speech such as this one is particularly good for the occasion since it talks about all the candidates in very general and noncommittal terms. While acknowledging each candidate's dedication and effort, it avoids indicating preference for any individual. Try this, and you will be pleased by the response from the candidates.*

81

TOPIC: **Closing speech for a creative parenting conference.**
AUDIENCE: **Adults; primarily parents with some educators.**

(SPECIAL NOTE: See the notes on speech #71 for an explanation of parenting and parenting conferences. This speech is an adjunct to the first one, and it would be used following completion of the program.)

Ladies and gentlemen:
I think that we may all agree on one thing. We have been privileged to attend a truly outstanding program this evening. I'm certain that you will wish to join me now in showing these participants just how we feel.

(Begin applause. Wait until it dies down; then continue.)

I know I speak for everyone in the audience when I thank the members of the panel for sharing their expertise and their insights with us this evening. I know that I have profited from being here, and in the name of us all, I thank you.

Tonight, ladies and gentlemen, we gathered together, because we were concerned—we were concerned about our roles as parents; we were concerned about our children; we were concerned about the future. That concern has manifested itself in the fact that we have proven our will, this evening, to open our minds to new ideas—to learn.

We know that we have done this tonight not for ourselves, but in the hope of being better parents for the ultimate good of our children and the betterment of their lives. This is, indeed, a rich and noble goal, and I applaud your efforts and those of our speakers this evening in that behalf.

Perhaps it is evenings such as this which are the first step. Through sharing our insights and concerns, we have come to an understanding of ourselves as individuals and the goals for our lives and those of our children. Through such an understanding, we can begin to work together in new and creative ways toward the realization of those goals.

We fully realize that it will take work and dedication, but we are willing to accept the task gladly. We start with faith in ourselves, faith in our children, and with a firm hope in what will come tomorrow.

Again, thanks to our guests who presented this evening's program, and a special thanks to you, our parents, for caring enough to come here and participate.

Thank you all, have a safe trip home, and good night.

SPECIAL DATA: *Time of speech: between three and four minutes. It has been our experience that the parents who attend functions such as these usually have a great deal of dedication to being a good parent. It is well, therefore, for the school administrator to acknowledge this in these closing remarks. Parents generally appreciate recognition of the difficulty of their task. In fact, whatever the occasion, it is always a good policy to thank the speakers on the program and then thank the audience for caring enough to attend. It has a definite carryover effect in the positive attitudes that are carried out of the auditorium.*

82

TOPIC: **Closing speech for a Sports Night activity.**
AUDIENCE: **Mixed audience; students, parents, teachers, alumni.**

Ladies and gentlemen:

The last award has been given out; the last student athlete has been honored; and the last speech of the evening is about to begin. This evening draws to a close.

Yet, as we all know, the end of each evening implies the beginning of a new day. What kind of day will tomorrow bring?

Judging by what we have seen here this evening, tomorrow will be a bright and fair day filled with hope, because these fine young people whom we have honored this evening will be a part of it.

The British have a saying which claims that their military battles were won "... on the playing fields of Eton." Eton is a school that has produced some of England's greatest military and naval heroes. The saying refers to the fact that many of those leaders believed that they achieved knowledge and perfection in tactics, decisiveness, analysis of the situation, quick thinking, and command as part of the sports they played at their school.

There is much to be said for that. This evening we have had a chance to observe these young athletes in a social situation, just as we often have had the opportunity to observe their prowess on the field. We can see the confidence, the poise, and the good-natured sportsmanship that their participation in sports has brought them. We cannot help but be impressed.

To them I say, "You do us proud!" Through your efforts; through your commitment; through your hard work, you have trained your minds along with your bodies; you have grown in every aspect of your lives; you are, indeed, a credit to our school, a credit to your parents, and a credit to yourselves.

Our thanks goes out to everyone who attended this evening and helped to make it the enjoyable experience it was—to our marvelous speakers, whose wit and insight entertained and stirred us all; to our coaches, whose dedication to excellence and the ideals of sportsmanship and fair play has truly inspired us all; to our parents—our long-suffering, loving, nurturing parents—without whose support and encouragement none of this would be possible; and to our student athletes, who, in the final analysis, made it all worthwhile.

Thanks to you all.

Have a very pleasant evening, and good night.

SPECIAL DATA: *Time of speech: approximately four minutes. In speeches such as this where the audience is composed of students and parents, the administrator's aim must be toward acknowledgment of student effort without forgetting the others who have contributed to it—namely, parents and teachers. This speech does just that, and it is well-received by the audience. Sports banquets or awards activities are one of the most frequent functions at which the school administrator will be asked to speak, and it is well to be prepared.*

83

TOPIC: **Closing speech for a student activities night.**

AUDIENCE: **Mixed audience; mostly parents, but some students and educators as well.**

(SPECIAL NOTE: As with the Back-to-School Night activity, we are giving two closing speeches. This first speech would be for an activity where the evening closes with an announcement over the public address system. In this case, the audience will not reassemble for ending speeches.)

Ladies and gentlemen, may I have your attention please.

At this time we conclude this seventh annual student activities night. It is the sincere hope of everyone here at Rock Township High School—the students, the faculty, and the administration—that your evening with us has been an enjoyable and informative one. Everyone has worked long and hard to show what we are capable of. If you have enjoyed yourselves and appreciated our efforts, then we are indeed content and grateful.

Have a safe drive home, and good evening.

(SPECIAL NOTE: If the evening's program is to end with the guests reassembled in a central location, then a more thorough summation is called for. The speech that follows would be for such an occasion, and it is meant as the final speech of the evening.)

Well ... this has been quite some evening.

Tonight, we have been privileged to view the efforts and achievements of our students. I think we may all agree that what we have seen has been truly outstanding. It was obvious that endless hours of work, study, and practice went into tonight's exhibits and presentations. I, for one, would like to thank them for their outstanding efforts, and I know you'll want to join me in that.

(Begin applause. Wait until it dies down, then continue.)

I also know that I speak for everyone when I give a special thank you to the faculty who have given of their time so unstintingly to make this night successful. And, I send a special thank you also to the members of the PTA who volunteered their efforts, and who are always willing to help.

To you, our parents and our friends, our thanks as always for coming and supporting our endeavors this evening. If you have enjoyed yourselves and have come to know us a little better, then we are indeed rewarded for whatever efforts we may have made, and this evening was truly a success.

Thanks again for visiting with us.

Have a safe trip home, and good night.

SPECIAL DATA: *Time of first announcement: forty-five seconds. Time of closing speech: approximately three minutes. Closing remarks should always be suited to the occasion. If the affair closes with a brief announcement over the public address system, then it must be short and to the point. A longer speech over such a medium would fast lose its audience. When facing the assembled crowd, however, it is wise to capitalize on the fact that they will undoubtedly be pleased with what they have experienced. Remember that the speech should be short here as well, as they are usually anxious to get home and share the memory of the evening with their families.)*

AFTERTHOUGHTS

There is a maxim among comedians and stage performers that goes, "Always leave them laughing!" Well, if we may paraphrase that statement, perhaps the administrator's maxim for closing speeches should be, "Always leave them thinking!"

As the leader of the school and the moderator of the program, the audience expects you to set the tone of the evening. You do this with your opening remarks. At the conclusion of the program, they also expect you to say a few words. What you say in those closing remarks can be just as important as what has gone on during the entire evening.

To merely stand up, thank the speakers, say goodnight, and then sit down, leaves the audience with a highly impersonal feeling. An administrator who summarizes or encapsulates the evening, who thanks the speakers in the name of the audience and then thanks the audience and praises them for their participation, who reflects upon the meaning of the evening's activity in some personal way, and then sends the audience off with something to think about and appreciate—THAT is an administrator who has created a warm and positive feeling in the audience, and THAT is an administrator who will be appreciated and remembered.

SECTION FOUR

Administrator's Speeches
for Laymen

There is not a profession in the world that does not develop its own jargon. Perhaps it is natural, working as we do with such a wide variety of topics and situations, that we develop short cuts that others in our position would understand. We speak of "giving the CAT" when talking of administering the California Achievement Test. We speak of raw scores and percentiles and stanines, and a host of other words and phrases with which we have become familiar over the years.

This is fine when speaking with other educators who understand the language, but it is often confusing and frustrating to anyone not familiar with what we are talking about. Indeed, use of that type of language with laymen (which, for our purposes here, we will define as anyone not engaged in education as a profession), may have a negative effect. What are those educators trying to hide? Why don't they speak clearly?

The school administrator is frequently asked to address groups of people ranging from parents of the students within a particular school to a meeting of the general public to a women's club to a civic association. The one thing that all of these engagements have in common is the fact that, in each case, the school administrator will be speaking to a group of laymen whose only association with education may be that they attended a public school in their youth or that they have children attending the public schools at the present time.

Consequently, the administrator must take particular care when presenting such a speech before laymen. The language must be of such a nature that everyone in the audience understands without feeling that they are being "talked down to." The administrator must project a confident, warm, and positive image; quite often the audience will judge the schools on the basis of their reaction to the administrator. Whether that is right or wrong does not have bearing here, for we have seen it happen too many times to negate it.

The speeches in this section are for just such occasions when the school administrator must face the lay audience. They are on a wide variety of topics, each of which we have found to be of interest and concern to laymen. Each speech has been used successfully, and will work for you.

84

TOPIC: **The parent—leader or guide.**
AUDIENCE: **Adults; primarily parents.**

Good evening, ladies and gentlemen.

I'd like to thank Mrs. Gorney for that fine introduction. Now all I have to do is live up to it. Yes, thanks a lot, Mrs. Gorney.

It was Mark Twain who wrote, "When I was sixteen, I was convinced that my father was the most ignorant man on earth. By the time I was twenty-one, however, I was amazed at how much the old man had learned in five short years."

Put another way, I remember a colleague of mine who was bemoaning his teen-aged son. He said to me, "You know, the hardest thing for my son to realize is that in another thirty years, he'll be as stupid as his mother and I are now."

We've all had the experience, haven't we? Here we are, people of vast worldly experience; people who have "been through it"; people who know what life is like "out there," away from the family and the home. And what do we want to do with that knowledge? Just one thing—we want to pass it on. We'd like to save our children, whom we love, from having to go through the hardships we had to endure because of our mistakes. If possible, we'd like to smooth the way; point out the pitfalls; guide our children over the rough spots of life.

So what happens? We give our advice; we counsel; we educate—and the darn kid listens, smile, and turns up the stereo another four hundred decibels! We tell our son, we tell our daughter what needs to be done, and the little so-and-so goes out and does the direct opposite.

And we watch; we watch and see them grow and try and fail and we think, "Why didn't you listen? Why didn't you do what I told you to do? Don't you know that I know more about life than you do? Don't you know that I only want what's best for you?"

There are times when the labels "Child Proof" and "Unbreakable" don't come on parents' hearts.

But, that's only half the picture.

There are also times when that kid whom you bore and nurtured and loved will turn to you and say, "I love you Dad," or "I love you, Mom."

129

There are times when you catch a secret glance of the kid who used to come in from play with skinned knees and dirty face and it strikes you that he has become a handsome young man; she has turned into a beautiful young lady. There are times when you see your child help another child, learn something he never knew before, come home bursting with excitement when the team has won the game, go around starry-eyed with the newness of first love. There are these times, too, and they are worthwhile.

Where then, lies the balance between these two kids, the one who fills your heart with grief and the one who melts it with love? Where do we begin to understand?

Perhaps we begin by going back ourselves and understanding *us* at that age. What was it like to be an adolescent? It's been a long time, and the years have a way of blurring with memory, accentuating what was good and fading what was not.

I'd like to read you one definition of an adolescent. Let's see if we can agree with it.

"Put the personality of a child in the body of a man, furnish a need to be loved and a fierce desire to be independent, allow a need to be self-directing but leave out any idea of what direction to take, add an enormous amount of love but also the fear that it may not be accepted or returned, give physical and sexual powers without any knowledge or experience of how to use them—take these and place them in a society whose values and achievements are essentially incomprehensible and certainly unattainable and whose concerns are seemingly misplaced and insincere. Do this, and then you have just begun to understand the problems of adolescence."

Can we remember back to those days—honestly remember? Do we remember how confused we were about so many things? How we hungered to do so much? How enthusiastic we were? How easily hurt we could be in so many ways?

This is essentially what our children are going through now. They are bursting with life; they want independence; they want to be on their own—while at the same time, they are scared to death; they want direction; they cling to the home.

If that sounds contradictory, it is because adolescence is contradictory. If we look at this time as a bridge between the child and the adult, then our children stand, at this moment, with one foot on each bank. It's a hard position to hold for any length of time. Very often, the strain shows.

What, then, is our position as parents? How do we become the gate keeper on that bridge? How do we direct the traffic?

Perhaps our answer lies in the definition of two words: "leader" and "guide."

A "leader" is someone who takes you through the museum, telling you where to walk, and what to look at, and what you should like; a "guide" takes you through the museum pointing out what is there, letting you stand where you wish within limits, letting you decide what is the best of the best. A "leader" tells you what you must do; a "guide" lets you choose between acceptable alternatives. A "leader" tells; a "guide" suggests.

How does that work out in terms of us, the parents?

Let's talk about socks. That's right, socks, the kind you wear on your feet. I'll set a situation for you.

I am taking my son to a theater to see a play. This is going to be an evening affair, and my wife and I are going to make a grand evening out of it—dinner in a good restaurant, the play, perhaps a snack afterward, the works. Naturally, we want to dress appropriately. I'm even going to wear my good suit, the one without the patches on the elbows.

It's almost time to leave. Mom has laid out junior's sports jacket, a neat pair of blue trousers, a clean shirt, and one of my best ties. I call upstairs for junior to hurry, and down he comes, the picture of elegance except for one thing. He is wearing lavender socks! Did I say lavender? I was wrong, they're more like a combination of hot pink and grape jelly!

And the battle is joined! "You are not wearing those socks!" I state. "Why not?" says he. With ultimate logic, I reply, "Because I said so!"

Thirty minutes and a great deal of table-pounding later, he goes upstairs to change the socks (I'm stronger than he is, anyhow) and comes down, ten minutes later, wearing the right color socks—with blue jeans and a sweat shirt!

Sound familiar? Of course, it's not socks with everyone, but the underlying principle is one that all parents can understand.

Now what happens if we change the scenario a bit? It's the same situation, but now it's earlier in the afternoon.

"We're going to have a great time tonight," I tell him. "By the way, do you want to wear your suit or your sports jacket? I want to know so I'll know what I'm going to wear."

He picks one.

"Do you want to wear the blue slacks or the black ones with that?" He gives his choice.

"Are you going to wear black or gray socks with that? Would you want me to pick a tie for you, or do you want to pick one of mine?"

And so it goes.

Look at what we are doing. I have ceased to lead; I have stopped telling him what to do; I have stopped challenging his drive for independence, but, at the same time, the choices that he is allowed to make and make freely are within the boundaries that I have set. Nowhere did I command; everywhere did I guide.

Like that guide in the museum who lets you stand wherever you want as long as it is within the proper space, so too, the parent can accommodate the child's need for independence; need to make his or her own decisions; need to be his or her own person, while still making certain that the decisions are within boundaries that the parent has set.

We are the parents. We have the responsibility. We are concerned, and deeply so, with the total growth of our children. Of course we must set the boundaries—a child without parameters is like a weed that will grow without any idea of form or shape or direction. Of course, we also must make an effort to develop independence of thought and action in our children. By allowing them to make intelligent choices within the limits we have set, perhaps we can teach and train and develop in them just that sense of independence and freedom, which will serve them all of their adult lives.

Is a parent a leader or a guide? Perhaps the answer is that we are both. We are the people who must lead our children toward their futures; we are the people who must guide them rationally and judiciously toward the independence of choice and direction that will assure that their futures will be happy and productive.

Certainly, let us set the boundaries within which our children must grow, but let's also try to guide their choices within those boundaries to avoid the confrontation of power; to give our children the chance to develop rather than fight against orders; to give them the chance to bring out that functioning adult who hides bneath the dirty blue jeans and the tousled hair.

We are their leaders; we are their guides; we are their parents. We try; we fail and fall; we rise to try again. That we stumble every now and then does not matter. That we pick ourselves up and try again means everything, for that implies a love that will not stop; that will not give up when the going gets tough.

It is that love—make no mistake about it—that will carry us through. We are here tonight because of that love; we try new ideas and new approaches because of that love; and with that love to guide us, we will not go far wrong.

Therefore, let each of us here tonight know that he or she is not alone. Together we shall try. Together we shall learn and share and grow.

And, together, we shall make a new and better world by giving to the future the children that we raise today.

There is hope—and you are it.

Thank you, and good night.

SPECIAL DATA: *Time of speech: about fifteen minutes. Obviously, this is a longer speech that would be given as part of a full evening's program. Its theme is aimed at parents. While it might be given at any function since it expresses basic truths that touch most people, it is most effective when given for a group of parents. Notice how it starts out with humor, becomes serious, and ends on a very positive note. Try it, and you will find that it is very well-received.*

85

TOPIC: **Communication; community; and the schools.**

AUDIENCE: **Adults; community members.**

Good evening, ladies and gentlemen, and thank you for that very warm reception.

I ran away from school. Oh, not recently, if that's what you're thinking; I was seven years old at the time.

You see, I was in the first grade, and the teacher told me that she was going to keep me after school. That was the first time in my school career that I was going to face a detention. It wouldn't have been so bad, of course, if it hadn't been for Raymond.

Raymond was a boy who lived in our neighborhood. I looked upon him as an older man of great experience. After all, he was in the fourth grade while I was in the first. One day before the start of school, he took me aside and gave me some very sage advice.

"Whatever you do," he told me, "don't let them keep you after school. They take you and lock you in the closet, and it's all dark, and the rats come and eat your toes."

You can understand, therefore, why I didn't want to stay after school, and you can understand and imagine my panic when I was assigned detention.

I sweated through the afternoon, as I recall, and finally came up with a plan. I raised my hand, asked to go to the lavatory, left the room, and promptly walked straight out of the school and straight home.

Now, when I got home, I couldn't bring myself to tell my mother the real reason I was there, so I said that I was sick and the school nurse had sent me home.

Meanwhile, back at the school, all they knew was that they had lost a student. Now, I can picture what they must have gone through, frantically searching the place, looking behind the boiler and in the furnace, trying to find the body.

Inevitably, someone must have realized that they had to inform the home of the "Disappearance." I don't really know what was said or how that was accomplished, but the next thing I consciously remember was being dragged back to school by my mother, protesting vehemently all the long, cold way.

Well, I was NOT locked in a closet. I NEVER saw a single rat. I had to stay after school for a week. And, I never spoke to Raymond again in my life.

With a start like that, how could I have done anything else but go into education as a profession.

Of course, a seven-year-old child does not consciously analyze a situation. At the time, it was horrendous, as I recall. Now, however, with so many years having fallen between that time and this, I laugh along with you at the situation.

I also like to take it out and study it every so often, because it lets me think about several very important facts.

What did I, as a seven-year-old, do that caused so much upset for everyone, including myself?

First of all, I believed a rumor. When Raymond told me the "horrors" of detention, I accepted that as unalterable truth. I never took the time to question what I had heard. I never took the time to find out what was so and what was not.

Next, I never communicated my concerns, my "fears" if you will, with anyone. So simple an action as sharing what I had "learned" about staying after school with my parents, the teacher, or even another student in the school might have alleviated my misgivings and most certainly would have prevented the entire situation from occurring. I kept it to myself, however, and that was a mistake.

Finally, I forgot that I had options. I ran from a situation which I saw as intolerable. I could not see, at that age, that I might have expressed my concerns; I might have talked out my fears; I might have stayed after school and found out for myself.

Of course, asking a seven-year-old to consciously run through these processes is asking too much. A seven-year-old mind can rarely handle those complexities.

It is not too much, however, to expect this process in an adult.

How might we apply this to a situation with which most of us here tonight are familiar?

As parents, we raise our children with love and concern for their well-being and growth. This includes educating our children to take a place in the adult world when it comes their time to do so. For the vast majority of us, this means enrolling our children in the public schools.

As part of that public school system, I am intimately aware of what goes on within those schools. For many of us, however, our only connection to the schools is the fact that we may have attended them ourselves as children. Granting that there is a distance between then and now, this can be the cause of some misunderstanding that, left unattended, can lead to difficulties for everyone.

Our schools are set up to serve you, the community. You support these schools in terms of your taxes, it is true, but you also support them in terms of providing input as to which direction they shall take. Your will, expressed through the board of education officials you freely select, helps to establish the curriculum, determine the extent of services, and even the quality of the education which your schools will supply to your children.

The twelve-year process, however, does not always flow smoothly. In any operation as large, as complex, and as vital as our school system, there is bound to be periods of misunderstanding. Even with close-knit families, misunderstandings are bound to occur, so we can only expect that this will also happen in the much larger extended family of school and community.

That these misunderstandings happen is not the problem. That these misunderstandings remain misunderstandings and are not cleared up to everyone's satisfaction most definitely is the problem.

One first-grade teacher I know sends a note home to every parent at the beginning of the year. It states: "If you promise not to believe everything your child tells you about me; I promise not to believe everything they tell me about you."

Certainly, we can all chuckle about this. We know from experience that children often misinterpret what has been seen or heard, or they embellish or extend what has been perceived. Any parent who has ever been called into his child's bedroom late at night because, as the child reports, there is an alligator hiding under the bed, will know the truth of that statement.

Of course children, especially younger children, come home with tales from school. Some of them can be very fanciful, while others can have a ring of truth, perhaps even the ring of very disturbing and upsetting truth. If your child came home and said that the teacher brought an elephant to school, cooked it, and fed elephant sandwiches to them for lunch, you would probably have to leave the room to keep from laughing in his face. If, however, your child told you that the teacher was making him stand in the corner all afternoon and wouldn't let him go to the boy's room, wouldn't you begin to get somewhat upset? I know that I most certainly would.

What can we do in situations such as this? Well, if we remember the incident of being called into our child's room because of the alligator under the bed, perhaps it will give us our first clue. That actually happened with me and my son, and when it did, my reaction was to get down on my hands and knees and search under the bed. I knew that no amount of logic and abstract thought would pacify a child who is convinced that under his bed lies an alligator waiting to attack. After I had searched thoroughly, poking into all corners, I invited my son to join me, and together we looked everywhere in the room. Not finding a single alligator, we concluded that the beast had probably left and would not be coming back.

The point is that we did not dismiss it as fantasy; we did not ignore it as a lie; we found out the facts of the matter. That is precisely our clue to handling disturbing tales from school. If you were at work or visiting a friend and someone told you that they had seen your spouse entering your house, obviously very ill, would you ignore it? Dismiss it? Of course not. You would call your home and find out. Well, ladies and gentlemen, the schools are YOUR schools; they educate YOUR children; YOU have every right to find out!

Your child tells you that the teacher won't let him go to the boy's room when he has to use it. Disturbing? Yes. Potentially harmful to your child? Yes, again. What do we do? You find out. You call YOUR school; you make YOUR concerns known; YOU FIND OUT!

I found out, because that problem with the boy's room was one which I faced with my son. What did I find out? I found that my son was telling the truth. The teacher refused to let him go to the boy's room. It seems that there was a major plumbing problem in that room, and for several days, certain elementary classes had to use the girl's lavatories under proper supervision. She wasn't denying him the use of a rest room, but she wasn't letting him use the boy's room, either.

Did I feel a little foolish? All right, I did, somewhat. But, I would have felt a great deal worse if my child was suffering and I did nothing about it.

As our children grow, we sometimes hear other rumors about our schools and what is done in them. These can be anything from drug pushers invading the hallways to a teacher spreading Communist propaganda in class. These are rumors that can be devastating to a parent whose natural love and concern is for the child's safety and well-being, and which can be devastating to a school system because of the mistrust they generate.

What is a rumor? Take a pillow to the highest steeple in town on a windy night. Rip it open and let the feathers fly where they may. Then, on the following day, try to find and collect each feather. That will give you some idea of how fast a rumor can spread and how difficult it is to stop once it has started.

What can we do to stem this tide? We have our answer. WE CAN FIND OUT! We can find out the facts of the matter. We can find out the truth of the situation.

Is this interfering? Of course not! We have said before, the schools are your schools. They belong to you just as surely as if you had laid every brick and driven every nail. You have a major investment in them, not only in terms of the taxes you pay, but in the lives of your children as well. We owe it to ourselves and we owe it to our children to protect that investment by not listening to rumor but by finding out.

And what will you find out? Because I am a part of our schools, I can tell you what you WON'T find in Rock Township Schools. You won't find a closed shop where no one will talk to you. You won't find yourself passed from secretary to secretary in a wild attempt to cover up or avoid responsibility. You won't find a place that belittles you or talks down to you or tries to give you a brush-off.

You will find a place that is proud of its accomplishments. You will find a place that will invite you to come in and see for yourself. You will find a place that will recognize your concern and do everything in its power to provide you with real answers that will satisfy you. You will find a place that cares about your child, cares about you, and cares about your interest. You will find that they are YOUR schools and are there to serve YOU!

If your concern involves a case of misunderstanding, we will do our best to clear it up to your satisfaction. If it involves a real problem, then I promise you that we will work with you to solve that problem. We care about the same thing, ladies and gentlemen—we care about our kids. Working together, there is nothing that we, you and I, cannot accomplish.

Certainly there can be problems in school. Certainly there can be difficulties, from drugs to bullies. Certainly, there can be improper actions on the part of teachers and administrators. Certainly there can be legitimate concerns about curriculum and expenses. But, just as certainly, there can be solutions and remedies if we will only work together for the benefit of our children.

If I could leave you this evening with only one word, it would be this—communicate. Do you have concerns about your child in school? Don't keep them inside—communicate! Is something happening in the schools that you see as potentially damaging? Don't fret about it—communicate! Do you have something that bothers you about a teacher? An administrator? A program? A condition of the building? A rule of the school? Don't sit and worry—communicate! Do you feel that something is wrong, terribly wrong, with the state of education in our schools? Don't tell your neighbor—tell us and communicate!

When we communicate, we share our feelings, and there is an exchange of information that can open the minds of both sides. Through this process of communication can come understanding, and with understanding comes a new commitment. A commitment to further communication; a commitment to finding out for ourselves the exact nature of the problem; a commitment to work together, the school and the home—two of the most powerful forces on earth—to seek for remedies; to seek for solutions; to seek for that common ground that will eventually allow our schools and our children to be the best they are capable of becoming.

We, you and I, the school and the home—we can communicate. We can work together. We can understand the problems, the concerns, the frustrations of each other. We can come to a new understanding and a new appreciation that will serve one purpose and one purpose only—the growth and development of our children.

It is within our grasp. For our children's sake, we can do no less than try.

Thank you, and good night.

SPECIAL DATA: *Time of speech: fifteen to sixteen minutes. This is a very powerful speech which "builds." That is, it starts off slowly and builds in power and impact as it goes along, culminating in a plea for understanding and communication. It is extremely effective, and if you deliver it with a great deal of conviction, it will serve you well.*

This speech could be delivered at a local civic or community group meeting where you might be asked to speak. Lack of communication between the home and the school is often a cause of problems in communities throughout the country; a problem that often manifests itself in failed school budgets and community opposition to school-sponsored programs. This speech was originally delivered to combat just such an attitude, and it is effective in sponsoring communications between the school and the community.

86

TOPIC: **The school and the future.**

AUDIENCE: **Adults; parents and community members.**

Good evening, ladies and gentlemen.

There is a story which goes that an old hillbilly family decided that they would send one of their members to school to get some education. Now, the lad they chose was the first member of the family who had ever gone to any school anywhere.

After the lad had been away at school for quite some time, he returned for a vacation and visited with his family. One night at dinner, curiosity got the better of Pa and Grandpa.

"What do they teach you at that school," asked Pa, "besides readin' and 'ritin'?"

"Well, Pa," replied the boy, "they teach me things like geometry and trigonometry, and...."

"Say something in geometry," interrupted the father.

The lad thought a moment and then said, "Pi R squared (πr^2)."

"That's ridiculous," exclaimed Pa. "Everybody knows that pies are round; it's cornbread that are squared."

"Let the boy alone," chided Grandpa. "Maybe that geometry ain't no good, but that trigger-nometry sounds like just what he needs. He always was the worst shot in the family!"

Of course, we all laugh at this story because of the obvious mistakes made by Pa and Grandpa as they failed to understand what the boy was talking about. We think, "My goodness, how could they be that uninformed," and we laugh.

Well, let me tell you something. I once tried to help my daughter with her math homework. After two hours of set theory, probability, and truth tables, I became so frustrated that had I been inclined the way Grandpa was in the story, I'd have taken my trusty rifle and shot the darn math book!

In short, that math was so different from that which I learned when I was going to school, that it was almost an alien language to me. The result was a great deal of frustration on my part and an injunction to my daughter to make certain that she paid attention in math class so that she could help me in the future.

In fact, the seeming complexity of the problems and theory behind them so intrigued me that I set out to discover just what was being taught in my daughter's class and why.

I found out, all right, and what I found out amazed me. I learned, for example, that she was being taught something called "binary notation." This is a process for recording numbers where it looks like this:

(Hold up a poster such as that shown in Figure 4-1.)

```
           1  =  1
           2  =  10
           3  =  11          84 =
           4  =  100
           5  =  101         1010100
           6  =  110


              BINARY NOTATION
```

Figure 4-1

Immediately, I was thrown into mass confusion. What were those ones and zeros supposed to mean? What looked to me like one million, ten thousand one hundred was supposed to be the number eighty-four? I didn't understand, and for a moment I became angry that my child was being subjected to something so meaningless. Outside of its being some sort of mind game, I could see no value in it. Therefore, I decided to ask an expert—my daughter.

"Oh, Daddy," she said. She always starts with "Oh, Daddy," when she has relegated me to something with the intelligence level of a mushroom. "Oh, Daddy, can't you see that the ones could stand for when a switch was on and the zeros could stand for when a switch was off?"

I admitted that I could grant this, but I didn't see what it had to do with the price of a math book at the local book store.

"Well," she continued, being very patient with the old man, "a computer doesn't recognize numbers. All it can tell is if a circuit is on or off. Soooo, this way you can enter any number into a computer and it can store it and remember it and do things with it. If we didn't have this kind of math, we couldn't have computers or calculators."

By that time I was admiring her intelligence and wondering if it was too late to trade her in.

Seriously, do you see the point I'm trying to make? Here was my daughter learning something perfectly rational and which would serve her understanding and use for a product that didn't exist when I was her age. They were teaching her a skill for tomorrow, which I could not see today.

Upon reflection, perhaps it is right that the school should be teaching her these things. There is no one who seriously doubts that computers are here to stay. In fact, everything which we can learn indicates that computers are the wave of the future. My daughter, as your sons and daughters, will be a part of that future. There is, consequently, a need for them to know these things.

Reflecting even further, it seems to me that the school was doing exactly what it should have been doing—preparing our children for the future.

Certainly, this has been a part of the school's function from the beginnings of public education. Indeed, as parents, we realize that no matter how knowledgeable we may be, we cannot handle the entire education of our children on our own. We also realize that the future of society requires an informed and educated populace. That is why we send our children off to school; that is why we provide them with an education.

It may sound a bit grandiose and heroic, but as I prepared to take a place in professional education, I learned that the purpose of our schools was to educate every child to the fullest of his or her potential and to prepare these children to take a place in the world they would inherit as adults. I believed that then, and over the intervening years, there is nothing that has convinced me otherwise. I still believe that today.

What children learn in school today must prepare them for what they will face tomorrow. Certainly, this is true in terms of the job or career that they will pursue in life, but it is true of living in society as well. Perhaps one child out of my daughter's math class will become a computer programmer, but the chances are very likely that the vast majority of them will have to live with and work with computers in their day to day lives as adults in tomorrow's society.

You know that I am a part of education, and you may take it with a grain of salt if you wish, but it is my honest belief that the schools of this nation in general and our township in particular are doing an outstanding job in that respect.

There are courses offered in today's schools that were not even dreamed of forty or fifty years ago. Today, a high school student can take a course in computers, both technology and programming; a student can study social issues that are as timely and provocative as this morning's headlines; a student can speculate and plan and investigate modes of living that were unheard of just a few short years ago.

Since most of you are my age or thereabouts, you will remember that you chose to enter a particular job or career for only a very few reasons. Maybe your father had a certain position and it was expected that you would follow in his footsteps. Perhaps it just so happened that your family knew someone who would take you in if you got the proper training within a certain field. Perhaps you did choose your own job, but, for the most part, it was probably a combination of being in the right place at the right time, or taking what was available.

Today the job market is becoming more and more selective. Tomorrow will bring jobs that will require very specialized knowledge and will need very special people to fill those positions. Consequently, in schools today, students are taking courses in careers. That's right, they are studying about what careers are available, what each requires in terms of education and experience, and the rewards that each job offers both in financial terms and in terms of personal fulfillment.

This would have been considered nonsensical when I started to teach. It is not in today's world, however, where an individual must know what is available if he or she is to receive the proper training that will allow him or her to gain access into that field. Today that is a fact of life, and the schools have stepped in to meet the challenge and to fill the need today for the choice tomorrow.

The student of today will be the citizen of tomorrow all too soon. To send a child into that world unprepared for what he or she will encounter would be nothing short of criminal. I believe that the schools recognize this and are doing their very best to see to it that our students will be able to meet the future in every way.

The noted anthropologist, Margaret Mead, once wrote, "the pattern of the future is change." All we have to do is to look around us to see the truth of that statement. Things are changing, sometimes so fast that we are hard pressed to keep up. We realize, however, that we must try, or society will fast leave us behind.

That is true of the schools no less than of the individual. If we, in public education, are to serve you, the citizens and children of the community, then we must also try to keep up with a changing world. We must change along with society in order that we may be a part of the world for which we prepare our children. This is not always easy.

We try new programs; we try new approaches; we try new disciplines; we try new techniques. Sometimes we succeed, and sometimes we fail, but, if we fail, we rise to try again. If life is ever-changing, then so must our schools reach out and try. If our job is to educate children for tomorrow, then we can do no less.

Remember the incident with my daughter's math class that I told you about earlier? Well, I have to tell you one more thing about that. As I was sharing that incident with a friend of mine, I found myself remarking, "They didn't do things like that when I went to school."

I stopped myself at that point, because it suddenly dawned on me that indeed they hadn't done things like that when I went to school because it didn't exist when I went to school; because when I went to school there was no need for that; because that was then, and this is now. No, they didn't do that when I went to school, but they are doing it now, and thank goodness that they are. Thank goodness that the schools have realized that my daughter needs that information for the life she will lead several years from now. Thank goodness that she is going to a school that has learned to change; that has learned to prepare its students for the future.

We live in a hectic, turbulent, often frustrating and discouraging world. We also live in a world that makes daily progress against disease, against social injustice, against the darkness of ignorance. We also live in a world that vibrates with promise—the promise of an exciting and fulfilling world of tomorrow for all.

It is the schools of this nation, in close and vital cooperation with our nation's parents, that will assume the job of educating today's children for that world of tomorrow. Working together, we can prepare our children to face that world armed with the knowledge, the skills, and the courage they will need.

Working together, we can give our children the future—and it will be bright, indeed.

Thank you, and good night.

SPECIAL DATA: *Time of speech: approximately fifteen minutes. There is often an attitude among parents and some community members that the schools are teaching "useless" courses. This stems from the fact that these people see the* *schools as they were, while we, the professional educators, know the schools as they are today. A speech such as this, which puts the role of the schools in preparing students for the future into a real perspective, can be very valuable. This speech could be used equally well before a group of parents and other concerned citizens, or for a group of businesspeople, such as at a Rotary meeting or a Junior Chamber of Commerce meeting. It is quite effective and generally well-received.*

87

TOPIC: **A program for gifted and talented children.**

AUDIENCE: **Adults; parents of children about to enter the program.**

> *(SPECIAL NOTE: The school was about to establish a special program for gifted and talented children. This was a new program, and it was to be voluntary for the children identified for the program.)*

Good evening, ladies and gentlemen. Thank you for coming here this evening, and thank you for your kind reception.

It is the beginning of the year, and the teacher is taking some information from the students. The teacher asks one child, "Whom shall we notify in case of an accident?"

The child thinks for a moment and replies, "I think I'd like you to notify the closest first aid squad."

It's a little later in the school year, and the teacher asks the class, "How many months have twenty-eight days in them?"

One hand goes up immediately, and the teacher calls upon the child.

"All right," she says, "how many months have twenty-eight days in them?"

"All of them," answers the child.

Of course we smile when we hear these answers, and there is the possibility that the child involved is being a classroom comedian, but it is just as possible that the child is merely thinking in terms that his or her classmates have yet to understand.

After all, if any of us were injured, the first aid squad is probably the first people we would want notified, and it is true that every month in the calendar does have twenty-eight days.

What we are witnessing is the fact that there is a complex thought process going on. We are seeing the child weighing the question and ponder the various deviations that could affect the answer. This is no easy task in an adult, and it is an amazing and wonderful thing to observe in a child.

Yet, we all realize that the greatest gold deposit in the world is nothing but rocks in the ground unless it is discovered and mined and processed.

So too, the mind with the ability to analyze, to approach a subject critically, to think in abstract and wonderful ways, will stay just another mind unless it is discovered and mined and processed.

You know, as an educator, I have often heard people talk about the various kinds of students we have in our schools. It is true that we have children who have serious problems learning and need specialized help. It is also true that we have children of more or less average ability who have rough spots every now and then, but who have the ability to get through. It is also true that we have children who could only be called bright, or extra intelligent, or gifted.

It is about this latter group that I often hear the most. "What a pleasure they must be to teach," people say. "How easy it must be to deal with them. Why, you could take those kids, put them in a library for a year, and they'd learn more than they could in any class."

When I hear that, my blood runs cold, because from the bottom of my very being I deny that statement.

A gifted child is not easier to teach than any other student. In fact, such a child may be more difficult to challenge than another student. The work of a normal classroom may prove too easy for such a child. The child grasps the concepts immediately, finishes the work quickly and is bored to death. Such a child needs almost constant challenges just to maintain a normal, interesting environment in a classroom.

The implication is also that a gifted child has no problems, and this is most definitely false. The gifted child is still a child. His or her problems may be different from another child's problems, but they are still there. The difference comes in approach. The gifted child is not likely to accept the dictum of "because I said so" as a reasonable answer. Rather, the gifted child will need special direction, based on logic, to solve his or her special problems.

And what of the contention that you could put them in a library, on their own, and they would learn as much as in any class? Well, it is true that the gifted child is blessed with a consuming curiosity, and it is true that he or she will try to find out about anything that takes his or her mind and requires an explanation.

The trouble with the "place-'em-in-the-library-for-a-year" theory becomes obvious if we think about a telephone. If you wanted to find out the times of performance at a local movie house or you needed someone to fix your furnace or you needed a special kind of carpeting for an area of your home, I doubt that you would pick up a telephone and dial seven numbers at random. Rather, you would get out the telephone directory, look up what you needed, and then call the correct location that would supply your need.

It is the same way with the gifted child. Knowledge, the capacity for learning, left on its own becomes a torrent of water. A flood spreads far and wide, but it sweeps everything in its way. Without direction, it goes where it wills, leaving havoc in its path. A river, however, that is channeled and directed, is a source of life for all who live along its banks. It has purpose and direction and fits into the ecology of the land.

I believe that the analogy holds when speaking of gifted children as well. Yes, they will learn on their own, but what will they learn? They, as well as any other child, need preparation for life. They need to have their learning directed into areas where they will receive challenges worthy of their abilities. They need the direction that will channel them into the type of learning experiences that will form the basis for a lifelong learning process; that will form the basis of the future life and work and productivity of the gifted child.

Vince Lombardi, the much-honored football coach, said that he wanted every player on his team "to be the best that he was capable of becoming." As parents and educators, perhaps we can agree that we want exactly that for our children. We want them to live up to their fullest potential; to be the best that they are capable of becoming. We want for them the fullest and richest and productive life for them that they are capable of having.

There is nothing wrong with this dream. In fact, it is a laudable aspiration for parents to have for their children.

Our problem is, and always has been, how to ensure that our children will receive the training, the education that will help us fulfill that dream; that will help our children become all that they are capable of becoming.

You all realize that your children have been identified as being gifted and talented. That is why you are here this evening. However, I will wager that you did not need the school to tell you that there was something special about your son and about your daughter. I will wager that long before any paper arrived from this building, you knew that your child was special, and you knew that he or she would need some special handling.

Therefore, it probably came as no surprise when you were notified of this meeting.

Your concern, now, has to be about what kind of program we intend your child to enter. Of course you are concerned about the learning of your child as much as you have always been concerned about his or her welfare from the minute he or she was born. In fact, that is highly commendable, and I have only admiration for the concern that brings you here tonight.

In a few moments, I shall be turning you over to Mr. Melchior, who has developed the program we want your children to enter and who will be teaching that program in our school. He will tell you the particulars of the program and try to answer your questions. I have every confidence that when you have heard what he has to say, you will agree that this program is something your child needs and from which he or she will profit greatly.

We, in the schools, are trying our best to educate every child for the future. We are trying our best to get each child to live up to his or her fullest potential. This program is one way in which we hope to accomplish that goal.

With your cooperation and for your children's sake, we can do no less.

Thank you for being here, thank you for listening, and, most of all, thank you for caring.

SPECIAL DATA: *Time of speech: thirteen to fifteen minutes. Within this speech, the speaker introduces another speaker who will explain the gifted and talented program to the assembled parents. If the speaker were to perform this task, he or she would do it at that point in the speech and leave the final paragraphs for the concluding remarks.*

Gifted and talented programs are increasing throughout our nation's schools. This speech informs and advises parents about such programs and the need for them, as well as attacking some of the more common myths about the gifted child. It is generally well-received and appreciated by the parents who attend.

88

TOPIC: **A life in education.**

AUDIENCE: **Adults; suitable for any group.**

Good evening, ladies and gentlemen. Thank you for having me here this evening. I must say, that was a very warm reception considering the fact that I haven't done anything yet.

Perhaps I should start out by telling you that for the past twenty-some-odd years, my life has been involved with education. In that time, I have seen thousands of children, stood before them, taught them, listened to them, and watched them grow.

Over those years, there has been accomplishment and frustration, triumph and tragedy, tears and laughter. Perhaps tonight I might share some of those times with you.

I remember the first time I set foot into a school as a teacher. Needless to say, I was a bit younger then as well as several pounds lighter and had hair a bit fuller. It was the first day of school, and I proudly stood by the door of my classroom as my students arrived. The halls had cleared, and I was just about to join my class when a much older teacher whom I had not met before came up to me.

"What are you doing here?" he asked. "The bell has rung. You should be in class with the other students."

"But, I'm not...." I started. "I mean, I'm a ... that is, I belong...."

"Look, kid," the teacher said, "I don't need any backtalk. Just get to your class!"

What could I do? I got in my class.

Do you know that for the next ten years, that teacher called me "kid"?

Well, it's been a long time since that first day.

In the musical, "The King and I," Oscar Hammerstein II wrote lyrics for a song, part of which goes, "It's a true and ancient saying, and a very special thought; that if you become a teacher, by your pupils you'll be taught."

Over the years, I have come to recognize the truth of that statement.

I remember one student. We had, in that class, a special "Parents' Day" activity. All of the mothers as well as a few fathers showed up for that one. All, that is, except one mother, who had never come to any other school function either. I imagine that you can appreciate how I felt. The other children proudly toured the room with mother or father, showing their accomplishments, being complimented and stroked in turn by their proud parents. This one child, however, sat alone in one corner of the classroom. No parent touched him; no one admired his work; no one patted his head.

I experienced two emotions at that point: a deep compassion for this child, and an emotion that I will not name for the parent who had left this child alone.

I went up to the child, put my arm around him, and said, "Harry, I'm sorry that your mother couldn't come today. I'm sure that she has a very good reason."

"Oh, she does," he smiled up at me. "When my Dad got sick, she had to go out and get a job. She works every day, and when she comes home, she helps us with our homework and then goes and visits Dad at the hospital. On Sunday she takes us to the park to play, and then we all go visit Dad. But, Sunday is her only day off, so that's why she can't be here today."

There was nothing I could do except to hug him. I had no words that could make me feel any less guilty for my thoughts.

Now, Harry was not the child's real name, nor will any of the names I mention today be the actual names of the children involved, but that was my first lesson that my students taught me. From that incident, I learned not to judge, and never to make assumptions.

That lesson stood me in good stead when I became a principal and had to deal with a situation that came up in one of our elementary classrooms.

It was shortly after the beginning of the year, and the teacher was in the process of dismissing the children. As they left the room to board their bus, she bid each one of them a good night.

"Good night, Mary," she said to one child.

"Good night, you ugly old hag!" Mary answered.

Naturally, I heard about that. It was disturbing, because, as you all realize, we can't have our children being so disrespectful. What I couldn't understand, however, was the fact that the teacher had reported that Mary was one of the best behaved children in the class and really seemed to have an affection for the teacher. Besides, there was also the fact that the teacher was an attractive young woman who had a most pleasant personality and a wonderful way with children. In all, it simply did not add up.

So, I investigated. I had a very informal talk with Mary and a discreet call to her home. What I found made me smile and reinforced the lesson I had been taught never to assume anything.

It seems that Mary came from a very loving home. The mother and father were deeply in love with each other, and, like many married couples, they often joked with each other.

For at least the past ten years, the father would joke with the mother. At the children's bedtime, he would kiss them all good night, and then kiss mother and remark, "... and a good night to you, you ugly old hag." The words were meaningless to the children, but the underlying warmth and love were felt deeply by every child, especially Mary. Mary did not know what "hag" meant, but she knew that her father loved her mother, so it must be something good.

Therefore, when Mary met her new teacher and grew to really like her, it was natural that she would wish to honor her with the words of love she had come to know—"Good night, you ugly old hag!"

I learned from that that children are very quick to pick up things from their parents. I remember one child I had in class when I was teaching. I gave Tommy an assignment and asked him how he was doing with it.

He looked up at me and said, "This is a hell of an assignment. I don't know if I can do the damn thing."

Well, that was a bit of a shock, hearing that language coming from a youngster. It was typical of his speech, I discovered. While he never came out with anything blatantly obscene, Tommy would utter vulgarities with a good frequency throughout the day.

I tried to break him of this habit with very little success, so I decided to involve the home. I made an appointment with the boy's father for the following day.

We met in the principal's office, and, after the introductions, I got right down to business and explained to the father the problem Tommy had been having with language.

The man's eyes grew wide as I spoke. When I had finished, the gentleman hung his head, ran a hand through his hair and looked up at the principal and myself.

He shook his head in despair and said, "That damned kid; I don't know where the hell he gets it!"

Not all problems have been that easy or humorous. There have been problems that break your heart; problems where there has been no solution; problems where the outcome has been tragic.

There was, for instance, my introduction to the drug problem.

During class one day, I noticed that one of my students, whom we will call Jim, had fallen asleep at his desk. Now, perhaps there is the streak of a practical joker in me, but I thought it might be a good idea to let my sleeper learn a lesson about not falling asleep in class. So, I cautioned the rest of the class to be quiet, and when the bell rang dismissing the class, they tiptoed out of the room very quietly. I stood at the door and cautioned my next class to be equally as quiet as they came in. They were, and the sleeper did not stir. When the entire class had assembled, or so my plan ran, I would wake the sleeper, and we would see how long it took him to realize that he was in an entirely different class. Then we would all have a good laugh about it, I would caution him to get more sleep at night, and I would send him on his way to his next class.

So, I waited until the new class had assembled with many a giggle and a shushing among them. I walked down to the boy's desk, stood over him, and in a booming voice, said, "… and what's the answer to that question, Jim?"

There was no answer, so I repeated myself a bit louder.

Nothing. There was no response.

In the back of my mind, a little doubt began to wiggle around. I reached down, took Jim by the shoulder, and shook him gently.

He fell. Rather, like an overstuffed rag doll, he unfolded from the desk and sprawled on the floor. He did not move.

I looked down at him. His lips were caked, and his face had a light blue pallor. I bent down and placed my fingers by the boy's mouth. I could not feel him breathing.

Jim did not die that day, but I will always remember kneeling beside him on the floor as several people worked feverishly over him to ease his breathing; to coax him back to life. The problem had been an overdose of drugs. It very nearly caused Jim his life.

I often stopped and wondered, after that, about what I might have done to have prevented that day; to have kept Jim from sticking a needle in his arm and almost wasting his life.

I suppose that if I had the answer to that, I would also be able to stop wars and ensure everlasting peace. The problem did bother me, however, and it continues to bother me to this day.

But I would not give you the impression that what happened with Jim was a usual occurrence in the schools, for it is not. Oh, certainly, if one went looking for that sort of thing, one could find it. I have met children who have been abused at home, beaten with sticks and chains; I have met children who were professional thieves at age ten; I have met children who were bullies, who delighted in causing pain, who extorted money from smaller children.

But that was just a very small part of all the children with whom I have come into contact. I have also met children who befriended another child when that child was alone and friendless; I have met children who gave up their lunches in order to feed a less fortunate child who might have gone without; I have met children who defended weaker children against bullies; who stopped a drug pusher who plagued a playground by reporting his activities; who stood up to incredible pressure to do what they believed was the right and proper thing to do.

In short, along with the crime and degradation, I have witnessed heroism, trust, faith, concern, morality of the highest degree, and cultivated senses of justice and truth on a far greater degree than one could ever find in a daily newspaper or on the evening TV news program. I have been privileged to witness all of this.

Perhaps it is because of my position as an educator, but I am often asked if I believe that the world of the future is going to be all right; if the children of today will make a decent future for mankind. I suppose they think that because I work so closely with the citizens of tomorrow, I have that answer.

Well, I don't have any hard and fast answer, because there are no easy answers to the problems of the world. All I can say to those who ask me that question is to tell them what I feel.

Over the course of my lifetime I have had the privilege of working with children. I have taught them in the classroom as well as serving them as a group within the school. I have dealt with their problems. I have shared their triumphs. I have watched them learn and develop and grow.

I have dealt with the worst of children; I have dealt with the best of children. I have seen children who breeze through school without a bit of trouble; I have seen children who struggled through a torturous and convoluted school career. I have met children bursting with health; I have met children who were so ill they could not hold a pencil. I have dealt with children whom I would have trusted with my life; I have dealt with children I would not have turned my back on. I have met and dealt with them all.

And I have come to understand that there is hope for the future; that along with the fear and despair there is also courage and hope. I have seen that courage manifested time and again in the children I have met, and I have read the hope of the future in their faces. Yes, there have been moments of failure, but there have been moments of triumph, too. Those moments of triumph have far outnumbered the bad times. Yes, I have seen the worst in human nature, but I have seen the best as well, and the memory of that sustains me at the bleakest of times.

I answer, then, that yes, I believe in the future, because I believe in children. I believe in the future, because in my lifetime, I have been privileged to live and work with those who will make up that future. A small percentage have caused me to despair, but the majority—the vast majority—have filled me with joy and hope and convinced me that tomorrow will be the best that humanity can make of it.

I have been in education all my life, and I would not change that for the world.

Thank you for listening, and good night.

SPECIAL DATA: *Time of speech: fifteen to seventeen minutes. As you must be aware from having read this speech, this is quite different from the others in this section. That is because a speaker should always suit his or her speech to the occasion and the audience. This speech was originally for a local women's club who wanted an educator's reflections on education. The result was the speech you just read. It was met with overwhelming approval. Certainly, every educator can appreciate and believe in the reflections of this speech. Delivered with such sincerity, it will be extremely effective.*

89

TOPIC: **Education and civic consciousness.**

AUDIENCE: **Adults; members of a local civic club; community members.**

(SPECIAL NOTE: Administrators are often members of local civic clubs or are asked to speak before such organizations. This speech is suited to just such an occasion.)

If there is a single quality with which all children are blessed, it is an active imagination. My childhood was populated with some very active fantasies, and I'd be willing to wager that so was yours.

I remember that one particular daydream I returned to again and again was the one in which I, of course, was king of the world. Oh, what a fine king I made! Single-handedly I solved all the problems of the world and made it a beautiful place in which there were no problems, no concerns.

That was, of course, a child's dream. As I grew and learned, I began to realize that problems were rarely simple and solutions could be more perplexing than the problems they aimed at rectifying.

In school, I studied government, our constitution, and the thoughts and dreams of our greatest citizens as expressed in their writings. And, as I studied, a wonderful thing began to happen to me. I began to see our country as a land born out of a sense of justice and striving year after year, decade after decade, to become the shining light of freedom that would be the beacon for the world. I quickly lost my childhood fantasy of being king of the world, but I gained a larger perspective that I was part of a viable, honest, and ever-changing society which had its problems but which recognized that fact and worked toward solutions.

This was the beginning of what could be called a *civic consciousness*. It was a knowledge that if I were part of the problem, I was also a part of the solution. It was a knowledge that the contribution of the individual to society was important and could make a difference.

Now, suppose for a moment that everyone could discover that fact. If everyone believed that what he or she did could make a difference in this world and strived to produce the best of which he or she was capable, what a world we would have.

I believe that such a world is possible. I believe that through education we can show each individual his or her own worth and his or her place in society which they, through their efforts, can shape and improve.

Nor do I mean formal education taught in our schools. Of course I believe that our schools are doing an admirable job of educating our children for life in our democracy; I am a part of that endeavor and I have dedicated my life to it. But, I also mean the education of which we are all a part, whether in or out of school.

Each of us is a teacher, for each person we meet may learn from us as we may learn from each person we meet. If we dedicate ourselves to teaching others the value of positive lives, the value of contributing to the society of which they are a part, then society as a whole cannot help but profit from it.

If we remember that we teach not only by words but by deeds, then we will live our lives as citizens of this great land in such a manner that they will teach others that every life is worthy, has merit, and can make a contribution to the society of which we are all a part.

It is within our grasp, and, for the sake of our nation and ourselves, we can do no less.

SPECIAL DATA: *Time of speech; about four minutes. This is a short speech, well-suited to any number of civic groups who genuinely espouse the positive approaches offered in this speech. You should find it well-received.*

AFTERTHOUGHTS

The speeches in this section have been longer and more involved than any up to now. This is because we are dealing with speeches that are part and parcel of an evening's program or entertainment. We feel that they address their topics well, make dynamic and dramatic points, and show a bit of humor along the way.

Moreover, these speeches are meant for people who have no professional relationship to education. They avoid "educationalese" and all the technical aspects of education. They speak plainly and in warm terms that everyone in the audience can identify with and understand. Whether you use one of these or make up one of your own for your "layman's" audience, if you incorporate these values, you will not go wrong.

SECTION FIVE

Administrator's Speeches
for Educators

While it is a certainty that the school administrator is in demand to speak before parents and civic groups, it is an equal certainty that he or she will be asked to address a group of educators somewhere along the line. Whether that group consists of colleagues within a school or district or a group at the county, state or even national level, the challenges are great, and the school administrator is expected to meet them.

Speaking to a group of fellow educators can often be the most challenging situation in which the speaker may find himself. While audiences of laymen are quite often willing and anxious to accept what the educator has to say, a group of educators may include individuals equally as knowledgeable about the various aspects of education that will be covered, and each may well have his or her own opinions about the subject.

Therefore, the school administrator faced with this challenge must deliver a speech that will capture his or her audience's attention; that speaks to the subject in a straightforward manner; that presents issues or opinions backed by facts; and, that is entertaining. That last aspect is particularly important, for the best material and research in the world will be skimmed over lightly if delivered in a dry and lifeless manner.

The speeches in this section are geared to meet the administrator's needs in just these situations. They are geared to all levels, from the faculty of a school to a gathering of educators in top-rank positions; they are on a variety of subjects from the use of speech in education to the most serious of educational topics that affect us all; where needed, they are backed up by the latest data available. They are also entertaining and will involve your audience.

Enjoy speaking to your audience of educators, and they will enjoy listening to you.

90

TOPIC: **Communication between educators and the public.**
AUDIENCE: **Adults; all educators; the faculty of a school.**

Good afternoon, ladies and gentlemen.

As I look out upon this solid group of participating, on-line, hands-on educators, actively engaged in the contingencies of employing structured techniques of cognitive development to various strata of developmental groups within the contingencies of real-time extrapolation of the successful manipulation of resources, I perceive the variety of social interaction which allows for peer group assumption of maturity levels concurrent with affective development and interactive with goal-oriented progress within the framework skill-manipulative orientation and perceptual computations.

Therefore, I have one question to ask—What did I say?

Forgive me for my little joke, but the opening paragraph of my speech just didn't make any sense. I'm positive that no one in this audience understood anything I said, because I surely didn't, and if there is someone here who did understand it, may I suggest that the special services team will be more than willing to provide you with corrective counseling.

Seriously, I wanted to open with a confusing, disoriented statement filled with lage words and grandiose phrases. As I began to speak, I was noticing your reactions. You were all very polite, and no one got up to leave, but I could see the confusion entering your faces, and I could almost hear what you were thinking: "Good Lord, what is he talking about? I'm an intelligent person, but I can't understand what he's saying! Is there something wrong with me? What have I gotten myself in for? When will I get out of here? When is he going to stop?"

And, I will tell you that if I were in your position, that is exactly what I would be thinking, too.

My madness has a method, however. Let's analyze the situation and see if we can gain something from it.

We were confused because we didn't understand. Because we didn't understand, we felt alienated; left out. Because we felt left out of something that we knew we had a right to be part of, we felt resentment.

161

Because we felt resentment, if that dull, dry, verbose speaker—me—had continued much longer, we would have turned him off in order to protect our own integrity. We would have thought about the upcoming report card grades; we would have started correcting papers we brought with us; we would have mentally planned tonight's dinner menu—anything to escape from a situation that had become intolerable, because we were alienated from it by verbose and incomprehensible language delivered in an equally incomprehensible manner.

I hope you will agree that that is a fair appraisal of our reaction.

Now, what has this to do with education? Everything, because education is primarily a job of communications. The root words of the term "education" are the Latin words *E* and *Ducas*, which have the meaning of "leading out of." In education, we lead out of darkness into light; we lead out of ignorance into knowledge; we lead out of misery into happiness. These are our primary goals as they are the objectives of all educators everywhere.

And how do we "lead?" While the complete answer to that is extremely complicated, perhaps you will allow me to simplify it—in order to lead, we communicate. We communicate ideas and bodies of fact and knowledge to our students; we communicate our feeling, our aspirations, our concerns to our students; we communicate our plans, our goals, our advice and direction to parents; we communicate our image as dedicated and professional educational leaders to the public and the community at large. Yes, to educate, we communicate.

But how do we communicate? And how does the general public perceive us as communicating?

Recently, I watched a TV program. It was a situation comedy that had been written by that marvelous and humorous columnist, Erma Bombeck. I am certain that you are familiar with her work and her highly perceptive insights into American family life. She has a talent for allowing us to laugh at ourselves as she probes to the heart of the Human Comedy.

In this particular show, a typical suburban mother had been called to school by the teacher to discuss something that her son had done. The mother was seated in the classroom, and the teacher began to talk to her. The teacher spoke entirely in what had come to be known as "educationalese," the use of hackneyed phrases and platitudes that are part of educational "jargon." At first, we saw the mother's reaction as this teacher prattled on in incomprehensible babble. Then, as the TV camera held on the teacher, a running translation in English appeared as a subtitle across the bottom of the picture.

For example, while I do not remember the exact words as I was laughing too hard, the teacher said something like, "We do perceive that your son has made progress with certain dimensions of physiological development along the lines of acceptable peer-group interaction." While she was saying this, on the screen flashed the interpretation: "He no longer wets his pants!"

Like so much of Ms. Bombeck's work, this makes us laugh because it strikes home with such clarity. I have seen many of you at work in the classroom, and I well know that you go to extraordinary pains to make certain that every child in your class understands what is expected of him or her in terms of behavior, what must be done on an assignment, and that he or she has understood the lesson just given. Certainly, in the classroom, we communicate with crystal clarity to our students. But, and I have seen this happen as well, when it comes to communicating with our students' parents, it is quite often another matter. Perhaps because we know our students better than their parents, perhaps because we wish to impress the parents with the seriousness of the situation, perhaps because we, in administration, foster that kind of speech in our reports and bulletins, perhaps for any or all of these reasons, we tend to lapse into that "educationalese" when we meet with the parents.

I have seen it happen again and again, and I freely admit that I have not been guiltless, myself. We sit down for a conference with parents, and, before long, the phrases—peer-group acceptance; perceptual difficulties; cognitive development—begin to appear.

What is the possible reaction of the parents, then, to this situation? To answer that, we need to think back to the beginning of my speech this afternoon. What were YOUR reactions to a situation where you were made to feel alienated? Earlier, we said that it sponsored in us a feeling of being left out, a feeling of personal unworthiness because we did not understand, an anger aimed toward the speaker, and a firm resolution on our part to "tune out" the offensive bore who stood before you.

If this is our reaction, then we can only assume that the parent, faced with a similar situation, must react in kind. Surely, the parent, faced with "educationalese," must find himself first wondering what the teacher or administrator is talking about; must conclude, either consciously or subconsciously, that he is being purposely left out of the dialogue; that this person before him must have something to hide or has some darker purpose for not speaking and communicating to him; and, finally, must come to the decision, for the sake of his integrity, to simply "turn off" the teacher or administrator with whom he is faced.

Who suffers from that situation? The answer is, "everyone." The teacher or administrator suffers from loss of parental support and, eventually, the support of the community at large for the schools who insist on keeping them in the dark; who do not communicate. The parent suffers from those feelings of alienation mentioned before, as well as from the frustration he feels as his child continues to face difficulties in school which he is virtually powerless to do anything about. And, most importantly of all, the child suffers because the liaison between the home and the school that might have worked so well to solve whatever problems the child may have been having, never gets off the ground. So, the home and school cease to communicate, and the child declines more and more. That's who suffers—everyone!

Yet, we in education are used to problems. We face them every day. If the problem exists, there is no one more apt to find a solution than educators.

Therefore, may I suggest that we all remember that we are the roots of our own problem in this respect. May I further suggest that our solution to the problem is as close as our classrooms.

If we merely treat parents and community members with the same approach we use with our students, we will have eliminated the problem of communication overnight. We speak plainly to our students, and we don't leave them until we are certain that they understand. Of course we are polite to them; of course we try never to insult a student or make that student feel lacking in self-esteem; but, of course, we speak our minds clearly and plainly as we seek not to place blame but to work together for a solution to a common problem.

We do this with our students, and it will work equally well when dealing with our students' parents. Let us speak to them in plain terms of what goes on in the classroom; if we have a problem with their son or daughter, let's tell them plainly what the problem is, what the child has done or continues to do, what effect it is having on the child and the other children in the class. Then, let us work with the parent to establish a plan, clearly understood by parent and teacher alike, whose goal will be to remedy the situation and help the child.

I firmly believe that in this world we get back what we give out. If we are obtrusive in our speech and confusing to the people we serve, then we must expect a lack of understanding and cooperation in return. But, if we make every effort to make ourselves plainly understood, and if we enter into meaningful communication, then we have every right to expect that cooperation between home and school which will help us help our children even better.

All we need do is to put ourselves into the other party's shoes. If we were there to talk about our child, would we want buzzwords and catch phrases, or would we want action? I think the answer is obvious. The first gets us nothing but frustration and lack of accomplishment, while the second implies two equal partners working together for the good of the child. That's what I would want for my child. I can do no less as an educator than try to provide that for the children within my care.

Let each of us resolve, here and now, that he or she will make as much effort toward clear communications with parents as he or she makes for understanding within the classroom. With such a resolve and with such an effort, we cannot fail but benefit ourselves, our parents, and our students.

Finally, let me say that in achieving the zenith of interpersonal relations whereby a necessary surcease of verbal intercourse becomes a necessity, I am struck by the vagaries of chance in which it is my quintessential desire that the audience participate to the utmost.

In other words, goodbye and good luck.

SPECIAL DATA: *Time of speech: fifteen to sixteen minutes. Proper communication between the home and the school is one of our pet concerns. This speech mirrors that concern and addresses the question in a straightforward manner. Nonetheless, it is humorous and entertaining, and the first paragraph never fails to set up the audience for a very practical example of what is coming. In fact, the reversion to verbosity at the end of the speech never fails to bring a laugh and a large round of applause. This is a speech that goes over well with the faculty of a school, no matter what the level of the school may be.*

91

TOPIC: **Discipline in the schools.**

AUDIENCE: **Adults; all educators; suitable for any group at any level.**

Good evening, ladies and gentlemen.

Do you remember the woodshed? That was the place, according to several reliable sources, where your father took you when it was reported that you had misbehaved. Once there, Dad took his razor strap, a rather sturdy leather device used for honing Dad's straight razor, and proceeded to apply it to the seat of your consciousness until you saw the light of reason and promised to mend your ways.

All this happened in the "good old days," of course. Dad worked from sun to sun and mother's work was never done. Mother ran the house, seeing to it that meals were hot and on time and that the children were clean and presentable. Dad went to work each day, made the money, budgeted it out, and saw to it that the children were instilled with proper moral values.

When it was reported that you, as a child, had misbehaved in some way, be it firing a spitball at a classmate or the all but unforgivable crime of "sassing" the teacher, it was Dad's duty to help you mend your ways and set you on the path to righteousness. Usually, this consisted of a trip to the woodshed with Dad and application of "razor strap" logic.

If you listen closely to the people who tell you of these times, they will assert that everything was better then. Yes, your dignity smarted from time to time, but you behaved; you listened. If you misbehaved in school, the punishment you received there was nothing compared to what awaited you at home. If nothing else, you learned to "respect" your elders; you learned to behave.

Nowadays, things are different. Today, they point out, if a child misbehaves, nothing is done. Not only is there no punishment in school, but, if you inform the home, the parents' reaction is often to contact their lawyer to see if they can sue you for cruel and unusual punishment because you kept their child after school. Yes, they will point out, things were definitely different, and better, back in those "good old days."

Now, I would make a safe assumption that there are few in this audience who have not heard this philosophy voiced; who have not heard the schools taken to task for weak or loose discipline; who have not been captive audiences to diatribes on the problems of discipline in American schools.

I say this, because year after year, in poll after poll, the problem of discipline in the schools continues to head the list of the American public's concerns about education.

It is only natural, therefore, that almost everyone has a solution to the problem. Chief among them, or so it seems to me, is the woodshed philosophy and the razor-strap logic.

There's only one problem with that. When was the last time you even saw a woodshed? When was the last time you used a razor strap? The woodshed has been replaced by oil, gas, and electric heating systems. The razor strap has given way to the safety razor with disposable blades or the electric contraption you merely plug into the wall. In short, the times have changed.

Nor do I assert that they have changed in terms of technology alone. Certainly we are living in an age of technological revolution. Television, computers, rockets into space—these and more have inalterably changed the way we live. Advances in medicine and medical care have lessened the infant mortality rate and added years to the average lifespan. The automobile, the train, the airplane have enlarged our circle of operations and made the world our back yard. Yes, technology has opened up a new and more physically pleasing and comfortable world to each and every one of us. But, that is only a part of the whole; that is only half of the picture.

Along with the changes and improvements in technology have come changes in the social aspect of our lives as well. While I would be a fool to state that bigotry and prejudice have disappeared from the scene, we continue to see new and hopeful signals that it is lessening. In those "good old days," such practices as separate facilities for different racial groups or job ads stating that no one of a particular nationality need apply were common practices. Today, when we see such things in old movies or read about them in books it makes us uncomfortable; it makes us flinch. And, it is that feeling of uneasiness, that flinching, which is the hopeful sign—the sign that those practices are relegated to the past forever.

In short, if we look at the totality of those "good old days," they don't seem so "good" after all.

Which brings us back to discipline in the schools. Was it really so "good" after all?

There is a song with which you are all familiar. The least I can do is spare you my singing of it, but you all know the words. They go:

> School day, School days,
>   Dear old Golden Rule days;
> Reading and writing and 'rithmetic
>   Taught to the tune of the hickory stick...

What does that mean? What image does it conjure up? What does it tell us about discipline and education in those "good old days?"

Let's look at it part by part.

The image that we get of the old-time schoolmaster comes to us from etchings and drawings of that time. We see him or her standing before a class. In the background is his desk and in one corner is a conical-shaped hat along with a long, thin rod—the "hickory stick" of the song. The hat was the "dunce cap." When a child couldn't learn something, failed a test or quiz, or had difficulty comprehending a subject, the child would be sat in a corner with this "dunce cap" upon his head. Thereafter, he became the object of ridicule and derision by his classmates. This "teaching device" actually told him how stupid and worthless he was. It must have really helped his learning. And the rod in the corner—well, that was taken from a hickory tree for a very sound reason. You see, hickory is a very tough wood. It has a great deal of flexibility, but it will not break easily. This made it ideal for its purpose. It could be brought down with stinging, searing force time and time again upon the flesh of a child with the certain knowledge that while the flesh may give away and blister and bleed, the stick would remain whole for the next time it would be used.

Did I hear a groan? Did I hear someone out there becoming ill at the thought of this practice? I certainly hope so. The thought of this turns our stomachs, as well it should. Indeed, if we, as educators, knew of a single instance of this type of barbarity, I have no doubt that each of us would not only be outraged, but we would be actively engaged in seeing to it that the perpetrator never taught in any classroom again.

By our standards and by our enlightened consciousness, such a practice would be as unthinkable as putting a razor strap on the bathroom wall to sharpen our electric razors or asking the heating oil delivery man to pour the fuel into a shed some fifty yards behind our house.

The times have changed, and society has changed along with them. We are faced today with areas of knowledge and perceptions that did not exist thirty years ago. Reading and writing and arithmetic continue to be the basics for all children. But they are only a part of the curriculum, and how they have changed. Children learn computer math; a child with dyslexia is no longer given up as hopeless, but can be taught to read; the literature taught in schools has begun to reflect the diversity and complexity of the society in which we live. Even foreign languages, once thought a luxury or a mark of good breeding, are fast becoming a necessity for communication and understanding in our ever-shrinking world.

So, too, has our philosophy and approach to discipline changed. If the goal of discipline is merely to get an individual to conform, to sit quietly and cause no ripple in the pond, to say nothing and speak only when spoken to and then in short sentences mirroring only what we have taught them to say, then perhaps the hickory stick and the razor strap were pretty good tools. Fear is always a motivational force. If, however, our goal in discipline is to instill self-discipline in the child that will serve the child all of his life, to instill in the child an appreciation for his own uniqueness and at the same time an appreciation of the uniqueness of those around him, to get the child to think and respond and respect the rights of others and develop to his fullest potential, then those tools we mentioned before are horrors which we cannot afford to have in any classroom.

But, let us not make the mistake that many people in the general public make. Let us not confuse the type of discipline we are talking about with an open license to allow children to do whatever they please. That is not what true discipline means. That is not what we, in education, wish to achieve.

Let us state, unequivocally, that one student who walks down the hallway of a school in fear of his safety or one teacher who pauses at the door of his classroom because he is uncertain that he will survive the class without injury, is one student too many; one teacher too many. A school that has become a battleground is no longer a school. A person who uses a knife to terrorize or harass another person is an enemy of society and must be removed from society for the good of everyone else. This is true whether the perpetrator is thirteen or thirty; whether it takes place in a back alley or a classroom.

But, fortunately, this is not the rule. This is the exception, the gaudy, screaming exception that makes the nightly TV news or the evening headlines. Of course, it only has to happen to you, personally, once, to have it affect your entire life and career. Therefore, we, as educators, must support every effort to get young criminals out of the schools and into places where, if they cannot be helped, at least they cannot interfere with those who can be reached; who can be helped; who can be changed into productive adults.

What the papers do not report, what the TV moderator does not tell you, are the stories that take place in the classrooms, the millions of classrooms across our nation, each and every day. They do not tell you about the bully who no longer picks on children because some teacher has taken the time to work with him day after weary day until a breakthrough occurs. They do not tell you about the child who no longer steals because his teacher cared enough to make a conscious and concerted effort to get him to change. They do not tell you about the daydreamer who discovered, with a teacher's help, the joy of learning. They do not tell you about the child with difficulties at home who is held and comforted and given the strength to overcome those home problems. This will never make your TV screen; this will never make page one of the local paper.

Of course they won't, because these triumphs aren't sensational enough; they don't chill your spine; they don't allow you to break out in derision of the system that produces them. Perhaps if we turned the tables and began to criticize the public, we might wonder aloud at an audience that prefers to hear about failures rather than successes.

It is true that the knife-wielding teenage terrorist is our failure, as much as the child who no longer takes his classmate's pencil is our triumph. If we concentrated on the first to the exclusion of the second, perhaps we might, in time, bemoan the state of life and long for a time when control was uppermost in everyone's mind.

But, let's not do that; let's not fall into that trap. Let's make every effort to keep it all in perspective.

We are educators. That's a proud word. Our task, our mission if you will, is to educate the children of America. We must see to it that every child who comes within our purview is helped and encouraged to reach out and strive to become the very best that he is capable of being. We must see to it that the child who stands before us becomes a productive and responsible adult. This we must do. We must teach.

And how do we teach? I contend that we teach more by example than all the assignments we may ever give from a textbook. We teach by the way we relate to our students as much or more than we teach by drills and practice exercises. We teach by personal warmth, care, and concern far better than with the aid of any film projector or tape recorder.

And what do we teach? Of course we can control a child by force. We are bigger and stronger. We can control that way, but what do we teach when we do? Do we teach the child that might is the right; that force and pain are the answers to all problems; that striking out physically is the only way to settle a difficulty? Is this what we teach? Of course we can ridicule and blame and point fingers. We have the intelligence to verbally destroy anyone in the class. We can control that way, but what do we teach when we do? Do we teach a child that he is unworthy; that he has not the capabilities of achieving; that he must stop trying and begin drawing attention to himself in negative ways which, if they do not bring praise, will at least bring notice? Is this what we teach?

Or, have we learned from the past? Have we learned that if we approach our students with love, they learn what love means? Have we learned that if we refuse to give up on a child, the child learns not to give up on himself? Have we learned that firmness based on concern for the child's welfare rather than concern for toe-the-mark conformity helps the child to internalize what has been taught by example and apply what he has learned to the rest of the world?

We hope that is what we teach, day after day, in class after class, to child after child.

It's not easy. Of course it's not easy. Anyone who told you it would be has lied to you. We know that. We work, we strive, we succeed and sometimes we fail. We get discouraged. We take upon ourselves the problems and concerns of our students, and sometimes the burden is overwhelming. We get caught up in the daily record-keeping chores and there often seems very little time to care about Billy and Mary and Jimmy. We listen to people criticize and blame and tell us what is wrong, and we get discouraged and downhearted.

Yes, this happens. We all know it. But, we know something else as well. We know that because we are educators and because we do care, we refuse to give up. We get knocked down and dirtied, but we pick ourselves up and dust ourselves off and we rush back into the fray. We fail, but we try again, and after the one hundred and first failure with a kid, we see a little glimmer, a small success, and we are back at it as hard and tireless as ever before. It may well be that the child will never know in his entire life what you have done for him, but you will know. You will know that because you taught love, that child will know how to express that love to others in his adult years. You will know that because you took the time and trouble to correct what you perceived to be a destructive habit in the child's personal growth, the adult will no longer display that habit. You will know that because you worked with that child not on the basis of pain and fear but out of concern, the adult will work with others on the same basis of care and concern. The child and the adult may never consciously realize what has taken place, but you will know. And, for a true educator, that is enough.

So, when we are faced with someone who bemoans the state of discipline in our schools; when we are faced with those who long for the days of the woodshed and the razor strap; when we are faced with a philosophy that aims at conformity at any price, let's hear them out. Then let's make our opinions known as well. Let's tell them that we subscribe to and praise a discipline that teaches love rather than fear. Let's tell them that control is necessary in every classroom, but that it must be a control based on reason and steeped in understanding, so that it will carry over beyond the bell ending the session, beyond the end of the school day, into the real world of the child's life now and tomorrow.

Let us tell them this, and let us tell them one other thing as well. Let us tell them that we are educators and we love our children. Let us tell them that love means discipline, but a discipline aimed at the total growth of the total child and a discipline grounded in doing what is best for the child, while reinforcing those values we hope to instill in the adult that child will one day become.

Let's make an effort to get that person to use the razor strap to sharpen kitchen knives, which will help to prepare the food that will nourish his family's bodies. Let's see if we can get him to chop that woodshed into kindling for use in the fireplace, where it will warm his family and touch their hearts and souls.

Thank you for listening, and good night.

SPECIAL DATA: *Time of speech: approximately twenty minutes. It is true that discipline in the schools consistently heads the list of the public's concern about education, so it stands to reason that the educator has heard from many sources about this topic. This speech is well-received, not only because it strikes a respondent chord in the audience's mind, but because it reaffirms the general principles of care and concern that drove most people to become educators in the first place. While there is very little humor in this speech, it is dramatic enough to hold the attention of any audience of educators.*

92

TOPIC: **Educators and public image.**

AUDIENCE: **Adults; all educators; almost all administrators.**

(SPECIAL NOTE: Although this speech is aimed primarily at public school administrators, there is no reason why, with modifications that will become obvious as you read it, it could not be delivered effectively to any group of educators.)

Ladies and gentlemen, good evening, and thank you for having me. It's a pleasure to join you.

A few weeks ago I went through a very humbling experience which I think it appropriate to share with you. I was working in my garden one Saturday morning when I heard some voices coming from the other side of a hedge. I recognized them at once as my son and several of his playmates. It became obvious that they were talking about their fathers and what they did to earn a living. What could I do? I eavesdropped.

I listened as one boy told how his father was a lawyer and helped people who were in trouble. Another lad described how his father worked hard at being a policeman and catching bad guys so they didn't hurt anybody. And, so it went. Each boy described how hard his father worked. Finally, it was my son's turn, and I must admit that I leaned a little closer.

"Well," said my son, "I don't think my Dad does any work; he's a school principal!"

Yes, I can laugh along with you now, but at the time, I can tell you that I experienced the agony of defeat.

Nor could I really let it drop. It bothered me that my son perceived his father as not working. So, later that day, I had a little talk with him. I asked him, point-blank, what he thought I did all day in school.

"I know," he said, beaming. "You walk around the halls."

Taking a very deep breath, I continued, "Well, sometimes. But, let me put this another way. Do you think your teacher works very hard?"

"Oh, sure," he answered. "Mr. Tomkins corrects all our papers, and he teaches us things, and he helps us work on projects, and he stays after school and helps us. Yeah, he works hard."

Now I was getting somewhere. "Well," I went on, "what does the principal of your school do?"

"I don't know. The only time I see her is when she's walking up and down in the halls. That's what you do, right?"

That agony of defeat was beginning to creep in again.

So, I explained what I did as a principal. I tried to keep it at my son's level of understanding, of course, and that wasn't easy as I tried to explain the intricacies of budgets, curriculum meetings, coordination of departments and monthly reports, and the dozens of other matters that concern us as administrators.

When I had finished, my son looked up at me and said, "I didn't know you did that. Wait 'til I tell the guys."

So, that problem was solved, at least temporarily.

But, it set me to thinking. I began to wonder exactly how we, all of us, were perceived by others outside of education. What, I wondered, was the public's opinion of what we administrators did all day in school. My son thought all I did was walk around the halls of the school all day, because that was the only time he had occasion to see his principal. To another student who might have behavioral problems in school, was a principal's job nothing more than waiting in the office for students who had misbehaved and then assigning detentions or suspensions? To the PTA president, was a principal's job nothing more than acting as an aide at fund-raising activities? In short, how well did the general public understand exactly what a school administrator did?

I didn't then, and I don't now consider this a frivolous question. As public school administrators, we are public employees. The public is our boss, and through their taxes and support, we get paid. It is also up to the public to approve or disapprove school budgets which might be necessary to implement the educational plans we have been instrumental in formulating for our schools. Unless they perceive us as performing valuable functions and working hard, might they not think twice about voting in a budget that would, in effect, increase the taxes they would have to pay out?

Look at it this way. Suppose you hired a gardener to landscape an area by your home. Now suppose every time you looked out your window you saw that gardener lying under a tree smoking a cigarette. Let's further suppose that two weeks go by and the only thing that happened to your property was the planting of one shrub. Now let's suppose that the gardener comes to you and tells you that before he proceeds any further, he wants a raise. What do you think your reaction would be?

We know exactly what it would be. We'd ask what he had done to merit that raise. We'd want to know what he had produced. We'd tell him that we didn't see him working; that we couldn't see any results. We might, indeed, be rather indignant that he would ask for a raise in pay when we couldn't see that he had done anything.

Is there not a parallel here? When the general public is faced with that voting booth in which they will approve or disapprove the school budget for the next year, might they not be asking, "What have you done to merit this raise?"

And, if their perception of our jobs, of the work we do, is relegated to an image of someone who occasionally leaves his comfortable office to aimlessly roam the halls of the school, how do you perceive that they will vote?

The answer is obvious. You don't pay for something you can't see and don't recognize as important.

Of course we know how hard we work. We know, only too well, the long days, the thankless plodding through paperwork, the endless meetings, the frustration, the disappointments, the long and laborious tasks that are the world of the school administrator. We know that our day begins ten minutes before we are ready for it and ends hours after we thought it had.

We know this because we are part of it; because we live it each and every day. We don't have to be told how hard we work. The public, however, does.

Let's face one overwhelming fact. The schools cannot exist without the support of the public, and, just as in our analogy with the gardener, they are not going to long support something which they perceive as unproductive.

Lest we get discouraged, however, I assure you that this is not an insurmountable obstacle; it is not a problem without a solution. Rather, it is a challenge to each and every one of us. It is a challenge which we can meet.

We are, after all, educators. We are in the positions we hold because we know how to educate; we know how to teach. Therefore, the answer is simple—let's educate; let's teach the public about what goes on in school.

That doesn't mean standing on the street corner and telling every stranger we meet how hard we work. But it does mean making a concerted effort to enhance our image in the mind of the public when the opportunity presents itself.

Take, for example, one of the best public relations tools an administrator can have—the parent newsletter. It is what its name implies. A letter-type sheet or sheets which is sent home to the parents of the children in a school. It can run anywhere from one to five sheets in length and can come out anywhere from twice a month to once every marking period.

What's in it? Anything and everything that will put the school in a favorable light.

Did your team win a game? Put it in. Is there a play or choral recital or special exhibit coming up? Put it in. Have the children in a particular class written some poems, made a special bulletin board, volunteered to do tutoring in a lower grade? Put it in. Has a teacher or administrator distinguished himself in some way, gotten a new degree, published something? Put it in.

In short, put in that newsletter all the good things that are happening around your school that would otherwise have gone unnoticed unless you communicated them to your audience.

Don't forget one other vital part of any newsletter—a personal message from you as the school's administrator. That is, perhaps, the most important and most difficult part of all. It is, however, the part that will do you the most good in achieving a positive public image.

The keynotes of that message must be honesty and sincerity. Here, you must speak directly to the parents as if you were talking to old friends. Picture the audience as sitting across from you at a table. They have just asked you what is new, and you are about to tell them. Since they are friends, you won't talk down to them or patronize them; you won't make everything seem rosy when it is not; you won't try to make them believe that your school, uniquely in this entire world, exists without problems. What you will do, however, is speak to them plainly and directly. You'll tell them what is good, what needs improvement, and what you are doing to bring about that improvement. You'll tell them what you have achieved and what you hope to achieve in the future. You'll tell them of the obstacles in your way and how you are going to surmount those obstacles.

The best rule of all is to be yourself. If you are normally humorous, be humorous. If you are normally serious, be serious. Just be yourself and let your personality come through. Share with them your hopes and aspirations; your triumphs and failures; your joys and your sorrows. Just be yourself.

Do you know what you will find? You will find an image beginning to form in the minds of the public about you and your school. If you have been warm, honest, and sincere with them, you will find that the image is one of warmth and confidence in their school and in you. That shouldn't be surprising, for what you have done is to make them a part of the school. You have made it their school instead of just the place where their children go for several hours every day.

And what will this mean to you? First, it will mean a good and basic rapport with the parents, which, as we are all well aware, pays dividends when we are faced with contacting them for any one of a variety of reasons. Second, it will mean parental and community support of your school. As parents become convinced of the worth of the school, it is only natural that they will tell others in the community who may not be directly connected to the school via children attending them. Good will spreads. Finally, it will mean support of you and the educational programs and plans you have made for your school. Put enough of that support and good will together, and—who knows—you may just see the next school budget passed overwhelmingly.

Of course it doesn't happen overnight. A good public image for you and your school is something that must be worked at. Besides public relations vehicles such as that newsletter, the administrator must take every opportunity to speak to groups of parents and community members. At sporting events, at school visitations, at school plays and art exhibits—wherever groups of parents and concerned citizens gather. Keep the speech short and simple, but let the same rules that guided your message in the parent newsletter guide you here as well. Be sincere and let your personality show through.

Get your message across. If, for example, you are at a school art exhibit, praise the students, the art teachers and the parents who helped to make this possible. Tell how you feel about the great job that was done. Just think what they could have accomplished if they had that new art room? In any event, with the less than perfect conditions they have at present, this show is nothing short of phenomenal, and they are all to be praised.

You get the idea. You can praise their accomplishments, show everybody there how great a school you have, and still get in your message to support the referendum that will allow your school to install the new art room. The message, believe me, is not lost on the parents. It will be carried over to the community at large as well.

I am well aware that this does not come easily. We are, for the most part, fairly refined individuals. It goes against our basic natures to brag or to say, in effect, look at what I have accomplished; look at what I have done for you and for the students of this school.

Yet, it behooves us to remember that the brightest diamond in the world, if it remains locked in some rock formation hundreds of feet below the earth's surface, will never be seen, never be admired, never be appreciated for the beauty it contains.

It is exactly the same thing for us and our schools. We are there every day. We see what goes on. We are aware of the fine quality of education that is taking place in our classrooms. We know of the selfless dedication of our faculty and staff. We see the growth and discovery that takes place in our children. We live the arduous and time-consuming work that is necessary on our part to shape the school into the vital entity that it is.

But, and this is the point of it all, unless others know about it, it will remain hidden. The school will remain "that place" rather than "our place." Parents and community members will remain cool. Budgets will come and the reaction will be "so what?" Like the diamond of which we spoke, the beauty of it all will go unappreciated and unsung.

Therefore, let us make a distinction. Let the distinction be between those who shout and fuss and draw attention to themselves in order to show the world how important they are and those who praise what is around them, point out what is good and fine, educate the community to the positive things that are happening in their schools. We are not the first, for we seek no sensationalism, nor do we seek personal aggrandizement. Let us rather be the second. We are but mirrors, reflecting for the public the image of the schools that we have come to know so well and which we feel a need to share with others. We neither need nor want people to tell us how fantastic we are, but we do need and want people in the community to recognize the schools for what they are—to see their accomplishments, to feel their needs, and, perhaps most importantly of all, to act in their behalf.

So, let us not think of public relations as something better relegated to a Madison Avenue advertising executive; as something akin to a toothpaste commercial on TV. Rather, let us see it for what is is—a tool, a very valuable tool, which is part of our kit of tools that we use to create, maintain, upgrade and build our schools into the finest places they are capable of becoming. This is part and parcel of our duty as administrators, a duty we cannot shirk if we are to accomplish our purpose.

We do not face an easy task. With sensational stories of crime and violence and degradation in the schools shouting at us from every news stand; with TV programs and magazine "exposés" on what's wrong with our schools exploding into the living room; with children running home to tell about the fight that took place in the halls without ever mentioning how that day they conquered fractions; with all these bombarding parents and the community, the community is well aware of the negative aspects of school. Our duty now is to educate that same community about the positive and good things that are happening. We must show them the good and the kindness and the dedication; we must show them the learning and the growth; we must show them what's right with our schools!

It can be done, but it is up to each and every one of us. Let us be spreaders of good news. Let us draw attention to what our schools are accomplishing. Let us tell everyone of our needs and our progress and our hopes for tomorrow.

We are educators—let us educate!

And, the very next time that someone comes up to you and says, "What's new?" for goodness sake—tell him!

Thank you for your attention, and good night.

SPECIAL DATA: *Time of speech: approximately eighteen minutes.*

Obviously, this is a formal speech to be given at some academic function. It can be cut to a shorter time and used effectively in a less formal setting, but its message is aimed at educators and the need for garnering public support for the schools through the effective use of public relations.

The message is very clear-cut and dynamic, and there have been favorable comments about its inspirational nature.

As we indicated at the beginning of this speech, with certain obvious modifications, this could be effectively delivered to any group of educators, not just administrators.

93

TOPIC: **We Are What We Teach.**

AUDIENCE: **Adults; all educators, administrators and teachers.**

Good evening, ladies and gentlemen, thank you for your very kind reception.

I'd like you to picture a scene. There is mass confusion in a small room; from the back of that room a booming noise echoes as a stack of boxes falls to the ground; sheets of paper are flying in the air and fluttering downward; in one corner, a child sits weeping; on a hard, wooden chair, a grown man sits with his head in his hands.

Is this the climactic scene from some Hollywood disaster movie? An air-raid shelter in a TV drama about a war? The part in a science fiction thriller where the aliens invade Earth? No, it is none of these. Rather, it is a fairly accurate description of what my classroom looked like some ten minutes after the opening of school on the first day of my teaching career.

I grant you, that was some time ago, but the memory is crystal clear. Indeed, I have spoken to hundreds of educators over the years, and if there is one thing we all have in common it is that memory of the first day in the classroom.

Understandably, things got better. I learned to organize and plan, to assign duties, to speak clearly and make myself understood, to head off potential discipline problems before they occurred; I learned how to soothe the pain, stop the hurt, control the class and get on with the business of learning. I learned as every teacher in every school has learned.

On that first day, however, I would not have given you two cents for my chances of lasting out the week. "Discouragement" was a positive word compared to how I felt as I dragged myself into the Teacher's Lounge at the end of that devastating day. I don't believe that I was ever at a lower point. Nothing had gone right—everything had gone wrong. I was a mess.

I suppose it must have shown, because an older teacher in the school came over to sit by me and had the mercy and sensitivity not to ask how things had gone. I don't how long she sat there before she finally spoke to me, but when she did, she said, "Today, I taught my kids that it's all right to make mistakes."

"What?" I mumbled, coming out of my fog.

"That you can make mistakes and still learn," she continued. "I had passed out books and given an assignment before I realized that they were the wrong books, much too difficult for them. I had to collect the whole batch, put them away, get out the correct books, pass them out, record them all over again, and teach and give a new assignment. It destroyed my entire morning schedule."

"But how did that teach them anything?" I asked.

She gave me a look over the top of her glasses; a look such as must have shaken many a potential classroom bully, and said, "Because I told them that I had made a mistake, of course. I told them precisely what I had done and asked for their suggestions as to how we could put away the wrong books and get the right ones in the best possible manner. They told me; I listened; we did it, and everything went fairly well. After it was all straightened out, I thanked them for their help, and we had a very productive talk about what to do when you make a mistake. It was an excellent learning situation."

"You mean," I stammered, "that you told them that *you* were wrong?"

"Young man," she responded, flaring her nostrils in my direction, "we are what we teach!"

I didn't quite understand the statement at that time, but I realized that she had taught me something. If she could make a mistake and profit from it, perhaps I could, too. I went home and thought about what I had and had not done in class on that first horrendous day. I planned for the next day; I organized; I discarded what had not worked; I tried to learn from what I had done wrong.

The second day was better than the first. The third was better than the second, and each day thereafter was better still. The classroom became a better place for me to be, and, by projection, it became a better place for my students as well.

The grand lady in question has passed away now, but her words stay with me, particularly that statement with which she ended our first conversation—"We are what we teach."

At first it confused me, because I took it literally. How, I would think, could we be history and math and English grammar? That's not me. I teach that to my classes, but I can't be equated with my subject matter. What had she meant?

I found out because of a very bad joke. I remember that a student came up to me and was anxious to share a "funny story" he had heard. You know how this happens—students always tell their teachers jokes. The story he told me, however, was obscene. No, not the type of obscenity with vulgar words and twisted sexual connotations—I think I could have handled that—but the type of obscenity which is racial in form; which denigrates and debases members of another race.

I remember that I wanted to be very careful in reacting to this child's story. It suddenly struck me that if I showed approval in any way, I was strengthening a racial prejudice that would grow into a destructive force in the child's life. At the same time, I was aware that open hostility and castigation on my part would have done no good either, merely showing him that I had more power and also showing him how to upset and "get to" me. So, I thought a while before I reacted.

I didn't smile or frown. I asked him to explain the "joke." I asked him if he thought that it was true. Frankly, the story had been anti-black, and I asked him if he thought that Mr. Harris, a very popular black teacher in our school, was like the person in the story. Of course, the child said no, and I asked him to put himself in Mr. Harris' place and consider how he would feel if someone told that "joke." Finally, I explained that the trouble with those and all racial and ethnic jokes was that they made everybody of a particular race or nationality seem stupid or bad, and that simply wasn't true. I put my arm around him and asked him what he thought he would do if he heard another story like that. I got the response I had hoped for, and I hugged him all the harder.

That was not the end of the incident, however. About three weeks later, I was standing hall duty when I overheard a conversation. One boy was telling another story very similar to the one I just described. When the first boy had finished, however, the second boy did not laugh. Instead, he began to tell the first boy what was wrong with racial jokes. He expressed himself in words almost exactly like those I had used three weeks earlier.

What was amazing to me, however, was that the lad who had just set straight his joke-telling companion was not the one I had spoken to earlier. Rather, it was a classmate of the boy who had been standing near my desk at the time of the first incident and must have overheard the conversation.

There is an old saying which goes that, in school, children learn not only what is taught, but what is caught. This boy overheard what I said to another student, and the message sunk in. He internalized it to the point where he was living it.

That set me to thinking. What if I had laughed at the first story or let it go or even ignored it? In doing that would I have taught my students that that kind of prejudice was acceptable? Would I have given tacit approval for that type of attitude and feeling in their future lives? If I had reacted in a prejudiced manner, would I have taught prejudice? I believe that I would have. I believe that in trying to overcome prejudice, I did, if only in this one boy.

The words came back to me: "We are what we teach."

Yes, we teach history; yes, we teach science; yes, we teach parts of speech and composition techniques, but yes, we also teach our opinions of life and the quality of it; yes, we also teach our hopes and fears; yes, we also teach a standard of morality.

Certainly, there is a difference in the way we teach these things. The first we teach with blackboard and textbook and questions and quizzes, while the second we teach in far more subtle ways. The second we teach in our reactions, in our attitudes, in our day-to-day lives, both inside and outside the classroom, in our daily dealings with our students and colleagues.

And the words come back to me now: "We are what we teach."

What, for instance, do you hate? Do you hate being inconvenienced? Do you hate having to go out of your way to help someone? Do you hate having to deal with someone who is "different" in any way? Do you hate children who plague you with questions?

If you do, then this is what you will teach your children. You will teach them not to care about others, because other people are only a bothersome inconvenience. You will teach them that "different" means "wrong," and the best way to handle a "different" person is to avoid him. You will teach that asking questions is stupid and a mark of stupidity, and the child will stop asking and stop learning.

But, now, what do you really hate? Do you hate injustice in any form? Do you hate bullying? Do you hate prejudice? Do you hate ignorance?

If you do, then this is what you will teach your children. You will teach them to be just in their dealings with others. You will teach them kindness and understanding for the people they will meet in life. You will teach them the necessity of love in a world where it is so badly needed. You will teach them the joy and the wonder of learning. This is what you will teach.

What's more, you will teach it without paper and pencil, without books and filmstrips, without lecture and test—you will teach it to them by living it in your own life and by being a real and active part of their lives while they are under your care.

And the words are stronger, now: "We are what we teach."

If there is a child in my room, and I dislike that child; I mistrust that child; I anticipate the bad that that child will do; I know how badly that child will perform on his classwork—then I will project that to the child; I will teach that child that he is untrustworthy; I will teach that child that he cannot learn; I will teach that child just how unworthy he is—and as certainly as the sunlight, that child will live up to my expectations of him.

If I have a child in my room, and I like that child for what he is or even for what he may be; if I strive to actively trust him and bring out the best that is in him; if I strive to fill him with knowledge, knowing that with help and understanding he can learn—then I will project that to the child as well; I will teach him that somebody cares about him; I will teach him that he is a person worthy of love; I will teach him that he can learn and that there is a joy in acquiring new knowledge; I will teach him to look at others in the same way I look at him—and that child, as surely as the one in the previous example, will live up to my expectations of him.

And the words echo in my mind: "We are what we teach."

As educators we have tried and succeeded; we have tried and failed. As educators, however, if we have failed, we have not given up, but we have tried again, and again if necessary, and again, and again. Through all this we have taught our students not to give up; to keep trying; to make mistakes, but to learn from those mistakes and go on. We have taught our students how to measure the square feet in a room, and, we hope, we have also taught them the measure of a full and productive life.

Teaching is a twenty-four-hour-a-day job. We are not teachers just for the hours we spend in the classroom; just for the days we spend in school. We are teachers after school, on weekends, and throughout our lives. We entered this profession willingly, because we believe in education and we believe in children and we believe in the future of which those children will be a part. If we project that belief in our personal lives, our students cannot help but learn that lesson well.

Let us hear the words: "We are what we teach."

I firmly believe that if we are kind, we will teach kindness, and we will receive kindness. If we make an effort to understand, we will teach understanding, and we will receive understanding. If we trust in the goodness of others, we will teach trust and goodness, and we will be trusted as a force for good in this world.

Most importantly of all, I believe that if we have within ourselves the capacity to love, and if we love our children every day, then we will teach love in the classroom in everything we do, and we will receive the love we teach in a thousand ways and with a thousand voices.

Of course it will not be easy. Of course there will be setbacks and times that will try our patience. Of course we will fail from time to time.

But, just as certainly, there will be successes and rewards that cannot be estimated in earthly terms. Of course, we can each resolve to do the very best of which we are capable in order to teach what we carry in our hearts as well as what we know in our minds.

Each of us has within that spark of compassion and concern and love that drove us into teaching in the first place. Each of us can fan that spark into a flame that will warm our classrooms and nurture our students now and in the future. We can teach them as one day they will be teaching others.

"We are what we teach."

And that can be magnificent.

Thank you, and good evening.

SPECIAL DATA: *Time of speech; approximately fourteen minutes.*

The simple truisms expressed in this speech are ones which we don't take out and examine often enough. This speech brings home what we all know as educators but do not express often enough.

This speech receives good reactions from all levels of education, both from administrators and teachers, for each seems to find within it something that touches their lives.

This speech should be delivered simply and straightforwardly, as it is dramatic enough of itself to carry the speaker.

AFTERTHOUGHTS

As we indicated in the introduction to this section, these speeches are aimed at educators. They involve education, and many times they refer to situations and aspects of school that only educators could fully appreciate. This does mean, however, that there is any reason why someone outside of education would not enjoy them as well.

The last speech in this section, for instance, was also given for a group of parents. It was announced that the speech had been delivered previously at a gathering of educators, and then it was given exactly as written here. It was tremendously well-received and prompted a very productive group discussion that followed.

Therefore, while these may be primarily aimed at only educators, you may find that some parts or even the entire speech may be suited to another audience.

SECTION SIX

A Variety of Speeches
That Inspire

Take an informal poll of your friends who are educators. Ask them why they entered education as a profession rather than something else. We would be willing to wager that a good percentage of them will say they became teachers because during their own education they met someone or had a teacher who inspired them to enter that field. We asked this once with a group of 100 educators and 73 of them claimed the inspiration of a teacher as a major reason why they became educators.

The quality of inspiration cannot be taken lightly. How many acts of heroism and valor have occurred because someone has inspired another? We will never know, of course, but we can well recognize that inspiration is a noble and powerful force when used for good and wholesome purpose.

Giving an inspirational speech can be difficult. What may work for one need not necessarily work for another. There are, however, certain basics that are part of all inspirational speaking.

First and foremost, the speaker must be sincere. He must believe in what he is saying and project that belief to the audience. Next, the speaker must believe that he is helping the audience. That sincere desire to communicate valuable insights and information to the audience will also be communicated and cannot help but be assimilated by the listeners. Finally, the speaker must be enthusiastic. This is really an outgrowth of the first two.

If a speaker truly believes in what he is saying, if he truly believes that he is doing the audience a valuable service by speaking to them and communicating his thoughts, then he will be enthusiastic. He will approach the audience and the speech with a certain inner fire that cannot help but warm the audience. Enthusiasm is catching. Let the speaker possess it, and the audience cannot help but react.

Within this section, you will find a variety of speeches, both entire speeches as well as beginnings and closes of speeches, that are "inspirational" in nature. If you find one that suits your purposes, if you can fully believe in its contents, if you are anxious to communicate it to your next audience, then you will have the enthusiasm that will enable you to deliver a truly inspirational speech.

94

TOPIC: **All-purpose inspirational closing for a speech.**
AUDIENCE: **Suitable for all audiences.**

> *(SPECIAL NOTE: The following anecdote is particularly applicable to any speech where you are urging your audience to do something, to try something new, or to deal with an existing condition. Further suggestions follow the anecdote.)*

...Finally, I would like to tell you a story. It's about a wise man who lived long ago and very far away. This wise man was very kind and loving and was, consequently, much beloved by the people of this ancient land.

In this same land, there was a nobleman, a prince, who hated this wise man. He saw the wise man as taking from him the love of the people. The people listened to the wise man, not the prince, and that angered the prince beyond belief.

One day, the prince said to his followers, "I have a plan whereby I can discredit the wise man; a way in which I can make him appear to be a fool.

"Each day, the wise man goes to the marketplace where he speaks to the people and gives them advice. Tomorrow, when the people gather, I will go to the square disguised as a peasant. In my hand I shall hold a white dove. When the crowd has gathered, I shall raise my voice above the crowd and say, 'Wise man! I have a simple question for you. This dove which I hold in my hand—is it alive or dead?'

"Now, while this appears a simple question, it is not, for if he says it is dead, I will open my hand and let the bird fly away. If he says it is alive, however, I will crush the bird in my hand and let it fall dead to the ground. Either way, he will be mistaken; either way he will appear to have made a mistake; either way it will appear that he cannot even tell the difference between a living and a dead bird; either way he will be discredited in the eyes of the people and will lose their love."

The next day came, and true to his word, the prince disguised himself as a peasant and, taking a white dove, he went to the marketplace. There he waited until the crowd had gathered and the wise man had appeared. He made his way to the front of the crowd and raised his voice.

"Wise man!" he shouted. "I would ask you a simple question. This dove which I hold in my hand, is it alive or is it dead?"

The crowd grew quiet, and all eyes turned toward the wise man. The wise man paused, looked at the prince, and said, "That which you hold in your hand. It is...what you make of it."

It is what you make of it. A wise answer from a wise man. Whether the dove which the prince held was alive or dead depended upon the prince and what he did with what he had.

Tonight, I have told you about a new idea, a new concept, and now I leave it in your hands. What will we do with it? Will it be alive to soar and grow and flourish, or will it fall to the ground dead and unused?

In the words of the wise man, "It is what we make of it."

SPECIAL DATA: *Time of anecdote; approximately two minutes.*

> *We think you can see the value of this anecdote when used as the conclusion of a speech. You have given your audience some insights or a plan or a program, and now you place it in their hands. From this point on, it will be up to them. Working together, you can see to it that the plan succeeds or fails, but it is really up to you. It is what you make of it.*

> *Used in this manner, this inspirational ending of a speech has a tremendous impact upon any audience.*

95

TOPIC: **Inspirational closing.**

AUDIENCE: **Adults; some parents, but primarily educators.**

> *(SPECIAL NOTE: Again, this is meant as the closing remarks of a longer speech. Originally, this was part of a speech on discipline in the classroom, and we incorporated it into our book* The New Psychology of Classroom Discipline and Control. *We feel that it is strong enough to be used either by itself or as the conclusion of many types of speeches. The poem used in the speech is original with us, and it really bespeaks what we feel.)*

...So we come to the end of this evening and the end of this speech. If I have been able to share with you some observations on classroom discipline and control that will help you in the daily running of your classroom, then I am rewarded, indeed.

I'd like to leave you with one final thought, however. As this evening ends, your classes continue. What has been done in the past is just that— passed. What will happen in the future, from this day forward, depends on you.

I have one final thing to share with you. It is a poem that expresses our view of the teacher's part in education. I call it:

LET IT BEGIN WITH ME

The world's a disgrace and a terrible place,
  Or at least say the prophets of doom.
With fear all around and no peace to be found,
  It's a landscape of darkness and gloom.

There's hunger and doubt, and who cares about
  All the suffering, trial and pain;
And there seems not a place in the whole human race
  Where a soul can be happy again.

But that's not for me, for I can't help but see,
  With the dawning of each brand new day,
That there's hope in the smile of every child,
  And I just can't help feeling that way.

For the child of today is the person, they say,
  Who will fashion the world that's to come;
And I know that I can in that life take a hand,
  Shaping those who'll make tomorrow run.

So I pray that I'll reach every child I teach
  With the finest that mankind can give,
And instill in these youth a love for the truth
  Which will serve them wherever they live.

Let me teach them to know understanding and show
  A respect for each person they see;
Let me teach them as they will teach others some day—
  And let it begin with me!

The French scientist Louis Pasteur once wrote, "When I approach a child, he inspires me in two sentiments: tenderness for what he is, and respect for what he may become." Let us take those words to heart and learn to live by them. Each and every child is someone special. Some breeze through school with little or no difficulty, while others find trial and tribulation at every turn. Some children we would gladly adopt as our own, while others cause us to pound our heads in frustration. Some days are perfect and filled with the joy of teaching, while others are exercises in frustration and pain.

This is life, but we can have our say in how we will approach our students and direct their learning while they are in our classrooms.

Let us set out now to implement a new psychology of classroom discipline and control that will serve us all by bringing out the best we all have to offer. Let each of us commit himself again to the principles of education. Let each of us say in his heart:

> Let me teach them to know understanding and show
> A respect for each person they see;
> Let me teach them as they will teach others some day—
> AND LET IT BEGIN WITH ME!

SPECIAL DATA: *Time of closing: about three minutes.*

We really feel that every educator believes in the sentiments expressed in that poem. Certainly, it touches something within each of us that channeled us into education in the first place. We have yet to use it without receiving extremely positive comments from the audience.

The poem alone, without the rest of the speech, is also very effective when used with groups of parents.

Whatever use you may put it to, if you believe in its message, others will as well.

96

TOPIC: **Inspirational opening for a speech.**
AUDIENCE: **Suitable for all audiences.**

Good evening, ladies and gentlemen.

We are here this evening to discover. For a brief moment, bring your minds back to the first time you ever "discovered" something on your very own. Perhaps it was when you were very young and entailed something as simple as discovering that an object could float in water. Perhaps it was later in life as you struggled with the multiplication table until that magic moment when you suddenly "discovered" the reason behind it, and it all became clear. Whatever the occasion was for you, try to think back to that time and remember what you felt.

Whatever it was, there was a joy and an exhilaration in that discovery. Your mind rejoiced in its new knowledge, and something that had been incomprehensible suddenly became clear. It was the joy of learning, and, for that moment, it brightened your life. I know that was how it was for me, and I'd wager that you shared a similar experience.

Tonight, we are on the brink of discovery again. Through the ideas and insights that will be offered this evening, we will be in a position to open our minds to new avenues that may well lead each of us to "discover" a new aspect of knowledge and understanding. It is an opportunity to be cherished.

For, that is what we offer: not answers, but opportunities. Opportunities to open our minds; opportunities to expand our perspectives; opportunities to exchange our ideas and in that exchange to come to new understandings and appreciations.

It has been said that man, uniquely of all animals, has the ability to think. Of all the powers with which we have been endowed, surely that must be the greatest. The ability to think and to reason has lifted mankind from the mud and sent him to the stars. We, here tonight, have the wondrous opportunity to use our minds to discover each other and to share in that unique exchange of ideas that brings about the fulfillment of knowledge.

With open minds, hungry for ideas, let us begin our journey to discovery....

SPECIAL DATA: *Time of opening; about two minutes.*

This opening is particularly suited to the beginning of a program or panel discussion on a "hot" or controversial topic, which was how it was originally used. It might also be used effectively to introduce a very dynamic speaker or even a speech of your own that might contain some material with which the audience may find exception.

This opening exhorts your audience to view what follows with an open mind. As we are all aware, when presenting something of a controversial nature, this is the best for which we can hope. Try it and see.

97

TOPIC: **Inspirational speech on athletics.**
AUDIENCE: **Adults and students; educators and parents.**

There is something that I am NOT going to tell you.

I am not going to say that it doesn't matter if we win or lose. If I said that, I doubt that anyone here would believe me anyway. We know that winning is better, far better, than losing. We know the joy and the exhilaration that comes with success on the field, and we know the pain and the hurt that comes with losing. So, I am not going to tell you that it doesn't matter who wins. We want to win. We will try to win. And, it is the fervent hope of everyone here that we will win.

We have practiced; we have disciplined ourselves; we have worked for this day. You all know what it has entailed. You know the endless hours, the sore muscles, the fatigue, and you know the courage it took to keep on trying when everything within you told you to quit. Yes, you have worked for this day, and now, it is yours.

We will go out there and work as a team, as one body, to bring victory to our side. In my heart, I know that it will be ours.

But, while I have not told you that it matters not if we win or lose, I will tell you that it matters more than anything else how we play that game. We will win today, but we will win because we are the better team. We will win because we will make less mistakes than they will. We will win because we have worked harder, practiced longer, and sacrificed more.

We will go out there and we will play a hard game. We will give it everything we have. But, we will also play a clean game. We will learn to respect our opponents. We will learn to match our strength against theirs, to pit our knowledge against theirs, to try our cunning in the face of theirs. We respect them for what they are, as we know that they will respect us for what we are.

Because of this, if we fall, we will work all the harder to get up and go on. If things look bleak, we will not despair but will try all the more. If we are on the bottom we will know that the only way we can go is upward, and we will scramble and climb all the harder.

If one of their players should fall, I know that our players will be the first to offer their hands to help him up.

This is what makes us great. This is what gives us the determination to strive. This is what will give us the dedication needed to win.

We are ready. We are willing. We are able.

Now—let's go out there and win!

SPECIAL DATA: *Time of speech: about two or three minutes, depending on audience reaction.*

    This speech could be used effectively in a number of situations. It is a natural pre-game speech. It could be used at a pep rally before the "big" game. It might be used at an athletic banquet held toward the end of the season. It might even be used in the locker room.

You will notice that it is not the win-at-any-price philosophy, which has been so roundly condemned. Rather, it encourages players to dedicate themselves to giving the best they have to offer while making certain that they play cleanly and with a respect for their opponents. This is generally understood and appreciated by parents and fellow educators who hear it. This speech also builds naturally to its climax, and with the last words, you will have the audience standing and cheering and the team inspired to play their best.

98

TOPIC: **The role of the teacher in the inspirational process.**
AUDIENCE: **Adults; almost all educators.**

(SPECIAL NOTE: Up until now, we have presented parts of speeches that are inspirational in nature. The following is a full-length speech originally given as part of an in-service program. It is, as you will see, readily adaptable to most situations involving educators.)

Good afternoon, ladies and gentlemen.

"A teacher affects eternity; he can never tell where his influence stops...."

With these words, written in his autobiography, Henry Adams honored all educators. Indeed, the thought that what we do in the classroom may have implications weeks, months and even years later in the lives of our students, is very sobering, and it places a real and very heavy responsibility on the shoulders of the teacher.

Yet, I know of very few educators who do not accept this responsibility and accept it willingly and gladly. Teachers constantly work toward inspiring their students and exerting an influence that will, as Henry Adams stated, "affect eternity."

But, how do we inspire? How do we fire up our students to do their best and achieve all of which they are capable? Well, there is one way. There is one key element in all inspiration that is available to all of us— the quality of enthusiasm.

I know of a teacher who has a unique way of teaching the Civil War. On one day, he dresses in the full uniform of a Confederate soldier and gives the lesson as if he were a participant in the battle. The next day, he is dressed as a Union soldier, and he retells the lesson of the previous day, but this time from the Union soldier's point of view. It is really amazing; even his voice changes when he assumes the different characters. Moreover, he gives not only the facts of the battle he is discussing, but he provides insight into what daily life was like for a soldier, what it was like to load his rifle, and what his family was like at home. As you can well imagine, his class is enraptured, and no one daydreams during these lessons. Indeed, so popular were these lessons that a problem arose when students began sneaking out of other teachers' classes and tried to sneak in to attend the lecture.

Eventually, other teachers began to ask if they could bring their classes when these lessons were given. The last I heard, he was giving his presentation on the stage of the school's auditorium to several classes who eagerly look forward to the day.

Parents of the children in this teacher's class report that it is not unusual for them to get requests from their sons and daughters for birthday or holiday gifts like Bruce Catton's *Army of the Potomac* or a book of the photographs of Matthew Brady.

Here is the case of a teacher who has truly inspired his students in a specific subject area due largely to his personal enthusiasm and verve.

Wait a minute. Are you thinking that I'm suggesting that the only way to inspire is to put on a costume and makeup and put on your own show? Of course I'm not; not all of us are suited to this type of activity. Teachers, in general, are gregarious, but we're not all "hams." If you will analyze the anecdote, you will see that the main factor in the inspiration was not the acting but the enthusiasm that this teacher felt for his subject.

Indeed, enthusiasm is the key factor in all inspiration. If we are enthusiastic about something—anything—that enthusiasm is communicated to those around us. If you have ever been with someone who is "hot" about something, you will know what I mean. There is something catching about enthusiasm. If you are on fire, your students cannot help but feel the heat.

How do you become enthusiastic? I feel that it is a three-part process.

First, you learn it. Know your subject matter. Find little known facts that will be of interest to your class. Look for examples of the application of what you teach in today's world. Know all you can.

Second, you love it. Become convinced of the value and necessity of what you are teaching. See it as a joy rather than a task. Look upon it as something about which you want to know more and more.

Finally, you live it. Bring your enthusiasm into the classroom. Enjoy your teaching and your class. Share your joy in the subject with your students. WANT to make them see the subject as you do and work toward that goal. Be happy about being able to teach others what you know.

Nor is this process limited to subject matter. A human being can learn, love and live such qualities as honesty, equality, brotherhood and truth. Enthusiasm for these and the other qualities that are the hallmarks of mankind at its best will also be communicated to a class as the teacher learns to live it.

In 1973, when the New York Mets won the National League pennant, a story came out that one of the players, Tug McGraw, coined a phrase that was adopted first by the rest of the team and finally by all the fans. That phrase was, "You gotta believe!" With that motto and the enthusiasm of the players, the team went from the bottom of the league all the way to the final game of the World Series.

That story has a direct relationship to our roles as teachers who are hoping to inspire our students. If you want to inspire—"You gotta believe!" "You gotta believe" that what you are doing is important and that your students will benefit from what you will teach them. "You gotta believe" that you can make a difference in their lives. "You gotta believe" that your students will love a subject or an idea as much as you do and then work because of that love.

If you do believe these things; if you act upon them; if you carry your personal enthusiasm into your dealings with your students; then you cannot help but communicate that enthusiasm to them.

If that isn't inspiration, I don't know what is!

Thank you, and good afternoon.

SPECIAL DATA: *Time of speech; approximately six minutes.*

Here is an inspirational speech about inspiration. The principles upon which it is based are sound, and the practices it suggests are firmly rooted in sound educational practices.

This speech would be effective as part of an in-service or as a part of the ceremonies at the beginning of a new school year. It could also be used with parents as there is no reason why inspiration must be limited to the classroom. With obvious modifications, it might even be presented to selected students, especially those in student government or tutorial programs where they will have the chance to work with other students.

99

TOPIC: **You can make the difference.**

AUDIENCE: **Adults; primarily parents and community members.**

Good evening, ladies and gentlemen.

When my son came home from his first day in the first grade, I asked him how things had gone.

"Terrible," he announced.

Naturally, I tried to get to the bottom of his difficulty, and finally the truth of the matter came out.

Looking up at me, he blurted, "There's three boys and ten million girls!"

That was then, of course, and today, I'm certain my son would relish those odds. Naturally, he exaggerated, but at that stage of his life, he literally felt overwhelmed by numbers.

That's an easy state to get into, incidentally. Just get stuck in any rush-hour traffic jam, and you can very easily feel overwhelmed by the numbers.

When we begin feeling that way, it's fairly easy to begin feeling insignificant. I'm only one car among all these other cars on the highway. What can I do? I'm only one citizen among all the citizens of this country. What can I do? I'm only one human being among all the human beings on this planet. What can I do?

Yes, it's easy to feel that way. When we perceive ourselves as tiny and unimportant; when we perceive ourselves as not mattering in the scheme of things; when we begin to look at what we do as incidental and insignificant in a cold and unfeeling world; when we do these things, it's easy to adopt an attitude of "Why bother? It doesn't matter anyhow."

Of course, we all feel that way from time to time—we wouldn't be human if we didn't. It is important, however, that we recognize this for what it is: a momentary setback; a time when the pressures of the world have gotten to us; a time when we are momentarily overwhelmed by the demands of the day-to-day world.

Because, we are important, each and every one of us, and what we do does make a difference. It makes a difference now, and tomorrow, and the day after.

Why should I vote in elections, for example? My vote is only a single mark among many. If I didn't vote, it wouldn't change anything. I'm only one person.

What is one vote? I'll tell you. Thomas Jefferson was elected president by one vote in the electoral college. So was John Quincy Adams. Rutherford B. Hayes was elected president by one vote. His election was contested, and referred to an electoral commission where the matter was again decided by a single vote. The man who cast the deciding vote for President Hayes was himself elected to Congress by a margin of one vote. California, Washington, Idaho, Texas and Oregon gained statehood by one vote. The War of 1812 was brought about by a series of events based upon one vote, and the successor to Abraham Lincoln, President Andrew Johnson, was saved from impeachment by—you guessed it—one vote.

We do make a difference, each and every one of us. If we give up, if we feel that we cannot make a difference, then the difference we make will be a negative one. If, however, we know that what we do now will have an effect tomorrow and tomorrow and tomorrow, then we will do our best at all times, and that best will make a positive and glowing contribution to the world.

If we believe this, then we won't try to be interesting; we will be interested. We won't expect to be pleased; we will be pleasing. We won't wait to be entertained; we will be entertaining. We won't wait to be loved; we will be lovable. We won't ask to be helped; we will be helpful.

That will make all the difference.

It has been said that to get anywhere in this world, you have to know someone important. I think that's true. You do have to know someone important—you have to know yourself.

Knowing yourself, knowing what you can and cannot do, and trying to do your best in each and every situation; believing that what you do today is important and will affect tomorrow; striving, with this in mind, to do what you can when you can; doing this will make this world a better place for everyone in it.

Just imagine a world filled with people who know that what they do will make a difference, and who strive consciously to make that difference a positive good for everyone.

That world is a reality within our grasp.

You do make a difference, and that difference is you.

Thank you, and good night.

SPECIAL DATA: *Time of speech; about three minutes.*

This is a type of "all-purpose" inspirational speech that can be used as part of a longer speech on the part played by the parent, teacher, administrator or student in the overall structure of the school, or it can be used by itself to almost any group.

It can be used effectively with students, educators or parents with equal conviction, for it bespeaks a positive philosophy that if internalized, cannot help but bring about equally positive results.

100

TOPIC: **Inspirational graduation speech.**
AUDIENCE: **Adults and students; a typical graduation audience.**

(SPECIAL NOTE: Generally speaking, all graduation speeches are inspirational in nature. They are, if you will, a transition between school and the adult world. As such, they must inspire the graduates and send them off into that world. Graduation speeches are also included in Sections Nine and Ten, and you will find that they are inspirational as well.)

Mr. Superintendent, Mr. Mayor, parents, honored guests, and the graduating classs of 19XX.

If you will look at the program you received this evening, you will notice that the first words on the cover are these: "Commencement Exercises."

The word, "commencement," often causes some confusion, and perhaps it is right and proper that we clear up that confusion. We know that the root of that word is "commence," which means to start or to begin. Yet, as I have heard from many of you, this is a graduation, which marks the conclusion—the successful conclusion I hasten to add—of your school careers. How can an ending be called a beginning?

The answer is obvious. Yes, this evening is an ending, a conclusion of a process you began some twelve years ago. A process called formal education. Throughout that time you have worked and studied and striven for this day; the day when you had completed your studies and would receive a certificate which attested to that fact. Now that day has come, and the conclusion of your schooling is at hand.

But, just as certainly, tonight is a beginning as well. This becomes just as obvious if we ask ourselves the question: What were those twelve years of education for? Why did we go through them?

Let me suggest that they were not to prepare you to end or conclude a portion of your life, but they were to prepare you to begin a new life.

After this evening, I will greet you not as a student in our school, but as a citizen of the world. You do not end your life as a student as much as you begin your life as an adult in an adult world.

With this new position which you assume tonight go many rights and privileges, it is true. But with it also come many awesome responsibilities and demands. The very fact that you have completed your studies and are part of this audience tonight, means that the last twelve years have prepared you to accept those responsibilities and to meet those demands. Certainly, that is the fervent hope of the faculty and staff of our school.

Therefore, take what you have learned and use it. Use it at this "commencement." Use it as you begin your new life as an equal partner in the world. Use it as you meet challenges. Use it now and throughout your lives. May it serve you well.

We, as educators, and you, as students, have each done our part. Now we stand at a gateway, on the other side of which is the world with all that it offers and all that it demands. As you say farewell to us, you say hello to tomorrow.

Grab hold of that tomorrow, and using what you have learned in the past, build it into a bright and shining future. It is the hope and prayer of everyone here that your pathway may be straight and true and that your destination may be golden with happiness and alive with vibrant promise.

Luck, success and happiness to the class of 19XX!

SPECIAL DATA: *Time of speech; approximately four minutes.*

As a general rule, graduation speeches should be kept short. This one reminds the graduates and all who may be in attendance of the significance and import of the occasion. It is also short enough to have impact while holding the attention of the audience.

If you use it, you would, of course, fill in the correct year of the graduating class and make references to the name of your particular school at appropriate places within the speech.

101

TOPIC: **Keeping a positive attitude in education.**
AUDIENCE: **Adults; mainly educators, primarily teachers.**

I'm going to start off with a statement with which you will all agree. It isn't easy being a teacher.

(SPECIAL NOTE: This invariably brings a round of applause when used before a gathering of educators. Therefore, wait until the reaction dies down before continuing.)

You see, I told you you'd agree with me.

Seriously, we all know the frustrations that teaching can bring. We know the day-to-day realities and the trials that plague us as we try to educate our students, a goal which we all share. We also know that it is important for us to keep a positive attitude that will communicate itself to our students and encourage them as they continue with their learning. We know this, but it is often easier said than done.

Frankly, it's not easy to keep a positive outlook and a high energy level over a sustained period of time. So much can happen to eat away at the enthusiasm and joy we once felt every time we set foot in the classroom, that it is easy to find ourselves discouraged. We know this from personal experience.

We try and try, and still there is the child who refuses to learn; we work and spend extra time and effort on helping a child with a behavior problem only to see him slip back into old habits; we do our best to teach and to inspire only to have someone who doesn't know the situation criticize and complain; we plan and plan for learning experiences that will be unique and inspirational only to have those plans dissolve before us when something happens over which we have no control; we try to teach effectively and concentrate on that teaching only to receive a note that we haven't been handing in our "milk purchases count" to the office on a daily basis.

Oh, yes, there are so many things that can lessen our enthusiasm. It is extremely easy to get discouraged and let this discouragement lead to "teacher burnout" or whatever they are calling it these days—that state where we go through the motions while the spirit lags behind.

But, I am here to tell you that this can be prevented; that we can maintain that positive perspective. All we have to do is to learn one thing—how to concentrate. That's right, concentrate.

We must concentrate on success rather than failure.

Recently, a teacher showed me two papers. Both had been written by the same student, about three weeks apart. Both were illegible. They were so filled with mistakes, bad handwriting, spelling errors that defied understanding, and a complete indifference to punctuation, that it was all I could do to even decipher what they were about. To me, there was no difference between them. They were completely discouraging.

I was about to commiserate with the teacher, when she said that she was very encouraged at the progress the student had shown. I must have been standing there with my mouth hanging open, because she quickly pointed out that on the first paper, the boy had used the pronoun "I" and had written it in the lower case. On the second paper, even though other mistakes were rampant, the "I" had been capitalized throughout.

Certainly, that was very small progress, but it was progress. The teacher was not telling me that I should ignore all the other mistakes, but that I must look at the success in terms of the child as well. That teacher's efforts had gotten that child to capitalize the pronoun "I" where previously he hadn't. That was progress and she was responsible.

I believe that this is the only way we are going to manage to keep our perspective. We are going to have to look for the small successes along the way. We have all been in education for many years, and we all know literally hundreds of teachers. We can all testify that there are no sudden miraculous successes in teaching. If we are waiting for a kid who has been a bully, a thief, and a genuine behavioral problem to suddenly throw up his hands one day and shout, "Gosh, Mr. Jones, you've saved me! I see the right path now, thanks to you, and I'll never misbehave again!" then we will wait forever. That sort of thing just doesn't happen.

What we can find, if we look for it, are small changes in the child's attitude. The child needed a pencil today, and he came to us to ask for one rather than stealing one from a classmate's desk. He still isn't bringing materials to class, but at least he isn't stealing them. A kid who always uses vulgar language in class stubs his toe and throws a book against a wall. He's still not controlling his temper, but he didn't say something obscene as he would have a month ago. That's real success!

Let us learn to look for success in little things. Let's not expect overnight changes. Let us know that it will not be easy, but that with application and concentration it can be done. Let us do these things, and we will keep our perspective.

None of us went into teaching for the money, and we all like to feel that we are doing a good job. Concentrating on success is one way to achieve that goal.

It is within the grasp of each and every one of us.

Because we are educators, we can do no less than try.

SPECIAL DATA: *Time of speech; about five minutes.*

This speech is extremely well-received by educators on all levels. Perhaps it touches a truth that we all know but have not examined for some time. This speech might be used to advantage during an in-service session, at the start of a new school year, or at any meeting that involves front-line educators.

As with other speeches in this book, with obvious modifications, it might even be used effectively with a group of parents at a parent/teacher workshop.

102

TOPIC: **Building education through the sharing of ideas.**

AUDIENCE: **Adults; all educators.**

Good evening, ladies and gentlemen.

I have just been very graciously introduced as the author of several books on education. If I didn't know me, I'd be impressed.

Actually, I'm not so much an author as I am a reporter. I look for the best in education, I find it, and I set it down on paper. I like to think that the books I write merely take the good ideas of teachers everywhere and share them with members of our profession.

It is about this sharing that I would like to speak to you tonight.

In most professions, there is a feeling of collective research. There is the "team effort," if you will, that says, "We did it!" when a breakthrough is announced. Why doesn't this hold true in education? First, we are a profession, and there is a great deal of research being done in the field. But, do we share it?

I have told you about my writing, and during research on any particular book, I must hear hundreds of statements like, "Oh, you don't want to put this in; it isn't good enough!" or "This is just something I do with my class; you want something better." Please understand, modesty is fine—in its place—but it has no place in education if it leads to the feeling that all the good ideas belong to somebody else or will be forthcoming from some great, unknown expert.

This is a tremendously self-defeating attitude. Most of the best creative educational thoughts come from the classroom teacher. After all, he is the one who has to make them work; she is the one who has to teach the class what they have to know. Their judgment as to what is or is not successful is the best example of clinical research available. The classroom teacher bows to no one when it comes to knowing what to do with a class. Consequently, we have to get rid of the idea that what we do individually is not good enough for our peers.

How do we reverse this self-defeating trend? We do it by sharing our ideas. We must share our successes and our objective evaluations of them, and we must offer positive suggestions for their adaptation. Then, we must offer constructive hints for overcoming any problems that we may have encountered. I realize that some of us may feel that this calls for us to act like some kind of expert. Well, what's wrong with that? When you use a particular technique, you know more about its ramifications at that particular moment than anyone else. I'm not suggesting that you show off—just share, because as others learn from you, you will learn from them.

Why not start compiling a notebook in which you write down your best techniques? Get others to do the same thing. Then, as your notebooks grow, share pages. If you have a couple of "gold star" techniques, why should your fellow educator not benefit from them? You may have been searching for one spectacular technique to stop an "itchy" problem once and for all. You notice that your friend never has that problem. Find out why. The technique he uses might be just the one for which you have been looking. Copying may be wrong for students, but it is not for the teacher seeking solutions to problems. This borrowing and lending of pages from your techniques notebook will add more jewels to each of your collections.

Another idea would be to start a central receiving file for these techniques. This could be a large notebook kept in the library or a series of filed material kept in the Teacher's Room. When something happens that will be of benefit to anyone else—contribute it. Before starting anything new, check that file. Someone may have come up with an idea that, with your adaptation and creativity, could really turn on your classroom. In this type of file, nothing is extraneous. A great technique that a kindergarten teacher used can be adapted to an eighth grade science class. All that is needed is the kindergarten teacher's evaluative comments, a particular need collectively shared, and the science teacher's creativity and ingenuity.

One final idea that has been used with great success is meeting together to discuss techniques, not because you have to, but because you want to. Call it "rapping," call it "brainstorming," call it whatever you please, but sitting down together on a regular basis and sharing and critiquing the techniques of yourself and others will produce a twofold benefit. First, it will keep you informed as to what others are doing, and, second, you will begin to get the feeling that you are a working part of a cohesive unit. It doesn't matter if you do it in the teacher's room, at someone's home over a cup of coffee, or even in a local bistro if you are so inclined, but it does matter that you share those precious ideas!

You can make a difference. You are an expert. You can be a teacher and a student at the same time. You can learn from others as others can learn from you. You can make life better for yourself, your colleagues, and your students.

Let us recognize our power to teach and to learn, let us come together as one body with the single goal of the best in education for our students, and, for goodness sake, let us share!

Thank you, and good evening.

SPECIAL DATA: *Time of speech: abut five to six minutes.*

This is another speech that is a natural for an in-service or opening of the school year for educators. The particular reference to writing at the beginning of the speech was included because that's how it applied to us. You would, of course, adapt it to your own situation.

This speech might also be used as the keynote to one of those "Good Ideas" conferences which are gaining in popularity among educators.

103

TOPIC: **How parents and the school can communicate.**

AUDIENCE: **Adults; mainly parents and community members and teachers.**

Good evening, ladies and gentlemen. Thank you for that warm reception.

I once overheard two women talking in a crowded bus. One woman said, "These new shoes I'm wearing are going to be the death of me."

"My dear," said her friend, "why don't we go to a restaurant where you can sit down and slip them off? Under the table, no one will notice."

"Look," said the first, "when we get through here, I have to get my car back from the garage and argue with the mechanic about the bill;

then I have to do the shopping that I didn't do yesterday; then I'll go home and look at the bills that the mailman has brought; then I'll have to clean up whatever the dog has knocked over during the day; then my husband is going to come home wanting dinner, it won't be ready, and we'll probably get into an argument."

"But, what has all that got to do with your shoes?" asked her friend.

"Just this," the woman answered. "The only pleasure I'm going to get all day long is taking them off, and I'm going to save it until I really need it."

I suppose you might say the point of view of that story is that we can look at things from many points of view. I told it to you, because that is what I would like to discuss with you this evening.

Beside the fact that we are all human beings, we here tonight have one other common characteristic. We are all involved with the education of children. Some of us do this as teachers and administrators of this school, and some of us do this as parents intricately involved in the raising of our children. Whatever the point of view, we are involved in education.

In order for a school to function as it should, it must be far more than a composition of brick and plaster and water fountains and heating units. Oh, certainly these are important for the physical comfort and well-being of its inhabitants, but these constitute only the material aspects of the building. A school must also be a place where minds can be opened to learning, where children are allowed to grow, where there is a free interchange of ideas in order that knowledge may flourish.

I think that we can all agree to that. It would indeed be a marvelous thing if that's what happened with every child who passed through the doors of the school. But, we as educators and you as parents well know that is not the case for all children. Some do find little or no difficulty, but there are others who find frustration and trial at every turn.

If I had the power to make a wish for each child that enters this school it would be that he or she does the best that he or she is capable of doing. This is not a unique wish. It is, indeed, the basic desire and goal of every teacher and every parent here tonight. No one wants to see a child fail. Everyone wants children to learn, grow, and succeed.

Yet, though teachers and parents share that common goal, there are times when the working out of that goal is not easy. There are times when roadblocks in many forms halt the wheels of progress. I suggest that many times these roadblocks are of our own making; that many times they are the result of a difference in point of view from both the teacher's side and the parent's side.

Quite frankly, there are parents and teachers who look upon a child's education as a twelve-year war between the two sides. The parent may view the teacher as a pedagogue who is unfriendly, unbending, openly hostile to his child, trying to teach too much or too little, and with no understanding of his child's needs, wants, capabilities, or sensitivities. The teacher may view the parent as overprotective, overtly hostile, awaiting any opportunity in order to sue the school, unappreciative of the teacher's efforts, and with no understanding of the other students' needs, wants, capabilities, or sensitivities.

Positions are drawn, and the battles ensue. It goes like this. Why should I, Mr. Parent, call that teacher? He'll only give me a lot of double talk, and then he'll take it out on my kid. Why should I, Mr. Teacher, call that parent? He'll only tell me I don't understand his child, and then he'll tell me I don't know what I'm doing and threaten to sue me.

So it goes. Each side, certain of what will happen if they approach the other, remains in the trenches and plays a waiting game of silence. Consequently, there is no communication. Neither side talks, they just sit and grumble. It would almost be laughable if it didn't have such tragic consequences.

Because, and make no mistake about it, the battlefield for this conflagration is the child's education. The teacher loses minimally through lack of parental support. The parent loses minimally through lack of teacher cooperation. The child loses maximally through lack of communication between the home and school, which forces the child to act without guidance, without direction, and without the limits in which children grow and learn the best.

If what I have said offends some parents or some teachers, I really do not care, because my point of view of education is from neither side. I want what is best for the growing child!

I have seen hundreds of cases where the teacher and parent sat enbattled and argumentative while the child floundered and all but screamed out for some recognition, from either side, of his needs, his wants, his capabilities, or his sensitivities.

There is an answer, and it is an answer as patently simple as what we are doing tonight. That answer is communication.

It is like the little boy who went to his father and said, "Dad, can I go over to Jimmy's house? Mom said it was all right with her if it's all right with you." Dad gave his consent, and the boy went to his mother and asked, "Mom, can I go over to Jimmy's house? Dad said it's all right with him if it's all right with you."

Divide and conquer. Sometimes I think kids must be born with that technique. But, consider for a moment, that that ploy could work only in a home where Mom and Dad don't communicate. If Mom and Dad talk to each other, discuss the day and the family, check with each other about what is going on, that "Mommy-Daddy" game could never succeed.

So, too, in education, there are relatively minor problems if only the home and the school communicate; if only they look upon the education of a child as a vital and ongoing venture in which they are both engaged; to which they are both entitled to have input; and by which they hope to produce a happy, intelligent, and functioning child. When this happens, when both sides are less interested in their fears and suspicions and more interested in the ultimate good of the child, then education will have the chance to flourish and the child will be allowed to grow in mind as well as body.

Then, indeed, we will be taking care of the child and of all his needs, all his wants, all his capabilities, and all his sensitivities.

Let's do it then, for our kids. Let's try to communicate. If we don't understand what's going on, let's make an effort to find out. If a child is doing poorly in school, let's communicate with the goal in mind of solving that problem. Let's get the home and the school working together in order that what is taught in school is enforced in the home, and that what is taught in the home is enforced in the school. This can be done if both parents and teachers enter into dialogues that clear up misunderstandings, that exchange insights into the child's developing personality, that build bases for quick and decisive action when the problems do occur.

Of course there will be difficulties. Life without problems simply does not exist, but there will be no problem that will be insurmountable, there will be no problem that is insoluble; there will be no problem that cannot be discussed and plans worked out for its solution.

Working together, as partners, for the common goal of what is best for the growing and developing child, gives that child the greatest head start in the world. With so many people working together, communicating, exchanging ideas and plans for his benefit, he cannot help but succeed in school and in life.

If I have communicated anything to you this evening, let it be that—through communication—this is within our grasp.

For our children's sake, we can do no less than try.

Thank you, and good evening.

SPECIAL DATA: *Time of speech; about eleven minutes.*

   This inspirational speech about the power of communication between the home and the school is very powerful if delivered with conviction, and we have had many favorable comments about it.

Do not worry about offending anyone with references in this speech. Both parents and teachers will invariably take the attitude that since they are at a school function, they are obviously interested in communicating, so you must be talking about those not in attendance.

104

TOPIC: **Striving for new solutions.**
AUDIENCE: **Adults; primarily aimed at educators.**

Good evening, ladies and gentlemen. I'm here to talk about problems.

Do I really have to tell you that you have problems in school; that you face these problems each and every day; that they can be frustrating, and wearisome and debilitating? I don't have to tell you that. If I stood here and enumerated the problems faced by the average educator, we'd get out of this meeting sometime around next Christmas.

Therefore, since we don't have to talk about the problems, let's spend some time talking about solutions. There are solutions, you know. They are available, and they are within your grasp. All you have to do is search for them.

If you listen to your parents, and especially if you listen to your grandparents, they will be quick to tell you that things were different back in those "good old days." Why, back then, if a kid misbehaved at school, he was dealt with swiftly and severely, and whatever punishment the school meted out was nothing compared to what awaited him at home. When parents learned that their son or daughter had "sassed" the teacher, father would take his trusty razor strap from the wall and walk the offender to the woodshed where he would forcibly apply moral principle to the seat of knowledge.

But, as Bob Dylan sang in a folk song of the 60's, "The times, they are a'changin'." There are very few woodsheds left, and you can't really find a razor strap outside of a barbershop anymore. Indeed, the people who expound upon the quality of discipline in the past see school as it was. We, as working professional educators, know what it's like now, today.

That our schools have changed is an evident fact and as inevitable as the progress of society itself. As the twentieth century unfolded, technology and mass media literally exploded upon society with a shattering impact. Not only was there more—so much more—to know and explore, but the general public watched history as it was being made and did so from the privacy of their living rooms. Along with technological advances came advances in personal lifestyles as well. People discovered a new social mobility, and the concept of the small town where one was born, reared, worked, married, reared a family and then passed on without ever venturing forth from the town boundaries, disappeared forever. The concept of personal freedom also advanced. People became increasingly aware of their personal and constitutional rights and their place in a modern society.

As a vital part of society, our schools changed as well. Today, our students are taking courses in subject matter that was unknown fifty years ago. Nor is it subject matter alone that has felt the effects of change. Reflective of society as a whole, students have begun to question the relevancy of what is taught and the efficacy of established rules of discipline. Where once schools thought it within their purview to dictate such variables as style of dress and personal appearance, courts throughout the land have ruled that no longer can such factors as length of hair or type of clothing or even factors such as saluting or not saluting our nation's flag be considered part of the educator's prerogative.

Moreover, those same parents who consistently choose "Discipline in the Schools" as their primary concern on those public opinion polls are among those who have brought legal suit against schools when they have felt that the disciplinary actions taken against their children were punitive or arbitrary or violated the constitutional safeguards of themselves or their families. Quite often, the courts have found that their concerns were justified and well-founded, and the schools have been required to take a hard look at their rules and codes.

Certainly the times have changed and will continue to change along with society. We, as professional educators, owe it to ourselves and our students to constantly investigate new avenues and approaches to all aspects of educational life. To the everlasting credit of our profession, most educators have done just that. Indeed, a majority of educators realize the need for new and effective methods of teaching and discipline and learning in general that are in tune with the needs of today's students and the structure of modern society. Many of the methods of the past are fine and work as well today as they did in years gone by, but many traditional approaches are being discarded. The reason, let's be quick to add, is not because they are old, but because they do not work.

This should be the task of every educator: getting rid of what does not work and keeping that which does.

There was a scientific experiment in which a mouse was placed in a maze with food at the end of one passage. Through trial and error, the mouse finally arrived at the food. When he had run the same course several times, the mouse no longer hesitated or turned down wrong corridors, but went directly down the correct path that led to the food. After a few more runs like this, the food was removed from the previous corridor and placed at the end of another passage. At first the mouse went to the old place. Finding nothing there, he retraced his path and investigated other passages until he found the newly-placed food. Thereafter, he had no trouble accommodating himself to the new route that brought the reward.

Now, the point of this story is that it shows the basic difference between mice and men. Eventually, the mouse will learn to seek other paths when the one he has always followed is no longer productive, while mankind will keep going down the same unproductive pathway forever.

There is a chilling truth in that anecdote. How often do we continue to do things in a certain manner just because they have always been done that way? Haven't we ever felt that our actions were not bringing the results we desired? Yet we continue to persist in our actions.

Let's make a checklist—a checklist for tomorrow. Let's examine what we are doing in our classes. If it works for us, then that is fine, and we must hold on to these methods and even share them with our colleagues. If some of the methods we are currently using no longer work, even though they may have worked in the past, then let us take a close, hard look at them and see if there are other passageways we can explore that WILL work and that WILL bring about our desired goals.

We will not throw out a method because it is old, but because it does not work. We will not adopt a method because it is new, but because it does work.

If we do this, we will become what we want to be; what we know we can be—the vital, concerned educator who plays such a dynamic and vital part in each child's life. We will have a classroom in which there is order and discipline, control and learning, but it will be a classroom that brings out the best qualities in both teacher and student, that allows for individual growth and differences, and that will make our task as an educator easier while ensuring that each student will receive the full benefits of our educational training.

It's certainly worth a try.

Thank you, and good night.

SPECIAL DATA: *Time of speech; approximately nine minutes.*

This speech is an excellent lead-off speech for an in-service session or a panel discussion on new ideas, or any activity in which teachers participate in order to learn new ideas and methods.

The analogy of the mouse is particularly apt to a situation where people may be reticent to try new ideas. It usually brings a laugh, but it gets people to think as well, and perhaps prepares them to at least listen to suggestions with an open mind.

AFTERTHOUGHTS

We cannot emphasize too much that the key to delivering a speech that is meant to inspire is enthusiasm. You can have the best material in the world, containing true gems of wisdom, but it will go unheeded if it is delivered in a dull and flat tone as if someone were reading a telephone book.

If, however, the speaker will FIRST become enthusiastic about his topic and THEN prepare and deliver his speech or one of the speeches in this section, then when he DELIVERS the speech, that enthusiasm, that joy, that concern cannot help but be communicated to the audience. The audience cannot help but respond and, yes, be inspired.

SECTION SEVEN

Dynamic Speeches for Retirements and Testimonials

Administrators are constantly called upon to speak at retirement dinners and testimonials for fellow educators. Whether the educator be a teacher or another administrator, his friends and associates have gone to some trouble to prepare this honor. Therefore, if you have been invited to speak, it is because of some special relationship you bear to the honoree. Perhaps you were the teacher's building principal, or perhaps you served with the administrator on several committees or even as a member of the Central Staff. Whatever the case, you know the honored individual, and you are expected to deliver a speech based on that knowledge.

Unless it is specifically stated otherwise, you may safely assume that you will be one of a number of speakers at the particular occasion. Consequently, retirement speeches and testimonials should be kept relatively short. In fact, as a general rule, these speeches should rarely exceed five minutes. If, however, you are specifically designated as the principal or only speaker, then your speech should lengthen accordingly.

Humor is always appreciated in these speeches, provided, of course, that the humor is warm and personal. If at all possible, the humor should be based upon some personal experience. Naturally, it goes without saying that the humor must never embarrass the honored person. It is always wise, however, to place the humor at the beginning of the speech and close with genuine and heartfelt praise or good wishes for the individual.

The following pages contain a number of examples of these types of speeches that are appropriate for these occasions. May you deliver them in good health, and may the retiree or honored guest enjoy them.

Retirement Speeches

105

TOPIC: **Retirement of a teacher.**

AUDIENCE: **Adults; mixed audience of laymen and educators.**

In a few days, Harriet Johnson will walk out the doors of Rock Township High School. When she does, however, she will not leave unattended. With her will march the accumulated memories of thirty-six years in the classroom—years filled with laughter and with tears; with comfort and with hardships; with pleasure and with pain.

That is inevitable, yet it is not the most important thing to us, her fellow educators, her colleagues, her friends. Rather, what is important is that we have had the privilege of knowing someone whose presence, like a delicate and rare perfume, will linger long after she has left. It is a presence that inspires us to overcome obstacles as she has done; that teaches us to fight for justice against impossible odds; that stirs our hearts and our memories and our spirits.

And, what will we remember? What will we say?

We will say that once in this sad and imperfect world, we knew someone who fought and conquered—who fought ignorance and conquered it with knowledge; who fought prejudice and conquered it with understanding; who fought hatred and conquered it with love.

We will say that once we knew a fighter; we knew a teacher; we knew a gentle, a strong, and an exemplary human being named Harriet Johnson, and, by God, it is WE who are the better for it.

SPECIAL DATA: *Time of speech; about two minutes.*

This speech was originally given to honor a woman who, many years ago, had been the first black teacher in an almost all-white school system, hence the reference to fighting prejudice. Personal anecdotes might be added at the beginning, but the speech, as it appears above, is a particularly strong closing and would not be enhanced by personal reminiscence.

106

TOPIC: **Retirement of an administrator.**

AUDIENCE: **Adults; educators, community members, and friends of the retiree.**

It has been said that "a thing of beauty is a joy forever," and while I would be the last person on earth to call Joe Morrison "beautiful," it does seem to me as if I have known him forever.

Joe, you and I go back quite a way, and I'm wondering if you remember the time when....

(SPECIAL NOTE: At this point, one or two anecdotes might be inserted based upon personal experience with the subject.)

Those were good times, that's for certain. Yet, as I think back on the days, and sometimes the late nights, that we have worked together, I find it almost impossible to recall a time that wasn't "good." Of course, there were times we disagreed; times we agonized together over difficult decisions; times we were so beseiged by work that there didn't seem time enough in the world to get it all done; times when budgets were defeated, enrollments were down, and we both wondered if it was too late to pursue some other career. Even so, looking back now with the perspective that only time can lend, all those occasions were "good times," mainly because you were there to share them.

Of course, I could speak of your intelligence; I could compliment your fantastic competence; I could point to you as a man of principles—a truly moral man whose honesty and integrity are unquestioned. Yes, I could do all of this, but all I would be doing is stating the obvious—obvious to anyone who has been blessed by knowing and working with you.

Instead, I'll just sum it up by saying that if I am proud of any single accomplishment in my life, it is this: Joseph Morrison is my friend and colleague.

No one can deny that you have earned your retirement, and there is no one who is not delighted that you will finally be getting some time for yourself. At the same time, there is no one who does not also realize that when you leave that administration building, there will occur a very real and palpable loss to this school district; that a part of what has made our school system the outstanding educational service that it is will have gone from us; that we will all somehow be the less for your absence.

We will miss you, Joe. We are thankful that you were here to contribute your thoughts and expertise to building our school system; we are honored that we have had the pleasure of being associated with you on a professional level; and, we are overjoyed that we may call you our friend.

Godspeed, Joe. May your retirement be filled with the sparkling and golden days you so richly deserve.

SPECIAL DATA: *Time of speech: four to six minutes, depending on anecdotes.*
This speech was delivered by a close personal friend as well as a professional colleague. The retiree had worked almost his entire professional life in the particular school district. The personal warmth of the speech is obvious.

107

TOPIC: **Retirement of a teacher.**

AUDIENCE: **Students and adults; students, parents, educators, community members, and other guests.**

(SPECIAL NOTE: The occasion for this speech would be an assembly or assembly-like program. The audience varies widely in age and background, although all have come to honor the retiring educator.)

We are gathered here today for a very happy and a very sad occasion. At the end of this present term, Mr. Halley will be leaving us to retire after a forty-year teaching career. It is a happy time, because we are glad that Mr. Halley is well and happy and will be getting some time to relax and enjoy himself. It is sad, because it is never easy to have to say goodbye to a friend.

Over the years that Mr. Halley has taught in our district, a number of students have passed through his classes. Several of these former students are here this afternoon. I'd like to introduce one of them now; a person who....

(At this point, the assembly program continues with short speeches by former students, colleagues, and those others designated to speak. Speeches by present students are also included. The administrator giving this speech now acts as Master of Ceremonies, introducing each speaker

and keeping things moving. When the last scheduled speaker has finished, the administrator continues...)

Before we hear from Mr. Halley, I'd like to share with you a thought I had as I listened to the speakers recall their association with him. It becomes obvious from listening to these speakers that Mr. Halley may best be characterized as a man who was always there when you needed him. He was there in the classroom to explain, to answer, and to guide; he was there for that extra help; he was there when you had a problem; he was there when you just wanted to talk; he was there when you needed advice; he was always there when you just needed a friend.

Many words have been spoken this afternoon, but I believe that I can sum up everything that has been said in just two words. Students of Rock Township High School, parents, faculty, and honored guests, I commend to your attention and your respect Mr. James Halley—Teacher and Friend!

(The administrator leads the applause and encourages the audience to rise, giving the teacher a standing ovation. The administrator goes over to the teacher, leads him to the podium, and discreetly steps back, still applauding, leaving the teacher to receive the acclaim and to speak if he should so desire.)

SPECIAL DATA: *Time of speech varies, according to the number of speakers and the length of the assembly. As a general rule, assemblies of this type should not exceed one regular class period. You will notice that the language is kept simple and direct because of the diversified audience. Assemblies of this type can be quite touching if handled properly. Also, taking nothing away from the contributions of the retiring educator, it is an excellent occasion for good public relations and positive news coverage.*

108

TOPIC: **Retirement of an administrator.**
AUDIENCE: **Adults; all educators, both teachers and administrators.**

There is no need for me to detail for this audience the difficulties and frustration faced by professional educators. We know only too well how demanding our profession can be. We know, firsthand, the pressures, the demands upon our time and resources, the drain upon our energies and intellects that are a part of a career as a professional educator.

Over the last twelve years, it has been my lot to share some of those demands with Wilma Bankhardt. My only regret from that association is that I have not had the pleasure of knowing her longer. Because she was there, the pressures of those twelve years lessened, the demands made lighter, and my energies replenished by her vitality, her great enthusiasm, and her extreme dedication and outstanding professionalism.

Wilma exemplifies the professional educator at her best. Whether during her eleven years as a teacher, her five years as a guidance counselor, her seven years as an assistant principal, or her fifteen years as a principal, the people associated with her could not help but benefit from her drive, her energy, her sense of humor which carried us through the darkest of times, her intelligence, her insight ... and her love.

Yes, her love. Because, if anything characterizes Wilma Bankhardt it is love—love for the children she has served so well, love for the ideals and goals of the profession which she chose, love for those who have served with her, and a love for life which has manifested itself in a brilliant career which has spanned thirty-eight years.

Thank you, Wilma. Thank you for your smile; thank you for your efficiency; thank you for those times when the most difficult of situations were solved because of your expertise and depth of understanding; thank you for caring; thank you for always "being there."

And most of all, thank you, Wilma, for being you.

SPECIAL DATA: *Time of speech: about three minutes. This speech could easily be expanded by adding anecdotes at the beginning or toward the middle to exemplify the qualities being detailed. Notice how the retiring person is addressed directly. This is a particularly effective technique and is used quite often in speeches of this type.*

109

TOPIC: **All-purpose poem for retirement.**

AUDIENCE: **Suitable for all audiences.**

(SPECIAL NOTE: The following poem could be used alone, or it could be the effective conclusion of a speech for a retired individual. If you can honestly mean everything that is in it and deliver it with sincerity, we have found it to be extremely dynamic and dramatic.)

> It seems it's been forever
>   Since the first time that we met,
> We've shared some days together
>   That we just cannot forget.
> There was work and there was laughter;
>   There were tears and triumphs, too;
> Successes and disasters,
>   But somehow we came through.
> Yes, we worked to make things last,
>   And yes, we had to strive;
> But, God, our blood ran hot and fast,
>   And, God, we felt alive!
> It's those moments we'll rely on;
>   They bespeak the way we feel,
> For we started out as iron,
>   But we ended up as steel.
> And now in days that yet will dawn,
>   Although we'll be apart,
> Those memories, we know, will spawn
>   A smile in our hearts.
> Now take our wishes with you
>   For Blessings from Above;
> For happiness in all you do;
>   But most of all—for Love.

SPECIAL DATA: *Time of poem: approximately one minute. If you think that this poem is a bit sentimental, remember that at a retirement affair, the mood is undoubtedly just as sentimental. Believe us, the effect upon the audience and the retiree will be substantial. If you use this poem as the conclusion of your speech, be certain not to add any comments after it. It is strong enough to stand on its own, creates a mood in the audience, and its impact would be lost by further commentary.*

110

TOPIC: **Retirement of a school nurse.**
AUDIENCE: **Adults; educators, friends and family.**

There is not a person here today who does not know the old adage, "A friend in need is a friend indeed." There is also not a person here today who does not recognize the truth of that adage. Indeed, we know it is true, because we have with us a person who embodies that statement; who is the living proof of its veracity.

I speak, of course, of Nurse Gina Capelli who retires today after a career that has spanned forty-two years of service, the last thirty of those years as a school nurse within our district.

Throughout those years, she has proven herself to be a friend again and again. Whenever anyone needed her, she was there. From the simplest of situations involving little more than a band-aid to the most horrible of accidents and the most devastating of illnesses, she was always there, working quietly, and efficiently, soothing the pain, giving encouragement, using her knowledge and her compassion to remedy the situation. That same efficiency, that same compassion, that same personal attention and care was there whether the incident was a scraped knee on the playground or the most complicated of broken bones.

You see, we've finally found Nurse Capelli's secret—she cares. Yes, she cares about each and every child in the school; she cares about each case that enters her office. I would venture to say that never in her career has Mrs. Capelli treated a "patient," but always—always—she has treated Billy, and Johnny, and Mary, and Fred. She has treated people. She has cared about each child. She has taken a warm and personal interest in every one of her thousands of children. And that, ladies and gentlemen, THAT has made all the difference.

Many words have been spoken here today, but perhaps the most eloquent words were those that were not spoken; that will never be spoken. No one will ever know how many children she has helped throughout her life; no one will ever know how much pain she has soothed, how many lives she has touched, how many personal problems she has helped solve. The legion of children who have passed through our schools and whose lives have been touched in some way by Mrs. Capelli's kindness and concern are not here today to speak for her, and yet they do speak. They speak in silence more eloquent than words. Theirs is the untold gratitude and love that fills our hearts; that allows us to swell with joy at the thought that Nurse Capelli will finally be getting the rest she so richly deserves, and allows us, as well, to feel that pang of regret that she will no longer be there.

On behalf of those voiceless children as well as everyone here, I wish you the health, happiness, and peace that you so richly deserve. May your retirement be filled with joy as your presence has filled our lives with riches beyond count.

SPECIAL DATA: *Time of speech; about four minutes.*
The school nurse is an important part of the structure of every school. Particularly if the nurse who has been in the district for any length of time, many parents and community members get to know her quite well. Her retirement, therefore, should receive the same amount of notice as that of a teacher or administrator. The speech above expresses some very basic feelings about the school nurse that are commonly held by educators, parents and community members.

111

TOPIC: **Retirement of a school custodian.**

AUDIENCE: **Adults; educators, friends, fellow custodians.**

The first thing I'm going to do is to promise not to make any jokes about how Bill really "cleaned up" in this job.

You see, Bill and I go back quite a ways, and from the bottom of my heart, I tell you it hasn't always been easy working with this man. I remember one time particularly...

*(Here would be inserted an anecdote or anecdotes, light and humorous
in nature, that reflects some personal relationship with the retiree.)*

I also remember that when I started out as a teacher about a million years ago, I was fortunate enough to come under the wing of an experienced, older teacher who gave me a piece of advice. "If you want to get anything done around here," he told me, "you have to remember two things: make sure your lesson plans are up to date, and make friends with the custodian."

Well, I always had trouble with those lesson plans, but when the head custodian is a man like Bill Peters, becoming friends with him was the easiest thing I ever did.

During the fifteen years that I have known him, Bill has maintained the school and kept it functioning smoothly in the face of impossible odds. There was never an emergency so large that he was not there to handle it nor a detail so small that he overlooked it. Bill takes pride in his work and in his school, and it just seems natural that we catch fire from him; that his pride becomes our pride as well.

And yet, Bill is also a man who knows, deep in his heart, that school is more than floor tiles and blackboards and brick. He realizes that every school has a soul, and that soul is comprised of the kids who come there day after day throughout the school year. I have had the privilege of watching Bill interact with these kids, and I have seen Bill's care and concern manifested time and time again.

I have seen him stare down the toughest bully who stood a full head taller than him; I have seen him work extra hours to construct a special ramp for some of our handicapped students; I have seen him take some of the worst discipline problems in school and turn them into kids who took pride in themselves and their school; I have seen him surrounded by kids struggling with each other for the chance to "help" our custodian. In short, I have had the honor to watch the love which Bill Peters poured out returned to him a hundredfold by the very kids he has worked with and served for so long.

My retirement wish for you, Bill, can be no less than this: as you have blessed our lives with your kindness, care and concern, may your retirement years be golden and warmed by the love we bear for you which you have so richly earned over these years.

Ladies and gentlemen, I give you a genuinely fine human being, Mr. Bill Peters.

SPECIAL DATA: *Time of speech; four to six minutes, depending on the length of the anecdotes used. A good custodian can often spell the difference between a functioning and a nonfunctioning school plant. It is also true that custodians interact with students, and a good custodian can be a factor in a positive school environment. Honoring the custodian at his retirement, therefore, should be part of every administrator's enjoyable duties.*

112

TOPIC: **Special retirement speech for a board of education member.**
AUDIENCE: **Adults; educators, board members, community leaders, etc.**

Tom Jeffries is about to retire, not only from his work as a businessman in our community, but from his position as president of our township's board of education. When I was asked to say something at this affair, it was suggested that, since I am an educator, I talk about that aspect of his life.

That presented a real problem. What do you say about a man who has been a continuing member of our board of education for twenty-one years, the last ten of those years as board president?

I could say that he has handled his responsibilities with efficiency and expertise that helped build our school system into one of the finest in the state, and I would be correct, for he has done that. But that is only a part of the picture.

I could say that he is a man who has made a deep personal commitment to education, reflected in the tireless quest for excellence and the hours of time he has spent not only in work on committees but in the schools, working alongside teachers and students, determining needs, constantly striving for the best for all the students, and I would be correct, for he has done that. But that is only a part of the picture.

I could say that he has handled a plethora of situations, some of them extremely delicate and volatile, with discretion, tact, compassion and competence, and I would be correct, for he has done that. But that is only a part of the picture as well.

Rather, I would paint for you the picture of a man of honor and principle who saw a need and did not shirk from his responsibilities in filling that need; a man who worked tirelessly and long to produce the best education for the children of this township; a man who has stood up for his principles time and again in the face of heavy opposition—in short, a man to cherish.

I think that Tom Jeffries knows the truth of the axiom, "You can't please everybody." As anyone who has ever attended an open meeting of the board of education will tell you, special interest groups abound. Whether in the form of groups of teachers, administrators, parents, concerned citizens or taxpayers' lobbies, if one thing is certain, it is that whatever you do, someone will disagree with you.

Into that situation, Tom Jeffries came and worked. He succeeded because he didn't please everybody. Rather, he worked consistently and unceasingly to do what he knew was best for the children of our community. With their interests paramount in his mind, he set about to perform the duties of a board member. It has not always been easy; his decisions have not always been popular; his was not a job filled with glory.

Yet, ask anyone in this township about Tom Jeffries, and they will tell you that he is a man who cares. Ask someone whose proposition Tom has had to vote against, and they will tell you that while they may not agree with him, they stand in total respect of his integrity. Ask us who have had to work with him, and we will tell you that the children of this township had a champion on the board of education, and his name was Tom Jeffries.

It is altogether fitting and proper that we should honor this man tonight, for over the years he has honored us in education by his selflessness, his devotion, and his care and concern.

On behalf of the educators and students of this township, I wish you a retirement filled with happiness, and I thank you for being there when we needed you.

SPECIAL DATA: *Time of speech; approximately four minutes.*

In any speech where you will be speaking before laymen as well as educators, it is best not to get too specific with educational detail. Educational references should be stated broadly enough that they may be understood and appreciated by all members of the audience.

113

TOPIC: **Benediction for a retirement dinner.**
AUDIENCE: **Suitable for all audiences.**

(SPECIAL NOTE: The following benediction is appropriate if you are asked to give a benediction at a retirement dinner.)

The sun rises and sets and day follows day. Before we are aware of it, time has slipped by and a career lies behind us. How can we measure that time? How can we put a value on it?

We are, for the most part, what we have done. The speakers here, tonight, have attested to the accomplishments and credits of our guest, and we have all been moved by the picture that has been drawn of dedication and service that have been the hallmarks of a rich and rewarding life.

We are thankful, therefore, that we have had the privilege of knowing someone like this. Our very association has helped our lives. We are thankful that such people exist in this world.

Go, and our love goes with you.

SPECIAL DATA: *Time of benediction: about one minute.*
This is a completely nonsectarian benediction that might be used with any audience. It is also a fitting conclusion to an evening devoted to honoring the retiree.

AFTERTHOUGHTS

No matter who is retiring or what your relationship may be to that person, your speech will be effective and appropriate if you do two things: mean what you say, and say it from your heart.

If you feel a special affection for the retiring person, then you don't need inflated words and grand rhetoric. Saying simply what is in your heart will be more effective than any wealth of words.

Practice your speech and try to deliver it without papers or note cards. Speak plainly and incorporate the retiree in your address. Say what is in your heart.

Follow these rules, and you will give a meaningful retirement speech that cannot help but be appreciated by everyone.

Testimonials

114

TOPIC: **Testimonial for a teacher who has won an award.**
AUDIENCE: **Adults; mixed audience of laymen and educators.**

I warned you, Bill; you can't say that I didn't. I distinctly remember taking you aside and telling you in my most fatherly—make that "brotherly"—manner that if you didn't stop this foolishness, some day soon you would be forced to sit at a dinner and listen while all sorts of people got up and talked about you in front of your back.

I did, ladies and gentlemen. I told him that if he didn't stop caring about his students more than he cared about himself; if he didn't stop spending extra hours preparing his classes to make them interesting, enlivening, and provocative learning situations; if he didn't stop giving of himself on project after project, serving as student advisor, going to bat for the underdog, helping and helping and helping; if he didn't stop all this, I told him, it was inevitable that it would lead to this very night.

Did he listen? No. He went right on seeing each student as an individual with special needs that he tried to meet; he went right on taking extra time to see to it that each student learned and was helped; he went right on sponsoring clubs and activities, working with students whom others had given up as lost, giving of himself even when he was tired, exhausted, and the situation seemed all but hopeless.

Yes, ladies and gentlemen, Bill Harrison went right on being a twenty-four hour teacher, a teacher whose day did not end with the final bell, whose work week did not end on Friday afternoon, whose commitment to the ideals of his profession did not end with the marking period or the term or the school year. He remained a teacher who was available to his students at all times—to help, to advise, or just to talk.

It was inevitable, therefore, that this path would lead you to your present predicament. There you sit, recipient of your Association's Teacher-of-the-Year Award.

You have no one to blame for it except yourself, Bill. In the final analysis, you will have to take the responsibility for being a dynamic and dedicated educator, for being loved by your students, and for being admired and respected by your colleagues. You are going to have to live with that, and—thank Heaven—so will we.

I know that I speak with the voice of hundreds of your students, your colleagues, and your friends when I say thank you—thank you for being ridiculous enough to care; thank you for being foolish enough to be dedicated; thank you for being a true professional in every sense of the word.

I can think of no better commentary than this: in this world, we deserve what we get. Bill Harrison deserves the award he receives tonight for he has earned it. And, while Bill may have this award, we take extreme pleasure in the fact that we have Bill Harrison to work with us and to be a part of our daily lives, and that is reward enough for anyone.

SPECIAL DATA: *Time of speech; about four and one-half minutes. This is a particularly effective speech that can be presented with great dramatic impact. Naturally, the audience understands that the administrator never really advised the teacher not to care, but in phrasing it in "tongue-in-cheek" style, you have a very warm, personable, and dynamic honor for this exemplary teacher. It is a speech that will be remembered.*

115

TOPIC: **Testimonial for a newly-appointed administrator.**

AUDIENCE: **Adults; educators and laymen—colleagues, friends, family members, members of the community.**

I have a question that I would like to ask: Why him? How come Thomas Connors has been appointed superintendent of schools for our district?

I mean, what has he done to deserve it? All he's done over the years is to be an outstanding teacher, an efficient vice-principal, a dynamic principal, and an extremely effective assistant superintendent whose insight and expertise have helped improve the quality of education in our schools. That's all he's done.

And what about the man, himself? All he has going for him is honesty, integrity, intelligence, compassion, wit and understanding. All that people can say about him is that he understands the problems of education and our district, that he is a tireless worker who adheres to the goals and objectives of public education, and that he is a man of dynamic talent whose ideas and ideals benefit all with whom he comes into contact.

Now, I ask you—honestly, are those any reasons to appoint Tom Connors as superintendent? Come to think of it—maybe they are. In fact, perhaps the wonder is not that Tom has been appointed superintendent, but that it has not happened long before now.

Tom, I know I speak for us all when I wish you the best of luck and success in your new position and tell you how much we look forward to working with you for the betterment of our system in the years to come.

I asked, "Why him?" I have my answer: because he is the best person for the job. Certainly, it is an honor for him, but it is we who are equally honored to have him with us.

Ladies and gentlemen, I give you Mr. Thomas Connors, superintendent of schools.

SPECIAL DATA: *Time of speech; about two minutes. This is a short speech that is well-suited to an educator who speaks as part of a much longer program. While this is certainly a testimonial, it could also serve as an introduction to the superintendent if he or she were going to speak.*

Notice the similarities to the previous speech about the teacher who is being given the award. Both employ a tongue-in-cheek style and should be delivered with a twinkle in the eye and a perceptible smile in the voice.

116

TOPIC: **Testimonial for a student.**

AUDIENCE: **Adults and students; teachers, friends, family members.**

Every so often, when we are scanning the entertainment pages of the newspaper, we come across a TV listing for a show that the networks have designated as a "special." When we see this label, we are aware that what we shall see if we tune in to the particular channel at the right time is not the usual fare, not the ordinary program that would normally be seen. Rather, we know that we can expect a program that is a cut above the regular, that has been worked on and produced in such a manner that it will, indeed, earn its title of "special."

In fact, that's a pretty good definition of the word itself. "Special" means out of the ordinary—a cut above the regular. Well, as we are all aware, TV is rather free with that word, calling some things "special" that you wouldn't look at unless you were tied down to the set. Yes, it's an overused word.

Therefore, when *we* use that word and apply it to a person, we had better make certain that the person we are so designating *is* out of the ordinary; a cut above the regular. We had better make certain that the person we are describing truly deserves the title, or the word becomes meaningless.

It is, therefore, with a great deal of personal happiness and some pride as well that I say to you that by anybody's definition, Kerri Martin is a very "special" person.

Whether as an honor student in our high school, as president of the student government, as actress in many school productions, as member of the forensic team, or as chairperson on various school committees, Kerri has proven herself worthy of that title. She is a very special person to her family, to her fellow students, and to the faculty of this school.

Now she has gone beyond the halls of our school and let her enthusiasm and drive guide her into the world community as well.

You all know the story, how deeply Kerri was touched when word reached us of the devastation caused by that earthquake and the plight of the homeless survivors. We all shook our heads and agreed that it was indeed a tragedy. So did Kerri, but, unlike the rest of us, she decided to do something about it.

Singlehandedly at first, and then as the head of a growing committee, Kerri spearheaded a drive to gather materials which would provide real relief to the victims. On her own, she investigated the means by which she could gather food and clothing and building materials and get them to the survivors.

As Kerri's commitment burned, those around her could not help but feel the heat and catch fire with her. Soon, she had organized students and teachers and parents and members of our community into groups that did more than hold meetings; more than sit around and talk—they worked.

The result was the tons of food, clothing and materials that were sent to those people in the time of their need.

For this service; for the hours and hours of work; for the nights and the weekends and the toil; Kerri asked for nothing in return. The knowledge that she had helped people in need was all the reward she needed.

But while Kerri may need nothing more, I think that we do. We who have worked with her on this project have a need to put into words that which we feel in our hearts.

We want to say "thank you," Kerri. Thank you for caring. Thank you for being the sort of person who sees a need and fills it. Thank you for being the warm, understanding, capable, tireless, courageous person that you are. Thank you for being out of the ordinary and a cut above the regular. Thank you for being "special."

And thank you for one thing more. Thank you for giving us, each and every one of us, the opportunity to say that for at least once in our lives we knew an example of the finest that humanity can produce. We knew Kerri Martin—a very special person, indeed.

SPECIAL DATA: *Time of speech; about three and one-half minutes.*

This is the type of speech that might be given by a principal about a student in his or her school or even a superintendent about a similar student within the district who had done something outstanding and was being honored for it. Particularly when a student is honored, there is a great deal of community good will involved. The administrator who gives an effective testimonial such as the one above will also participate in that good will.

Whenever you deal with speeches about students, it is best to forget attempts at humor and concentrate on the accomplishments of the student.

117

TOPIC: **Testimonial for a coach of school athletics.**

AUDIENCE: **Adults and students; teachers, parents, students and others.**

There has been, of late, quite a bit of talk in medical circles about the dangers of something called "stress." "Stress" occurs throughout life and, according to medical findings, it can have some devastating results. Doctors now tell us that stress can cause everything from headaches to acne to ulcers and heart attacks.

Of course, I do not dispute their findings. I will say, however, that if it is true what they tell us about stress, then this man, sitting to my right, should be the world's first walking and talking ulcer, for I can think of few jobs as filled with constant stress as that which Coach Ronald Harris does each and every day.

Coaching is a roller-coaster job at best. When a team is winning games, the coach becomes a cross between Superman and a Saint. When the team loses, it seems that everybody has some piece of advice to give, and some of it is far from complimentary. There are schedules to contend with, medical problems to deal with, and a group of eager youngsters to train into a cohesive unit. There is strategy to be planned and implemented. There are a thousand little details that mount into one gigantic headache. And, all of this must be dealt with under the knowledge that when the team takes the field, it is the coach who is two short hours away from being a hero or an object of scorn.

That's enough stress for anyone, and we cannot help but have respect for someone who handles that situation day in and day out and not only manages to stay perfectly healthy, but does the job in an exemplary and extraordinary manner.

It is just such a man that we are here to honor this evening.

Coach Ronald Harris is a man who works with tension and remains calm. He is a man who takes chaos and achieves order. He is a man who deals with hundreds of kids of varying backgrounds and temperaments and produces a team that functions as a single body upon the field. He is a man who works hard, gives of himself, never gives up, and, in that process, manages to uplift and inspire any boy lucky enough to have him as a coach.

And, we must ask ourselves, how can he do this? How can he be such an integral part of these stress-producing situations and emerge as a pillar of strength and concern? How can he work and work and work, see a player or a team fall, and resolve only to work the harder for the next time? How can he spend those long, extra hours working with each and every player to try and shape that player into the best person he is capable of becoming?

How? The answer is simple. It is as simple and as wonderful and courageous as the fine athletes he produces. It is this ... Coach Harris cares.

Yes, he cares. He cares about each and every boy on that field. He cares about the morality and personal growth of the individual boys more than the mere winning or losing of the game. He cares that each boy gives his best. He cares that his teams strive for excellence while keeping their honor. What other definition do we need—that is love, and that love is returned by his boys and manifests itself in the drive and vitality that has been evidenced in the superlative record of the season just finished.

Therefore, it is proper and fitting that we have gathered together this evening to tell this man a thing or two. To tell him that he has earned our respect; that he has earned our admiration; that he has been judged in the heart of everyone here and found to be the worthiest of men.

For your years of concern and toil, for your never-ending dedication to the goals of your profession, for your tireless efforts on behalf of the youth of this school and this community, we honor you this evening.

But, know this, Coach, and know it well—it is really you who honor us by being here tonight, by being on the field with our boys, and by being the person that you are.

For everyone here, thank you, Coach Harris, from the bottom of our hearts.

SPECIAL DATA: *Time of speech; about three and one-half minutes.*

Coaches who have been in a school system for some time usually acquire quite a following in the community, particularly if they are good, such as the subject of the speech above. Therefore, it is quite often the administrator's duty to reflect that community feeling, particularly when the coach is to be honored in some way. The preceding speech is an example of one that could be used for any exemplary coach, whatever the sport may be. You could give specific references to a particular season's record or game, if it seemed appropriate.

118

TOPIC: **Testimonial for a superintendent of schools.**

AUDIENCE: **Adults; educators and laymen, community members, board members.**

When I think about Dr. LeBarron, I cannot help but think of the first time we met. I had come ...

(SPECIAL NOTE: At this point, you insert a remembrance or anecdote based upon your personal association with the subject. Make sure that it is warm and human.)

... needless to say, we have been friends ever since.

It's been a while since then, and a great deal has happened in both our lives as well as in education in general. Indeed, we have all seen educational philosophy and methods change and we have all been affected by those changes. All we have to do is to think back to the schools of our youth to have that fact made amply evident.

Yet I would like to think that there are some things that do not change; that will never change. I would like to think that honor and truth will always be a part of every curriculum. I would want to believe that dedication and efficiency will always be needed and will continue to be a reward in themselves. I would like to think that a life devoted to serving the youth of a community will still have merit in the eyes of that community.

And I do believe these things. I believe them because it is my privilege to work with people who practice these virtues as part of their daily lives.

And the foremost of these practitioners is sitting here beside me—the man whom we have come to honor, Dr. Louis LeBarron, our superintendent of schools.

If you asked him, of course, he would answer that he couldn't see what all the fuss was about. He would tell you that he just did his job.

That is part of what we have come to know about this man.

We have come to appreciate his humility along with his dedication, his efficiency, and his devotion to the highest standards of education for the youth of our community.

Yes, you can ask him what he has done as superintendent of schools, and he will answer that he has merely done his job. But, if you should ask us, the people who have worked so closely with him, we will tell you of the countless hours he has spent pouring over data, analyzing situations, agonizing over budgets. We will tell you of a man who weighs each decision in his soul and puts a piece of himself into everything he does. If you should ask the students, both those in school today as well as those who have passed through our system, they might well tell you of a man who was always there; who was always willing to listen; who became involved with their lives; who attended their sporting events, their plays, their concerts, and even their social events—they would tell you of a man who cared about them.

Yes, Lou, you can tell us that you have just "done your job," and we will tell you that we believe you. You have "done your job," and that has meant an improvement in educational quality throughout our district. You have "done your job," and the lives of those around you have been made richer and fuller. You have "done your job," and thank God that there was a man like you to do it.

Yes, Lou, you can tell us that you have just "done your job," and my voice in answer will be the voice of everyone here tonight—of our entire community—as I tell you, "Well done, Dr. Louis LeBarron, superintendent of schools, well done, indeed!"

SPECIAL DATA: *Time of speech: three to five minutes depending on the length of the anecdotes used.*

An excellent and a very dramatic technique to use in speeches of this type is to pose a question, either directly or indirectly, and then answer it. In the speech above, the indirect question of "Has he done a good job?" is posed and then answered with dramatic effect. Of course, it might also have been stated more directly. For example, the speaker might have said, "Dr. LeBarron would answer that he has merely done his job. Well, we might well ask, 'Is that true? Has he merely "done his job?"'" Thereafter, the speaker would proceed to answer that question by detailing ways in which this superintendent has been exemplary in his duties.

Both the direct and indirect question-answer method have their advantages. Which do you like better?

119

TOPIC: **Testimonial for a principal.**

AUDIENCE: **Adults; educators and laymen, community members, parents.**

The first time I met Stan Jacobs, I entered his office in school and was amazed to find a large bowl of goldfish on his desk. I asked him if raising fish was a hobby of his. He answered that it wasn't, and, in fact, he didn't particularly like fish. Naturally, I asked him, if he didn't like fish, why did he have a bowl of them on his desk in his office?

He looked up at me and said, "Being the principal of this school, I just felt that I needed something around me that opens its mouth without complaining or yelling about something."

Later, after I got to know Stan a bit better, he invited me to dinner one evening. Not wanting to inconvenience him or his lovely wife, Virginia, I asked, "But, Stan, does your wife know I'm coming for dinner?"

"Of course, she does," Stan answered. "Why, we argued about it all last night."

Seriously, it has been a while since Stan first came to our district as principal of the then-new high school. In the years that have intervened, I have gotten to know him rather well, and I am very proud, indeed, to count him among my very close friends.

Being a new principal in a new school is not an easy task. It takes someone very special to handle it at all. It takes someone extraordinary to handle it so well that he can bring order out of confusion and, in a very short time, have the physical plant functioning smoothly, an effective curriculum established, and a school spirit built within the school and community. Yet, Stan Jacobs did just that, and by the end of its first year of operation, there was no one who did not point to our high school with pride.

Now it is the tenth anniversary of this school. Stan Jacobs remains its principal, and, thanks mainly to his untiring efforts, our school remains a place where learning takes place every day, where there is justifiable pride evident in students, faculty and community; where a record of academic, athletic and cultural accomplishments continues to mount.

And, how has he done this? How has he built our school into the exemplary place that it is?

He has done it with a warm and genuine sense of humor that uplifts all with whom he comes into contact and that makes even the darkest hours a little bit brighter for his being there. He did it with his insight, his expertise, and his fantastic competence. He did it with his unique qualities of care and concern for each and every individual who came within his purview. He did it by seeing each situation as a challenge and rising to meet that challenge.

Therefore, I am delighted to be a part of this evening's activities in honoring this outstanding human being. I am proud, indeed, to add my voice to that of the community in singing his praises. I can think of no one who deserves the honor more.

So, for everyone here, let me say, "Thank you, Stan." Thank you for coming to us. It is we who have benefited from the association.

SPECIAL DATA: *Time of speech; abut two and one-half minutes.*

This is a speech given by someone who is obviously a friend of the honored guest. Because of that relationship, he can have a little fun with the subject as evidenced by the humor at the beginning of the speech. You should not attempt humor, however, if it is widely known that you are not personal friends with the subject but maintain merely a work relationship.

Whether you use humor or not, it should never be used at the conclusion of a speech of this type. The conclusion of every testimonial should be composed of warm and heartfelt praise. To end a testimonial speech on a note of humor, whether or not it is at the expense of the subject, tends to lessen the impact. A speaker builds a mood. It is built from the start to the end of a speech. If that mood is one of warmth and praise, it would be disastrous to break it with humor.

120

TOPIC: **Testimonial for a guidance counselor.**

AUDIENCE: **Adults; educators primarily, but also some community members.**

I wonder what Janet Zanoff was like when she went to school? I don't mean that I wonder if she threw paper airplanes or cheered for the team on Saturday afernoons. I mean that I wonder what she conceived her life as an adult would be. I wonder if she ever thought about what she would be doing in twenty or thirty years. I wonder if she ever went to her guidance counselor for advice and guidance.

If she did, and if that guidance counselor advised her to enter education as a career, then she must have had a counselor almost as good as the counselor whom Janet would become.

We are here tonight to honor Janet Zanoff for her dedication and work as a guidance counselor within our district. It is not an honor that we bestow lightly. It is an honor that she has richly earned through years and years of service to the youth of our community.

A guidance counselor is inundated with work and pressure as few other individuals in education. Not only are there tests and records to maintain, scheduling with which to contend, and endless correspondence to answer, but there is a further factor that can be devastating.

A guidance counselor deals with people. She deals with their hopes, their dreams, their insecurities, their fears, and—most importantly—their futures. It is, indeeed, a heavy burden for those who care.

And Janet Zanoff cares. She cares about "her kids," as she often calls them. She cares about their lives and their problems and their futures. She cares that each and every student live up to the best of which he or she is capable of becoming.

Ask "her kids" and they will tell you. They will tell you that she is a person to whom you may come and share your trials without fear that your deepest thoughts or feelings will be scorned or belittled or go any further than her office. They will tell you that she is no pushover; that she can't be "conned" or lied to; that she never offers pity but always offers help. Ask "her kids," and that is what they will tell you.

Ask me, and I will tell you of how hard and relentlessly she works behind the scenes for the good of every student. I will tell you that it is easy to be a hero when the band is playing and the crowd cheers you on, but that Janet Zanoff sticks by her convictions and works for the good of her students when there is nobody to see her do it, when it means hours of solitary work, when it means going up against seemingly impervious stone walls. I will tell you that she fights for her kids when no one, not even the student involved, will ever know what she has done.

Yes, I will tell you this, and I will put a name to it. It is courage; it is concern; it is love.

For, if I had to sum up Janet in one word, it would be that word—love.

Janet Zanoff loves her work, she loves what she does, and she loves her kids, each and every one of them. They, in turn, cannot help but be touched by that love and carry it with them into the world that will be a better place because of it. And, one other thing. They return that love to Janet as do all of us here present.

We love you, Janet Zanoff. This honor is but a token of that love. Take it now, as you must take our love, day after day, for the rest of our lives.

SPECIAL DATA: *Time of speech; about four minutes.*

This is a particularly warm and personal speech that has great impact upon any audience. Obviously, the recipient of the praise must be well-known and deserving of it, but if this is the case, then this is a speech that will carry with it a dramatic impact that will not be soon forgotten.

While this speech is about a guidance counselor, it could be adapted to other situations where the subject has given of himself or herself in the service of others. In such a case, necessary adjustments would be made.

121

TOPIC: **A testimonial poem.**

AUDIENCE: **Suitable for all audiences.**

> If your life were an open book,
>   The pages would be tinged with gold.
> And we would read a story there
>   To be remembered and retold.
>
> For we would read of how you gave
>   To each and every one you met
> The fullness that your heart could give,
>   The love that no one could forget.

> And you would take a special place
> > Within our minds and our hearts, too.
> A place we'd often come to dream
> > And there, with love, remember you.

SPECIAL DATA: *Time of poem; less than a minute.*

Admittedly, this is a sort of "all-purpose" poem that could be used to advantage in a variety of speeches. It would work particularly well in a testimonial-type speech. It rather bespeaks a common feeling of warmth toward someone who is admired, and it conveys a great deal of feeling in a relatively few words. It also has a very favorable impact upon the audience.

AFTERTHOUGHTS

There are certain characteristics that testimonials and retirement speeches have in common. They are both meant to honor some individual, and they must both be warm expressions of good feelings toward the subject. Since they will undoubtedly be delivered before an audience, they must be pleasing and understandable to that audience as well.

Therefore, keep in mind that when composing a speech for a retirement or a testimonial, you should avoid "inside" jokes that might not be understood by the audience; you must never tell an anecdote (even if it's true) that embarrasses the subject; you should use humor only with a subject who is a personal friend; if you use humor, it should always be at the beginning of the speech; and, you should honestly mean everything you say.

If you follow those suggestions and speak what is in your heart with clarity and conviction, you will give a retirement or testimonial speech that will be remembered by everyone, and particularly by the subject of the speech, for whose benefit it was given in the first place.

SECTION EIGHT

Dignified and Meaningful Eulogies and Memorials

Delivering a eulogy is probably one of the most painful tasks that falls within the duties of the administrator. Whether it be a student, a teacher, or a fellow administrator who dies, if you are asked to speak at the services and deliver a eulogy, you can easily assume that the situation will be loaded with emotion, and it will be a difficult task for you. Yet, as we all realize, none of us would ever turn down such a request, for if the family has turned to you, you cannot do less than respond.

A memorial service is hardly pleasant, either, but memorials are at least blessed with the distance of time. Memorials can be held weeks, months, and even years after the passing of the individual, and time, that greatest of all healers, has had the opportunity to work. Nevertheless, as much care must be taken to delivering the memorial speech as went into the eulogy, for you are still dealing with an emotional situation.

There are some general rules regarding eulogies and memorials which, if they cannot make them pleasant, will at least make them fitting and appropriate.

Obviously, under no circumstances must humor enter into a eulogy. It doesn't matter how well you knew the person—keep humor out of it. Humor should also be kept out of memorials EXCEPT UNDER VERY SPECIAL CIRCUMSTANCES, which will be detailed later in this section. Keep the eulogy and memorial short, rarely exceeding five minutes. Speak about the person and accomplishments of the person. Keep it positive and never speak about how much he or she suffered. If at all possible, try to end it on a note of hope or with a look toward the future. These general rules will go a long way toward helping with any eulogy or memorial.

The biggest aid in any eulogy or memorial will be *your sincerity*. If you had a genuine affection for the person, and you speak of what is in your heart clearly and simply, you will deliver a better eulogy or memorial than could be matched by volumes of inflated prose. Let your heart be your guide, and you will not go wrong.

The following pages have several examples of effective eulogies and memorials. We have selected them because we feel they are both dignified and simple and do the best in a trying situation. It is our hope that you may never have to use them, but if you do, we hope you can find something appropriate.

Eulogies

122

TOPIC: **Eulogy for a teacher.**
AUDIENCE: **Mixed; family members, friends, colleagues.**

Mrs. Franklin, Bobbie and James *(deceased teacher's children)*, members of the Franklin family, ladies and gentlemen...

When we, at school, heard of Greg's passing, we were saddened beyond belief. There was a feeling that passed among us, a feeling that his death has left us with a void that can never be entirely filled. The student body, the faculty, and I cannot help but sense this to our abiding sorrow.

Our only consolation is the knowledge that we were privileged to know and work with Greg over the years. During that time we came to know him as a person of intelligence and integrity, always eager to help, whose life and career were, indeed, an inspiration to us all.

We also take comfort in the fact that a part of him will continue to live, reflected in the lives of the students he has instructed and guided over the years. As a teacher, he gave of himself, perhaps the greatest gift of all, and those students who were fortunate enough to fall under his dynamic tutelage will carry his ideals, his knowledge, and his moral principles into the world, and the world cannot help but be made a better place because of it.

Our hearts and our prayers are with you at this most difficult of times.

SPECIAL DATA: *Time of eulogy; about two minutes.*

Note the address at the beginning of the eulogy. The first person addressed is the surviving spouse, then the children of the deceased, then any special person of note who might be attending such as a mayor or congressman, and finally the members in attendance, addressed as "ladies and gentlemen."

Note also that this is short and simple, detailing the deceased's contributions and the affection of those with whom he worked, and dignified, adding dignity to an already exemplary life.

Remember, there is never any audience reaction following a eulogy or memorial, only silence. Therefore, deliver your speech, acknowledge the family with a nod, walk over to them and say a few personal words, and retire to your seat.

123

TOPIC: **Eulogy for an administrator.**

AUDIENCE: **Mixed; family members, friends, colleagues.**

Mrs. Sumner, Veronica, Mayor Jones, ladies and gentlemen...

There are some things in this world that, try as we may, just cannot be adequately done. One of those things, for me at least, is to express adequately what I feel about the passing of Dr. Arthur Sumner, superintendent of schools.

Arthur and I worked together for many years, and it was my honor to count him among my friends. He was a man of exceptional warmth and wisdom, and his loss leaves a void in all our lives that will not be readily filled.

I knew Arthur as an outstanding administrator, a man whose natural abilities of leadership inspired and enlivened those under his purview to their finest achievements. He was universally liked by teachers throughout the township as well as by his fellow administrators. Indeed, he earned the respect of everyone with whom he came into contact.

Arthur was a man you cannot forget. For us who are left, he will continue to live in our memories and our hearts.

We know that he has gone to the rest that he has so ably earned, and I think he knows that we will carry on in the manner which he taught us throughout his exemplary life.

SPECIAL DATA: *Time of speech; about two minutes.*

This is another very short eulogy, but is to the point and warm. Of course, the deceased's accomplishments in life could have been detailed, much like the middle part of a testimonial, but it is just as effective in this shorter and more direct format.

124

TOPIC: **Eulogy for a student.**
AUDIENCE: **Mixed; family members; friends.**

Mr. and Mrs. Gennert, Tammy and Jean, members of the Gennert family, ladies and gentlemen...

All of us at Rock Township High School, faculty and students alike, were both shocked and overcome with grief at the untimely passing of Robert Gennert. Bob, as he was known to us, was a student of whom we all thought highly; a boy to whom we pointed with pride as a student at our school.

Various members of the faculty who had Bob in class or knew him through his many school activities have spoken to me and asked me to convey their sense of loss and their deepest sympathies. This I do, and I add my own. Bob shall be missed by us all.

The loss of a child is one of life's greatest sorrows. When it is someone of the quality of Bob Gennert, it is a real tragedy for us all.

Mr. and Mrs. Gennert, we are aware that there are no words which are appropriate, but please know that we join you in your grief.

Our sincere and deepest sympathies to you in this time of loss and sorrow.

SPECIAL DATA: *Time of eulogy; about two minutes.*

While people do not like the idea of a loved one dying, they are somewhat prepared for death in an adult and especially an adult of advancing years. No one is prepared for the death of a child. Our careers in education have brought us to too many funeral homes to visit the families of students who have died. It has never been easy, and there are never the right words. If you must deliver a eulogy for a student, it is essential that it be short, sincere, and to the point.

125

TOPIC: **Eulogy at a class reunion for deceased classmates.**

AUDIENCE: **Adults; members of a particular class and their escorts.**

(SPECIAL NOTE: Administrators are often invited to attend class reunions. They may be asked to speak on many subjects related to the class, including delivering a eulogy for those members of the class who have died since graduation. Dr. Chester B. Ralph, a fine educator, has been kind enough to give us the following eulogy, which is highly dramatic and appropriate for the situation.)

Ladies and gentlemen...

It has been a little more than _____ years since we last met as a class at _____ upon the occasion of our graduation. It is inevitable, in that span of years, that many of our teachers and classmates will have been taken from us.

It is, therefore, altogether fitting and proper that we should pause in this hour of levity and reflect in our own lives the memory of those who have died.

I ask that we now bow our heads in silent meditation, and each of us, in his own way, pay tribute to the memory of those who do not answer when their names are called.

(SPECIAL NOTE: When all heads are bowed, the speaker recites the following poem.)

> Now the hour of reunion has arrived,
>   In this room of mirth and cheer;
> And silence descends as if from heaven,
>   Upon the group assembled here.
> Slowly die the fire's last embers,
>   As the night grows still and serene,
> And we toast our absent classmates
>   Who have passed beyond the screen.
> We behold with eyes grown older,
>   With eyes that have a magic scope,
> Life's abandoned fires that smolder
>   On the distant trail of hope;
> And our memories are beguiling
>   When the lights are soft and low,
> For we see our classmates smiling
>   As they smiled long years ago.

So to you, our absent classmates,
With our hearts and hands held high,
We drink a toast to your sweet memory
That will never, never die.

SPECIAL DATA: *Time of eulogy; about three minutes.*

On a personal note, we were out of high school less than a year when no less than three of our classmates had died from various causes. It is sad, but it does happen. Therefore, it is best to be prepared for it.

If you are ever in the situation where you use the eulogy above, be prepared for its impact. It is extremely dramatic, and its dynamics are added to by the nature of the gathering. There will be no applause, and we have personally witnessed occasions where several adults had to leave the room to compose themselves following its delivery.

It is a highly dramatic tribute to deceased classmates, and should be delivered simply without any attempt to embellish it by vocal dramatics.

126

TOPIC: **Eulogy for an educator.**
AUDIENCE: **Adults; family members, colleagues, friends.**

Mrs. Fernman, members of the Fernman family, ladies and gentlemen...

We are the slaves of words. All too often, they are all we have to express those wordless feelings that so fill our minds and hearts. Yes, words are all we have, and yet, at times such as this, they are simply not enough.

We use a word like "sorrow," but what does it convey? We are faced with a situation, here, where each of us, in his heart, must face a personal loss. Each of us will feel it and carry it and live with it, because someone we cherished so much has been removed from our lives. And yet, all we have is a word like "sorrow."

We try to describe what we felt for our friend and colleague and again we are stuck with words. We use a word like "honor," but what does it really mean? Why, we all stand as living proof of the greatness of our friend. We saw his dedication; we were witness to his care and concern; we stood in awe of his great wit, intelligence, efficiency, and tact; we whispered prayers of thanks that we were privileged enough to be associated with a person of his worth. We LIVED our friend's "honor," yet all we have is the word, which seems inadequate to do him justice.

And to sum up what he was and what he did, we use a word like "love," and what can that possibly convey? We saw our friend pour forth love on a daily basis. We knew of his care and concern for the children who came within his purview. We saw the gentleness and warmth and compassion with which he handled every situation. We were privy to the hours and hours of work he put into perfecting his skills in order that he might be the best he could be to help those who needed his help. Our hearts swell with the memories of how he lived that word—that word "love."

Certainly, there are other words that we might use—words like dedication, intelligence, efficiency, morality. All of these and more would fit him, and a lexicon of superlatives would not be enough, for here was a man who bespoke the best definition of each term.

Yet, we are heartened by the fact that rather than words, we will use our memories, those images that are inscribed within our hearts, to keep that part of him alive within us that we knew so well and to cherish the legacy that he has left for us all—that legacy of love and honor which was his life and which, in truth, can never, never die.

SPECIAL DATA: *Time of eulogy: about two and one-half minutes.*

This is a somewhat different type of eulogy which establishes a theme (in this case, the inadequacy of words) and carries that throughout the speech. This can be an effective technique.

You will notice that nowhere in the speech is the deceased's name mentioned. Rather, he is referred to as a "friend." Some speakers believe that this is the best approach since, they claim, everyone is only too aware of the subject anyhow. Others claim that this makes the eulogy seem rather formal, and that frequent mention of the subject's name makes for a warmer and more personal eulogy. It's up to you. What do you think?

127

TOPIC: **Eulogy for an educator (second version).**
AUDIENCE: **Adults; family members, colleagues, friends.**

Mrs. Hansen, members of the Hansen family, Dr. Springfield, ladies and gentlemen...

When we heard of the passing of John Hansen, there was no one who was not deeply saddened.

We were touched by his death, I know, because we had all been so deeply touched by his life—a life of dedication and service that spanned over thirty years as a hard-working, conscientious educator.

An educator of the quality of John Hansen holds a very special position in society, as we all know, and all the amassed superlatives that literature has used to describe outstanding educators could very easily be put together for a vivid description of the life of John Hansen.

Intelligent, dedicated, caring, supportive, courageous—these are adjectives that could be synonymous with John Hansen, and yet, they are more than words—they are the virtues that John lived each and every day.

Honor, morality, conscience—these are words that others used to describe John Hansen. Yet, more than words, these were qualities that were part and parcel of the man. He taught them as he lived them.

But, while John bespoke the epitome of the best that education has to offer, he belied the image of the educator as meek and mild, for he was a fighter—a person who would not give up. He fought for his students, striving against all odds to bring learning into the lives of each and every one. He fought for his school, striving always to improve what was already fine and good and shaping it into the finest it was capable of becoming. He fought for the children of this township, overcoming obstacles and raising the quality of education until we have the outstanding product that we have today. Yes, John Hansen was a fighter and a winner.

This was John Hansen, a man who left a mark on his chosen profession which we, in that profession, may well point to with justifiable pride.

As he was a man who lived a life worthy of respect, so we respect his memory; as he was a man of honor who brought honor and dignity to every situation he entered, so we honor his name; as he was a man who touched our lives and left us the better for the association, so his passing touches us now and leaves a void in our lives, a void that may close with time, but one that can never be made completely whole.

Therefore, we do now what we must: we pledge ourselves anew to those principles of education which were the guide and measure of John Hansen's life. We pledge that we will try as he tried to live up to that standard of honor John Hansen has left to all of us as his living legacy.

That dedication, inspired by his life, will spur us on to new achievements. Those achievements will remain as the living proof that John Hansen continues to live in the hearts of those who knew and loved him.

SPECIAL DATA: *Time of eulogy: slightly over three minutes.*

This eulogy is almost exactly like the one that preceded it. It uses words as a predominant theme and goes on to explain how they are more than words but qualities which the deceased exhibited in his life.

We feel this eulogy is much more personal than the preceding one, however. Here, the subject is mentioned by name several times throughout the eulogy. Moreover, specifics of his life and career are enumerated. Finally, his contribution to education and the effect which it would have on his fellow educators is spelled out.

128

TOPIC: **Eulogy for an educator who has met an untimely death.**
AUDIENCE: **Mixed; educators, family members, friends, colleagues.**

(SPECIAL NOTE: One of the saddest of life's occurrences happens when someone who is relatively young and healthy passes away unexpectedly. When this happens, and you are asked to deliver a eulogy, you might consider using the following, which concerns an educator who met with an untimely death.)

Mrs. Carson, Mr. and Mrs. Carson (deceased's parents), Betsy, Mayor Bradley, dear friends...

Adlai Stevenson was once asked to comment about a man who had met with an untimely death. His analysis was this: "It is not the years in a life that count; it is the life in the years."

Harold Carson has been taken from us. We know this to our abiding sorrow. While death is never welcome, we are, at least, prepared for it in a person of advanced years or someone who has fallen victim to pervasive illness. Therefore, we are doubly devastated when it occurs in someone of Harold's years and someone of his amazing vitality.

But, it is not of death that I would speak today. Rather, I would choose to speak of that vitality which I mentioned just now. I would tell you of a man who, to paraphrase Mr. Stevenson, filled his years with life even if his life was not filled with years. This is what I would speak about.

I would tell you of the Harold Carson I knew. This was a man who was comfortable wherever he went and with whomever he might be sharing his time. Whether it was before a class or a meeting of principals or the board of education or a civic or community group; whether he was with students, teachers, administrators or community leaders—whatever the circumstances; whoever the people—Harold Carson met the situation *and* the people with an enthusiasm, a concern, an energy, and a positive attitude that could not help but affect those he was with; that could not help but influence the situation and aid in bringing out the best in everyone. When Harry tackled a job, he did it with that vitality that made you realize he was not going to let go until the job was done, and inspired in you a confidence that it *could* be done, and that it was worthy of being done, and that you could have a hand in its completion.

Furthermore, perhaps one of the best indicators of that vitality and efficiency that we could note would be that while there were people who disagreed with Harry, Harry had no enemies, for there was no one who disagreed with Harry who did not respect him as well. Indeed, Harry Carson was respected as a man of honor and integrity. He was someone who could be trusted; he was someone to whom you could always go and find a willing listener with a receptive ear; he was someone who could be counted on to offer help in each and every case.

THIS is the life of which I would speak; THIS is the vitality; THIS is Harold Carson.

Now, too soon, he is gone. We can't fully comprehend it yet; it hasn't sunken in. But, we shall—we shall. Our lives shall be emptier for his absence, because they were made fuller by his presence.

And so, we honor his memory; a memory that each of us carries inscribed in his mind; a memory in which Harold Carson yet lives—the vital, intelligent, warm and humane person we all knew and loved so well.

And we resolve, here and now, to cherish that memory and nourish it. To keep the spirit of Harold Carson alive, and use it as a guide to spread those principles of honor and morality in which Harold Carson believed; to spread them throughout our own lives. In so doing, may we know that once we had the honor of knowing someone like Harold Carson, and that has made us better people and the world a better place to be.

SPECIAL DATA: *Time of speech; slightly over four minutes.*
    We feel that this is a particularly good eulogy, for it acknowledges the untimeliness of the death in direct and simple terms, yet manages to pay a powerful tribute to the deceased.

AFTERTHOUGHTS

Of course, the greatest eulogy ever written might be in the speaker's hands, but if it is delivered insincerely, if the speaker does not believe what is being said, if it is "tossed off" as "just another speech," then it will be as empty and meaningless as reading the back of a cereal box.

Conviction in a speaker's voice and genuine sorrow and concern in his heart, on the other hand, will mean more than any dearth of finely wrought words. It will mean a warm and genuine eulogy that will be remembered.

Whether you choose from the eulogies we have just presented or use them as models to write your own, if you say what is in your heart and keep in mind the feelings of the family of the deceased, you will be fine.

Memorials

129

TOPIC: **All-purpose memorial poem.**
AUDIENCE: **Suitable for all audiences.**

> So many days have passed, and yet
>   The memory remains.
> And still of soft and silent nights
>   You come to us again.
>
> We see you as we knew you once;
>   You seem to smile, and then
> We see ourselves there at your side
>   As often it had been.
>
> And we return the smile you give
>   And cherish in our hearts
> The thought that we had days to share
>   Before we had to part.
>
> And we find that time has not erased,
>   Nor has its passage paled,
> That warmth we held for you in life;
>   That love that has not failed.
>
> And so, dear friend, we keep you close,
>   Although we are apart,
> And visit with you daily in
>   The visions of our hearts.

SPECIAL DATA: *Time of poem; about one minute.*

This poem fits in well in any memorial speech. It is reflective of a wide variety of emotions about the person being remembered. Since it does not specify a particular individual, it can be effectively used for anyone. Just make certain that it is delivered with warmth and understanding.

If desired, it could easily be changed to first person address. Be sure to make the necessary pronoun changes throughout the poem.

130

TOPIC: **Benediction for a memorial service (first version).**
AUDIENCE: **Suitable for all audiences.**

Dear friends...

Upon occasions such as this, we are only too aware of the fragility of these shells we call our bodies. But, also upon occasions such as these, we sense that there is more to each and every one of us than muscle and flesh and bone. We sense, with a very special clarity, that these are but dressings for the mind, the spirit, the soul, if you will, that truly defines who and what we are.

There is something eternal in that thought; something within us which reaches for life beyond our physical beings.

We feel that here, today, for as we turn our minds and hearts to the memory of our friend, we know that he lives within us, and we know that somehow, and somewhere, his spirit continues to glow with the brilliance he manifested while he was among us.

As he honored us with his life, let each of us honor him within our hearts and minds.

SPECIAL DATA: *Time of memorial benediction; slightly over a minute.*

This particular benediction might be called a "nonsectarian" version of a benediction. You will notice that while it does mention immortality in an oblique manner, it does not mention the Almighty at all.

Please do not mistake us. We believe in God and certain religious principles, but in some situations where you might be speaking before people of widely divergent principles and beliefs, a benediction such as this, which phrases things in humanistic terms, might well suit the bill.

131

TOPIC: **Benediction for a memorial service (second version).**
AUDIENCE: **Suitable for all audiences.**

Dear friends...

Let us bow our heads, and each in his own way remember the subject of our gathering today.

I ask You, dear God, to hear us now. We ask Your blessing on our gathering here, today. We have met to remember our friend, Jesse Burke. It was Your will that he be taken from us, and we must accept that and take refuge in the thought that he is with You and at rest.

Grant that we may carry on the work that he pursued while he was with us. And, as Jesse's life of service and giving to others was pleasing in Your sight, may what we do, inspired by the quality of Jesse's association with us, be equally pleasing and blessed by You.

And may the soul of Jesse Burke rest in peace.

SPECIAL DATA: *Time of memorial benediction; about one minute.*

This second version directly mentions God and has pronounced religious overtones. It is more like what a clergyman would deliver than an administrator, but we thought that we would provide this version as well. You will know your audience, and only you will be able to judge what would go best before them. If you do choose this one, you will find that it is simple but effective.

132

TOPIC: **Memorial to an educator.**
AUDIENCE: **Suitable for all audiences, but better before adults.**

Dear friends...

We are gathered together today to pay tribute to someone whom we all knew very well.

It was one year ago today that our friend, Jane Bennett, died.

When I think of Jane, my mind is flooded with images. I see her in the classroom, bending over a child, explaining and helping that child to learn. I see her at rehearsal of the student plays which she so loved to direct and which she did so well. I see her getting up upon that stage to show the kids how a particular scene should go. I see her performing in the Parent-Faculty Variety Show, and I see her coercing several of us here to overcome our reluctance and join her in that activity. I see her working on school dances, tacking up decorations and showing the students a dance step or two in the process.

These things I see when I think of Jane Bennett, and I see even more.

I see her in my office, fighting for one of her students in whom she believed. I see her standing up for what she believed in against all kinds of odds. I see her working on committees to improve and revise the curriculum. I see her speaking before the board of education in behalf of her profession and for the welfare of the students in the face of budget cuts.

This I also see when the image of Jane Bennett floats across my memory.

I see these things, and I smile. I remember her vitality and enthusiasm, and she is back with me once more. I remember her commitment to education, her dedication to the ideals of teaching, her deep concern for each and every child, her expertise both in and out of the classroom, and I am proud of her.

And then I realize that she exists now only in my memory.

Yet, she is still real; still a part of our lives. She lives on in the lives of those students she guided and in whom she helped forge those principles of morality which she, herself, embodied. She lives on in our lives as her memory inspires us to strive, as she did, for all that is good and worth having for ourselves and others. She lives on as an educator, as our teacher, for by her life she taught us lessons in courage and concern, in dedication and commitment, and in efficiency and trust that will serve us all in our personal lives.

It was the hallmark of her life that Jane Bennett gave of herself in all situations. Now, it is our turn.

We can give to Jane Bennett the pledge that, in our lives, we will strive to help our students as she would have; we will fight for the best in education as she would have fought; we will always work for the best we can be, because she has left us a sterling model to be our guide.

Because of this, our students and those students not yet born will learn and grow.

Now—THAT is a memorial Jane would have loved.

SPECIAL DATA: *Time of memorial; about three and one-half minutes.*

This is an exceptional memorial that should be used to honor an exceptional educator. It bespeaks the finest sentiments about someone who gave a lifetime in service to education, and affirms her contribution in realistic terms and in terms of the present rather than the past.

As a tribute, it is outstanding. As a definition of the finest in education and dedication it is also unparalleled.

133

TOPIC: **Memorial for a group of individuals.**
AUDIENCE: **Suitable for all audiences.**

(SPECIAL NOTE: It is tragic, but it does happen that several people from a school system may meet with disaster, as during an accident on a school-sponsored trip, an explosion in school, etc. The following memorial is for such an occasion.)

Dear friends...

We gather together today on the anniversary of one of the greatest tragedies ever to befall our school system and our community.

It was a year ago today that a bus filled with fifty eager, excited and happy students set out from our school for a day that was to be filled with learning and fun. As we are all aware, the bus never reached its destination. The chaperones and twenty-eight of the students ended up in a hospital, some with extremely serious injuries that affect their lives even today.

Twenty-two students never returned.

At first, the magnitude of the loss refused to register. It was simply too much tragedy to comprehend. It was as if the shock of the news was so great that we were numb in the face of the onslaught. I remember the silence in the school when we first heard; a shocked, deadly silence that was more devastating than the loudest and most piercing of screams.

Then, with time, the full impact slapped us head on, and a sorrow beyond words, a grief that could never be adequately expressed settled upon us, and we came to understand the true meaning of the loss we had suffered and the emptiness it had left behind.

Then came the question; the inevitable question that mankind has surely asked from time immemorial; the cry that erupts from the depths of sorrow; the question—Why? Why had this happened? Why had our children been taken from us? Oh, certainly, we knew the mechanics of what had happened, but our question went deeper than that. It struck at the rationale of it all; it asked the cosmic reason why twenty-two of our children had to be denied life.

While that may be a universal question, the answer to it has always been personal in nature.

No one person can say "Why" it has happened, but each of us, in his own heart, must come to terms with it and find an answer in his own way. For some, it is slow in coming; for others, it never arrives, but, if it ever does, it will come in the sanctity of the individual heart that loved, that cherished, and that felt the loss. It is there and there alone that peace may be found, and it is there that each of us must seek an answer.

And we come, at last, to this very day. Time has passed and day has surplanted day. The seasons change as before; spring follows winter. Yet, it is not the same—not the same—for our children are not here to smell the crispness of the winter's air or to marvel at the beauty of the spring flowers, and that has made all the difference.

We pause now, in the day-to-day operation of our lives, to remember them as they were—the vital and laughing children we all knew. There is still sorrow for their passing, and we know that time will never fully erase the pain nor fill the void, but there is also the joy that we had them for a while, and our lives were made fuller by that association.

We will resolve, therefore, that they will not have died in vain; that we will keep them alive in our hearts and cherish their memories; that our love for those around us will be made stronger by the special bond that we will always have with them, our children.

We say this, and we tell them, sleep, sleep, our children, until that time when we may awake with you to face a new and a brighter day.

Sleep with our love.

SPECIAL DATA: *Time of memorial; slightly over four minutes.*

The type of tragedy detailed in this memorial has to be one of the worst disasters to befall a school system. Yet, as experience has taught us, it does happen. When it does, it will be difficult to say and will certainly be highly charged emotionally. Group services and memorials after the event become the rule.

The memorial above is powerful and touching, and we know that we would have a difficult time delivering it in the circumstances described. It would, however, be extremely effective and dynamic for everyone in the audience.

134

TOPIC: **Memorial for an administrator.**

AUDIENCE: **Adults; educators, community members, board of education members.**

Ladies and gentlemen...

I knew Dr. Helen Grayson for almost seventeen years. In that time it was my pleasure to work with her on numerous projects involving the quality of education within our district. I got to know, firsthand, the very real contributions she made during her tenure as superintendent of schools to our school system.

I remember her dedication to excellence. She was a person who would accept nothing less than the best for the children she served. She would also accept nothing less than the best from those who worked with her, which was only fair, since she set just as high a standard for herself. Indeed, it was a hallmark of her life that she drove herself harder than those around her.

I remember driving home late one night from another appointment I had and passing by the administration building. I spotted the lights still on in her office, and I went into the building to see if anything was wrong. It was just past eleven, and there she was assiduously working away at her desk. I reminded her of the time, and I further reminded her that she had to give an extensive presentation on the budget the following day. I suggested that perhaps she should get some rest. "Besides," I added, "you always do so well; you have nothing to worry about."

She looked up at me, as I remember, and shook her head.

"Bill," she said to me, "don't you know by now: it takes a great deal of effort to make something look effortless."

Nor was that midnight working schedule an isolated incident. She never was a "nine-to-fiver" in the sense of calling an end to her day when the clock indicated that the rest of the world had gone home. She was a person highly dedicated to the ideals of her profession, and she knew that they required hard work to accomplish. She did not shrink from that duty, but pursued it with a fervor which saw its fruition in the slow and steady improvement of our school system during her tenure.

Moreover, she was a fighter who would stand up to a board of education and fight for the restoration of budget cuts or stand up to a pressure group if she felt some moral principle were being violated or stand up to any pressure from any quarter if she believed that what she was doing was the right thing to do for the children of this community.

And, indeed, it was the children who were her primary concern. First, last, and always—the children. With all her work and with all the demands upon her time, she always saw to it that there was time for them. Whether it was a football game or a kindergarten classroom presentation, she made the time to be there. Often, she would visit a school just to be with "her kids" as she called them. Never—never in her career did she lose that contact with the children in whose behalf she worked so diligently.

Dr. Helen Grayson was a person whom you had to respect. She gave you no choice in the matter. Her life of dedication, her hard work, her tireless efforts in behalf of quality education, and her relentlessness in pursuing her ideals could not help but be noticed by everyone around her. Even if she sat on the opposite side of an issue from you, you were struck by her conviction and her morality. You simply *had* to respect this fine woman and outstanding educator.

Therefore, I am more than happy to be able to add my voice to others tonight in honoring this fine individual, this sterling example of a dynamic and dedicated educator. Her passing saddened us all and left us with a palpable void, the effects of which we still feel today. Yet, while she was with us, she left us an outstanding example, a blueprint if you will, of how to carry on after her.

Her life left us who carry on after her better people, better administrators, better educators. We stand as the living memorials to her as we fight for the standards that she established.

We cannot forget her, and the world cannot help but be a better place because she was once among us.

Thank you.

SPECIAL DATA: *Time of speech; about five minutes.*

This memorial for an outstanding administrator was written originally as part of a longer ceremony. The speaker concentrates on his association with the deceased. Other speakers would tell of other phases of the person's life, etc.

You will also notice that this speech contains a slight bit of humor in the part about her telling him that it took effort to make things look effortless. It seems fitting here, because it is warm, and it was well known that the speaker had a friendly relationship with the deceased. The ending of the memorial, however, is kept strictly serious.

Be very careful about the use of humor in a memorial speech. For example, it would not matter how close you were to the subjects of the disaster outlined in the previous memorial. The use of ANY humor in that case would be inappropriate and a gigantic mistake. Use humor very sparingly, if at all, and only in those situations where there cannot be the slightest objection to its use.

Believe us, if you are merely sensitive to the situation, you will know when and when not to use it and to what degree it should be used.

135

TOPIC: **Memorial for an individual student.**

AUDIENCE: **Mixed; adults and students, family members, others.**

Students of Rock Township High School, honored guests, and particularly the members of the Miller family...

Bob Miller was a student at our school. He was a junior here and deeply involved in many aspects of school life. Whether as a player on the basketball team, as president of the stamp and coin club, or vice-president of our student council, Bob was vitally involved in his school. He was almost universally popular with students and faculty, and during the times that I worked with him through his duties on the student council, he impressed me with his intelligence, his good common sense, and his concern for others—qualities of which we might all be justifiably proud.

It was, therefore, with the deepest of regret and sorrow that we learned of the accident that took him from us. There was no one in the entire school who was not touched by the tragedy.

We gather here today, to pay honor to his memory and to show, in a very real way, the high regard in which Bob Miller was kept by us all.

One of the people who knew Bob best was...

(SPECIAL NOTE: The administrator now introduces one or a few people who speak about the deceased student. The speakers should be few in number and a mixture of students and adults, preferably faculty members. Their speeches, particularly those of fellow students, should be discreetly screened for appropriateness. When all the speeches are completed, the administrator steps forward once more.)

Finally, I have here a plaque, which was commissioned by the student council. The name "Robert J. Miller" is inscribed on it along with the dates. It further states, "A student of our school. He left his mark upon us ...nor shall we forget." It will have a prominent place in our school that we and those who come after us may know what we felt for Bob. Mr. and Mrs. Miller, please accept this in Bob's memory and with our love.

(SPECIAL NOTE: At this point, the administrator goes to Mr. and Mrs. Miller, presents them with the plaque, and shakes hands with them. IF it has been arranged beforehand that Mr. or Mrs. Miller or both wish to speak to the assembly, then the administrator would gently lead them to the microphone, and discreetly step back allowing them to speak. If they indicated that they did not wish to speak at all, then after handing them the plaque and shaking hands, the administrator would step back to the microphone alone. Whatever the case, there will be applause when the administrator goes to the parents, and when finished with the presentation, the administator should join in the applause. Whether the parents speak or not, when the administrator returns to the microphone, he concludes the ceremony.)

Bob Miller was a credit to his friends, his school, and his parents, We who were privileged enough to know him, knew that he was a special person, indeed. We have seen fit to honor his memory this day. As we leave here, let each of us resolve to cherish his memory in our own way, that he may continue to live within our hearts.

Thank you, and good afternoon.

SPECIAL DATA: *Time of memorial program; five to fifteen minutes, depending upon the length and number of speeches given.*

This is an example of a memorial assembly program which might be given in a school where a student has died. The memorial above attempts to outline the procedures an administrator might follow in order to present an assembly.

The keynote to the success of the assembly would be planning it thoroughly beforehand. The parents should be notified well ahead of time. If they have objections to it, the matter should not be pressed. Nor should they be pressed into speaking if they do not want to. They should be informed as to precisely what will happen. For example, if they were not aware that a plaque was to be presented, and this so got to them emotionally that they had to be escorted off stage, it would not be well for anyone.

If, however, they know what to expect, and exact plans for the progression of the assembly are made and noted in advance, it can provide a very fitting memorial and an appropriate vehicle for faculty and students to express their feelings to the parents.

136

TOPIC: **An administrator's introduction to a memorial ceremony.**
AUDIENCE: **Adults.**

Ladies and gentlemen...

Because we are human beings and part of the family of mankind, we are aware that in the midst of life, there is death. As the poet John Donne wrote, "each man's death diminishes me, because I am a part of mankind." But, while death is universal, we are also aware that the lives which led to death differ drastically in quality. We realize that some people live their lives with such honor and morality and dignity, that at their deaths it is only fitting that those around them stand up and proclaim that this was a life worthy of note, worthy of respect, worthy of honor.

When this happens; when a particular life shines forth as a beacon to everyone of just what can be accomplished in this imperfect world; when a life is so lived that mankind is, indeed, shaken by its loss—when these things happen, then it is only right and proper that something be said about it; that the quality of that life be extolled so that everyone may know that this was a life one could point to with pride and hold up as a model to those who will come after.

That is the purpose of our gathering here today. Our colleague, our companion, our friend—Thomas Safick—has left us. We who stay behind remember what his life was like and what he gave. We have little choice but to gather together to express our regret that he is gone but, more importantly, our thanks that he was with us, an example to us all of just how fine a person can be.

SPECIAL DATA: *Time of memorial introduction; about one minute.*

Quite often, the administrator is asked to act as "moderator" of a memorial ceremony. If this is the case, the administrator will be expected to present a memorial speech, but he will also be expected to introduce other speakers and start the ceremony off and keep it going.

The speech above would be a good introduction and start of a memorial program. Thereafter, the administrator would introduce the speakers at the program and officiate at any further ceremony such as the dedication of a tree or a plaque.

The administrator should then reserve his memorial speech for last on the program. Following that, if there is to be a benediction, it should be given. If there is no benediction or after it has been given, the administrator should then dismiss the gathering. A simple phrase such as, "thank you all for coming, and good afternoon," would be sufficient.

When done properly and organized efficiently, such a memorial ceremony can be a fitting and touching tribute.

AFTERTHOUGHTS

If we could leave you with one idea firmly established about memorials, it would be this: Do your homework. By that, we mean that anyone who speaks at a memorial should take the time to work out or adapt a speech so that it will be personal and reflective of the life being honored. Certainly, you can use one of the speeches in this section, but be certain to adapt or alter it so that the personal and individual qualities of the subject come out.

You must also do particular homework if you are in charge of the entire memorial program. If everything is well-planned in advance, it will run smoothly. Just make certain that you have seen to every detail such as whether or not a relative of the deceased will speak, where the speakers will sit, etc. Planning is the keynote to efficiency.

Finally, if you will merely say what is in your heart, there is no one who can possibly fault your efforts. That is the final secret of all eulogies and memorials—sincerity. With it, all tasks, even something as draining as a speech of this type, are possible.

SECTION NINE

Special Speeches for Special Events

As every administrator knows, there are occasions that do not necessarily fit into one of the headings in this book. That is specifically the reason for this section in which we investigate some special speeches for special occasions.

For example, there will come the time when you retire, and you become the object of the retirement speeches of others. You will be expected to say something after all the other well-wishers have finished. It may well be that you will be the recipient of a testimonial, and you will be in the same position. As an administrator, you will be expected to say something, however brief, at the annual graduation ceremonies. And what about those "Sports Night" functions, or those dinners, or the faculty holiday party? Each and every one of these "special events" requires that the administrator be prepared to speak and say something meaningful as well as fitting.

Therefore, within the pages of this section, you will find fitting speeches on everything from a "quick" graduation speech to a highly effective speech about a life in education which might be effectively used at your own retirement dinner or at a testimonial for you. As with all the other speeches in this book, they are all ready to go and have been proven effective under rigorous conditions.

The key to the effective use of any or all of these speeches, of course, is personalizing them for your presentation. Change the names of people and places to fit your specifications, add personal anecdotes and stories where you find them appropriate, deliver them from your point of view and in your personal style, and you will have a speech that will be remembered.

Good luck, and have fun.

137

TOPIC: **Administrator's address to a graduating class.**

AUDIENCE: **Mixed; adults and students, educators, parents, friends.**

Members of the board of education, Dr. Parsons, members of the faculty, honored guests, parents, and members of the graduating class of 19XX...

Tonight I have a gift for you all—my speech will be short.

I am keeping it short, because I fully realize how eager you are to "get on with it." You are eager to get those diplomas for which you have worked so hard; you are eager to join your families and your friends to share your joy with them; you are eager to get started with your plans for the future.

And this is as it should be, for a graduation, far from being an end, is the beginning of all your tomorrows. Over the past several years you have worked and studied, practiced and played, and grown—grown mentally as well as physically—and now you are here, ready to begin your lives as members of the adult community.

For some of you this will mean a job and the responsibilities of family living. For others, this will mean college and further years of study and preparation. Whatever course YOUR future takes, it is my sincere hope that you will look back on your years here as having prepared you to meet and deal with the challenges that life will present.

On behalf of myself and the faculty and staff of Rock Township High School, I wish to each and every one of you the happiness of a productive life, the respect of your fellow human beings, and the love of your family. May the future be yours.

The best of luck and congratulations to the Class of 'XX.

SPECIAL DATA: *Time of speech; about two minutes.*

A graduation ceremony that drags on and on can seem interminable, and the audience can get very restless, precisely because of the reasons outlined in this speech. It is wise to leave the longer speeches to the principal speaker, if there is to be one, and to keep all other speeches short and to the point.

This is the type of speech that fills the bill for the administrator. It says everything that needs to be said, turns the attention of the class toward the future, conveys the message that the school has prepared them for that future, and wishes them the best of luck and happiness, and all in less than two minutes.

138

TOPIC: **Acceptance of retirement.**
AUDIENCE: **Adults; colleagues, friends, family.**

(SPECIAL NOTE: The following speech would be one given by the subject of a retirement dinner. When all the speeches have been made and the gift or gifts have been given, the audience usually expects the recipient to say a few words. This speech is when the person about to retire rises to address the audience.)

Well, I was going to start out by saying, "my friends," but after some of the jokes that have been made at my expense tonight, I think I'd better just say, "ladies and gentlemen...."

You know, I was watching closely as these people came up to speak tonight. Most of them I have known for almost all of my adult life. I was absolutely shocked, therefore, when I looked at them tonight and realized how fat and bald they had become.

And what they said! At one point, my wife poked me in the ribs and asked me who they were talking about. I told her that I didn't know, but if it turned out that they were talking about me, I was going to sue the superintendent for not giving me a better salary.

Seriously, however, I did have a difficult time listening to those speeches. They paint a picture of a life spent in education, and they were flattering in the extreme. For all those kind words, I am grateful, and I thank you. From my heart, for all that love, I thank you.

Yes, I have a life of thirty-five years in education to look back on, and I know that the memories from those years will remain with me in the days ahead. Of course, not all of the times were good times, but neither were they all bad. Rather, they were like all of life, a mixture of hills and valleys, ups and downs, that make up a span of years. Yet, as I look back even now, the unpleasant fades into the background, and that which was good and worthwhile remains vivid and clear.

And there was so much that was fine. I have seen students grow and mature; I have seen our school system grow and develop; I have seen education itself grow into a powerful and dynamic profession. That I was a part of it all, however small, gives me the greatest of pleasures, and I am thankful that I was allowed to be there.

Now I am stepping aside, but I am not stepping down. Education has been my life, and I fully intend to keep abreast of all that is happening. I also fully intend to visit from time to time just to keep in touch and, of course, to see to it that all of you keep on your toes.

And, while I do look forward to my retirement and to finally having the time to pursue some personal interests and, most importantly, to be able to spend more time with Arlene, my wife of thirty-seven years, whom I love dearly—while I do look forward to all of this, I know that I shall also miss my daily contact with all of you, my colleagues and my friends.

Because, and make no mistake about it, if some of the things that have been said about me this evening are true, it is because I have, in my professional life, been fortunate enough to be surrounded by some of the finest educators this country has produced; people whose dedication and drive and expertise could not help but rub off on me. I have learned from them, and, for that tutoring, I shall be eternally grateful.

For all that has been said this evening and for all that has been done, you have my deep thanks; for all the toil and care and concern that I have witnessed you give for the good of the children of this land, you have my respect; and, for all that you have been, are tonight, and will be tomorrow, you have my love.

Thank you for everything, and good evening.

SPECIAL DATA: *Time of speech; about five minutes.*

You will notice that this speech started out very humorously. It also contains slight but very warm digs at the speakers who were obviously friends of the subject. This was effective because of the very special relationship between the speaker and the audience. The warmth and the love in the latter part of the speech are evident.

This is the type of speech that will have an audience on its feet applauding at the end.

139

TOPIC: **Administrator's address to a gathering of alumni.**
AUDIENCE: **Adults; the alumni of the school and their guests.**

Ladies and gentlemen...

I have a very important announcement. If any of you in the audience feel the need to use the lavatory facilities, I expect you to first raise your hand and wait to be recognized.

(*SPECIAL NOTE: We have personally used this line with all types of adult audiences, and it never fails to get a big laugh and set everyone at ease.*)

Seriously, though, surely there must have come a moment in your life, as it comes to all of us, when you turned your mind toward the days of your youth. It was inevitable in such a reverie that you returned to the school that played such a major part in your life at that time. Indeed, it is inevitable that you and your school are intrinsically a part of each other. We can only hope that association was happy and beneficial, and that you are eager to learn more about your school and your fellow classmates.

Well, here you are, back once more. This time you travel the halls of the school as an observer rather than a participant. You will find no one who is going to tell you to stop chewing gum or send you to the office for smoking in the lavatory. What you will find, however, are memories around every corner.

You met your boyfriend or girfriend by the water fountain; you joined the rest of the guys around that locker; there's the table where you ate lunch with the rest of the gang. They are all here, these memories of the time when this was your school.

Yet, in a very real sense, this is still YOUR school. You have become a part of it as it has become a part of you that can never be erased.

This will always be your school.

Welcome back!

SPECIAL DATA: *Time of speech; about a minute and a half.*

An active and involved alumni can do a great deal of good for a school. Where one exists, it is quite common for the current administrator to be invited to speak. The speech above would be the welcoming speech for such a gathering. Notice that it is kept short and identifies the audience with the school.

140

TOPIC: **Address to faculty about news coverage.**
AUDIENCE: **Adults; all educators, the faculty of a school.**

Ladies and gentlemen...

Recently, with a change in editorial policy at our local newspaper, we have been fotunate enough to receive increased coverage of school events. With this increased coverage, we have had an excellent opportunity to present ourselves and our school to the residents of our district. I know that many of you have been asked to write articles on your extracurricular activities, activities of note in your classrooms, and even opinions about such topics as the current budget and board of education elections.

While what you write, if you choose to write, is strictly up to you, I thought that I might take this time to share with you some suggestions that have served me well in the past. I think you will find them worthy of your consideration.

First, emphasize the positive. We have many outstanding students and activities in this school. Many things happen here that are fine and noble. The public should be aware of these as they happen.

Second, don't hide the negative. If something unfortunate happens, please do not try to cover it up. That will only make it seem worse. Present it honestly. State your opinion of the incident in a positive manner, however.

Next, make certain that you tell the whole story. It is essential that we present all sides of an issue. If, for example, 50 students stage a demonstration on the front lawn, make certain that you mention the other 500 students who stayed in class and did not join them. Above all, let's keep our perspective.

Finally, if you are in doubt, if you are not certain what effect a story or comment will have on the school, the system, or you personally, then for goodness sake, check it out first. No one is going to think the less of you because you took time to see to it that what you had said or written was factual and did not hurt anyone. In that regard, I would be happy to offer any help I could, and you have an open invitation to consult me at any time.

Remember this: we don't have to manufacture news. There are enough positive, energetic and fine activities going on in our schools to supply many news stories.

Let's let the public know the good things that are going on in our schools.

SPECIAL DATA: *Time of speech; slightly over two minutes.*

This speech would be delivered at a faculty meeting where the administrator had to address a situation that had potential for becoming harmful. In this case, it was the fact of unedited and unchecked news releases going out of the building to the local newspaper.

Notice, however, that the speech is kept very positive and upbeat. At no point is anything said that might be interpreted as negating an individual's right to freedom of expression. Rather, it is a genuine and warm appeal to make certain that the whole story is told and that the positive as well as the negative is emphasized.

141

TOPIC: **Administrator's address at a "Sports Night" dinner.**
AUDIENCE: **Mixed; adults and student athletes, family, friends.**

Ladies and gentlemen and the athletes of Rock Township High School....

We have had an outstanding dinner, made all the better because we enjoyed it together.

Indeed, it is being together that makes so much of what we do in life worthwhile. I don't have to tell you that, because you are well aware of what is meant by "team spirit." During the school year, when you get out on that playing field, there is no one who does not recognize the fact that you function as a single unit, as a team. Because of that and because of the practice, dedication, and hard work that you have put into making that team the best it could be, you have achieved victory after victory. We here tonight are proud of you.

But, understand something. We would have been just as proud of you if you had not won a single game. We would have been proud of you, because you learned how to work together for a goal that was bigger than any one person. You learned to cooperate for the good of all, and that has made you the outstanding young men and women whom we applaud and admire.

Nor is what I am saying merely words. This dinner tonight stands as testimony to what we feel.

But there is another feeling here tonight; one which you should share with us as well.

Along with the pride and respect we feel, there is the realization that we are all part of a much larger team, a team in which everyone here plays a very important part. The name of that team is humanity.

We are all part of the family of mankind, and, as such, we all have a team position to play. From your teachers and coaches who instruct you, to your parents who raise you, care for you and love you, to the members of the opposing team who give you a challenge in order that you may perfect yourselves and your skills, we all play a part in a game called life.

Because we all play our parts, because we all function as members of that team, we can strive to be the best of which we are capable of becoming. In doing that, the team, mankind, cannot help but be the better for it.

Therefore, while I and all of us here assembled applaud your efforts as athletes during this past season, we also applaud your efforts as human beings. We applaud your dedication; your spirit of sacrifice for the good of others; your willingness to work together for that common goal. These are qualities that are none too common in the world, and when we find them in people such as you, it is only right that we acknowledge them.

We are well aware that what you accomplished on the playing field is only the forerunner of what you will do in life. That gives us renewed hope for a bright and positive future for all of mankind.

So, to all the members of the team—to everyone here and elsewhere who had a hand in this night—I say "Well done—well done, indeed."

Thank you.

SPECIAL DATA: *Time of speech; about four minutes.*

"Sports Night" dinners and end-of-the-year or season banquets are quite common. Administrators are usually expected to attend and to address the assembly. The speech above is one example of an appropriate speech for such a gathering.

All speeches of this nature should be upbeat and give credit to the students, their parents and teachers.

142

TOPIC: **Education as a career.**

AUDIENCE: **Mixed; mainly students, but possibly adults as well.**

> *(SPECIAL NOTE: With the increased emphasis on career education in our nation's schools, educators are often called upon to speak at various occasions about education as a career. Whether you are one speaker at a "Career Day" program or guest lecturer in a classroom, here is a speech that will serve.)*

Good afternoon, and thank you for the opportunity to speak to you about education.

I have to be honest with you, my career in education did not start out very well. While it may be difficult for you to picture, when I started teaching, I was a very young man, and, since I was starting off in a high school, I didn't look too different from some of the students in the school, particularly the seniors.

On the first day of school, I got there very early, prepared my classroom, and went to stand by my classroom door as the students arrived. Everything was going well, and most of the students had arrived when the bell rang for the start of homeroom period. Well, I noticed that not all the seats in my classroom were filled, so I stayed out in the hall, looking for some students who may have lost their way.

All at once, an older teacher whom I did not know or recognize came down the hall, spotted me pacing in front of the open classroom door, and rushed up to me.

"What are you doing in the hall?" he roared at me. "Didn't you hear that bell?"

"Yes," I said, "I did, but...."

"Don't give me any backtalk, kid," he went on. "Students are supposed to be in homeroom. Get where you belong!"

"Wait a minute," I tried to explain, "I'm not a kid. You see, I was just...."

"I don't need explanations. I just need you in a room. Right now, kid, or you're going to get a week of central detention!"

With that, he spun me around, directed me rather forcibly into the classroom, yelled out, "And stay there!" and slammed the door.

That is how I was introduced to my first class.

Many years have passed since then, but I still remember that situation. I have many other memories as well from a career in education, and most of them are memories I would not trade for any price.

If any of you are considering making education your career, however, there are some things you should know.

Perhaps the greatest fallacy about professional education is the idea that anyone can teach. I am here to tell you that simply is not true. I have seen some really tough character who entered education quit or leave in the middle of a school year because the pressure had gotten to them. I have seen people with a great deal of knowledge who were unable to communicate that knowledge to their classes. Not everyone can teach. It takes some special qualifications.

First of all, you have to like young people. Now, don't mistake me. That doesn't mean that you have to enjoy rock music or be able to boogie on the dance floor. What it does mean is that you have to believe that young people are the hope of the future. You have to believe that you can make a difference, and a positive difference, in their lives. You have to like being with them; be willing to listen to them without condemning; and give advice without preaching. You have to get a kick out of helping kids.

If you have this qualification, then the next thing you need is knowledge. You have to know the subject you are teaching. What's more, you have to know it inside and out.

Then, you have to know how to communicate. You have to be able to get that knowledge across to a roomful of students, some of whom may be painting their fingernails or gazing out the window at a beautiful spring day. You learn that students learn at different rates, and that what may be easy for one student may be incomprehensible for another. You have to be able to communicate to both of those students. Not only must you communicate with students, but quite often you must meet with parents or groups from the community, and you have to be able to make your ideas clear to them as well. Yes, you have to know how to communicate.

Finally, you must have specialized knowledge in teaching skills. I'm not talking here about how to make out an absentee report; that varies from school to school, and anybody can learn how to fill that out. Rather, I am talking about how to make up a test that is fair to the highest and lowest student in your class. You have to know how to present a subject in such a manner that the majority of the class will retain it. You have to know what to do when a student gets sick in class; how to spot potential trouble that may be harmful to students before it starts; how to get to the kid who is "turned off" to everything, including school.

How you get this knowledge, and what is specifically required to become a teacher, varies somewhat from state to state. In our state...

(SPECIAL NOTE: At this point, you would detail specific requirements for teaching certification and/or teaching within your district. It would be an excellent device to have some handouts.)

...and those are the basic requirements.

Now, many people who enter education as a teacher may feel, after a while, that they want to help young people in some way other than in the classroom. I speak now about positions such as guidance counselor, principal or even as a superintendent of schools; positions where, while you are not teaching, you are helping young people with their lives and life choices, are seeing to it that they get the best education they can, and are seeing to it that the school or the system runs efficiently for the good of those students.

Such positions are called administrative positions, and they require an entire range of knowledge above and beyond that of a classroom teacher. They also require state certification in certain areas.

(SPECIAL NOTE: Here, again, you would tell of the special requirements for a supervisory certificate as well as some specific requirements for an administrative position within your district.)

Whatever course your career in education may take, you can be certain that it will have its rewards and its drawbacks. I will tell you frankly that I still do not feel that educators are adequately paid. You can look forward to about two hours work at home each night after school just involving paper work of some kind. At times, discipline problems in a class may make that class frustrating. There are reports to be handed in. Sometimes it seems as if all people want to do is complain either to you or about you.

I will not lie to you. A career in education has its drawbacks. Aside from the pay and the hours and the complaints, there is the emotional involvement as well. I have seen kids whom I thought had a good chance at success destroy themselves with drugs, and I have been powerless to help. I have gone to the funerals of kids who, just a short time ago had faced me in the halls of the school. I have seen all this, and it has gotten to me.

But, I have also seen a kid begin to learn where before he did nothing but disrupt class. I have seen ideas enter a mind and change a life for the better. I have had a person come up to me to tell me how what I had done in class had changed his life. I have seen terrible personal problems solved silently and without anyone knowing about it, because I and others worked behind the scenes. I have been able to establish programs that I knew would benefit kids who weren't even born yet.

Yes, the rewards of a career in education are great, too.

Let me sum it all up. I started out by telling you what happened on the first day of my career; now let me end by telling you something that happened just recently.

I was shopping one Saturday recently when I heard my name called. I turned around and was faced by a young man of about twenty-one years. He came up and shook my hand. I have to tell you that I searched my memory, but I did not recognize him. Finally, I told him so.

"I'm sorry," I said, "I realize that I probably know you from school, but I simply do not remember you."

"That's not surprising," he said, "since we only met for one day."

I must have looked puzzled, because he continued.

"About five years ago, our science teacher, Mr. Jenkins, got sick and you had to take over the class."

I was beginning to remember. The teacher had, indeed, taken ill unexpectedly and had to leave the school. It was the last period of the day, and I stepped into the classroom to take over. Science was not and is not now my subject, and my knowledge of it was limited. Therefore, I had no idea of what I was going to do with this unexpected science class. Then I remembered about the book I had been reading which told about a man named Gregor Mendel, who had discovered the laws of heredity. So, I told them about that, and as I spoke, I became more and more enthusiastic. I really tried to get them to appreciate the story as I had. Finally, the bell had rung, the class had left, and that, I thought, was that.

It wasn't. The young man before me continued.

"I was in that class, and when you told us about the work that Mendel had done, you made it sound so interesting that, after the class, I just had to get a book on it. One thing led to another, and I'll be graduating from college this June with a degree in biology. When I saw you, I just wanted to say thanks."

With that, he turned and left. I never saw him again, and I still don't know his name.

But, I'll tell you one thing. THAT is one reward of a career in education that I'll take—any time!

Thank you, and good afternoon.

SPECIAL DATA: *Time of speech; ten to twenty minutes depending upon inserted material and audience reaction.*

This speech concentrates on a career in public education from elementary to high school level both as a teacher and as an administrator. If you wish to add teaching or administration on the college level, it would be an easy task.

As an overview of education as a career, it fits the bill, for it details not only requirements but rewards and drawbacks as well. Notice that it ends on a very positive note, and that the language is kept relatively simple, since it is intended as an introduction to education as a career for a group of young people.

143

TOPIC: **Kickoff speech for a fund-raising event.**

AUDIENCE: **Mixed; adults and students, educators, parents.**

(SPECIAL NOTE: The financial situation being what it is, it is not surprising that schools have money problems. There is simply not enough to go around to everybody. Therefore, schools raise money for special events not covered in the budget in ways that they have for many years. They hold fund-raising events. The following would be a kickoff speech for one such project.)

Faculty and students, parents, friends...

Whenever you start talking about money, everybody has an opinion. Some people will tell you that you don't need money to enjoy life. Others will tell you that that is true, but that you do need money to stay alive to enjoy the life that you don't need money to enjoy. Whatever is said, almost invariably the conversation will end up with the cliché, "Money is the root of all evil."

While that may be true, one social critic observed, "The lack of money is the root of all evil."

I don't know how true that is, but I do know this: The entire class represented here this evening has the once-in-a-lifetime opportunity to travel to Trinidad to perform in a cultural festival there, and, without money, they are not going, and THAT is far from good.

(SPECIAL NOTE: At this point, the speaker would briefly detail exactly what took place that occasioned the particular event or trip or whatever for which the money is needed. It need not be long, since most of the people would know the story anyhow.)

Which brings us to this very night. We know that we need funds. We know how much we need, and, thanks to the help and support and quality thinking of the committee organizers, we know how to go about getting it. Looking out at you tonight and seeing in your faces the enthusiasm and dedication that I do, I have not a single doubt but that we will work on this project, we will raise the money, and we will go and have a great time.

But, now it is time to do more than plan, more than think about it, more than talk—now it is time to act.

And act we will! In a few moments, I will be introducing you to the committee chairperson, Mrs. Petersen, who will explain in detail the procedures we will undertake to raise that money in time. I have had the opportunity to look them over, and I will tell you that they are ambitious and will require a great deal of hard work from everyone here tonight.

Let me also tell you that I firmly believe that the money will be raised and that our class will be on their way.

It has been said that anything worth having is worth working for. What we want for this class is worthwhile, and I know of no one here who is not willing to give of his time and effort to see it accomplished.

Whatever happens, you should know that rarely have I been prouder of a group of people than I am of you tonight. So many people see a task ahead which is large and overpowering, and they merely give up. They say, "I can't do it," and, sure enough, they can't. But, not you. No, not you wonderful, enthusiastic group of fighters. You see the task and say, "When can I get started?" We tell you that it is a huge undertaking, and you tell us that the largest mountain can be removed one stone at a time. We tell you that you will be working long and hard hours to get this done, and you tell us that you are not afraid of work and that you are anxious to get to it.

With an attitude like that; with the drive and excitement that is evidenced here tonight; with the dedication to each other which also bespeaks your love for each other—with all of this going for us, WE CANNOT FAIL.

ONWARD TO TRINIDAD!!!

(SPECIAL NOTE: At this point the audience will be very vocal. Wait for the applause to die down, say something like, "Now, let's get to it," and introduce the next speaker or the next segment of the program.)

SPECIAL DATA: *Time of speech; five to seven minutes, depending on amount of material inserted and audience reaction.*

The purpose of a fund-raiser kickoff speech is to fire up the workers, instill in them the conviction that the job can be done, and exhort them to action. It is not that you must become a cheerleader, but this must be an address of great conviction on your part and must "get to" the audience.

144

TOPIC: **Budget speech to the public.**

AUDIENCE: **Adults; mainly community members.**

(SPECIAL NOTE: School budgets are notorious for the way in which they get voted down by the public and the amount of furor they can engender in open meetings. The following speech is representative of one where the administrator defends the budget before a group of community members who, if not openly hostile, are not disposed toward new taxes and therefore, not in favor of it.)

Ladies and gentlemen…

Let's get right to it. We are here to speak about the school budget for the 19XX-19XX school year. I fully realize from the other people who have spoken this evening that there are people in this audience who are not in favor of it. That is, of course, their right as citizens of this community. I am in favor of it. I believe it is a good budget. In fact, I believe it is the best that we can have under the circumstances which I intend to detail for you. I do not ask you to agree with me; I do ask that you hear me out. If we have the right to disagree, then we each have the right to make our side known. I know, because I know and respect this community, that you will grant me that right.

Before I go saying something that isn't true or lest any of you accept a rumor that has no basis in fact, perhaps it would be wise if we both took a closer look at exactly what we are talking about.

This is the proposed budget for the coming school year.…

(SPECIAL NOTE: At this point, the administrator would explain the budget, preferably using a chart or some other visual aid. Don't merely detail how much is to be spent in each area, but tell what IMPROVE-MENTS there will be within each area. For example, "…and the establishment of that lunch program will mean the children will never have to walk in freezing rain or face the dangers of traffic at lunchtime.…")

...this, then, is the budget of which we are talking.

I hope you will agree with me and see it as I do—as a budget without "fat" in it in any way; as a sensible solution to some problems that have been causing your children trouble for some time now; as something that will cost money, but will pay dividends in improved student services and improved learning for our children.

I have not closed my ears to the community, nor have I closed my eyes to the situation of the economy. Yes, I am aware that these are hard times. Yes, I am aware that this budget will mean an increase in property taxes. Yes, I am aware of how much is involved.

But, some say, "Cut the budget." I ask, "Where?" Is it salaries? The salary guides for this district are public record. They are not exorbitant. They are comparable to every other community around us. Just last month, a community group published an open letter about the high quality of teaching in this township. Do we now go to the teachers and say, "You are doing a marvelous job, so we are cutting your pay."

All right, some say, "Cut the budget," and I ask, Where? Is it in services? If it is, then we must legitimately ask, "With whose child do we start?" We can cut down on transportation by making the children walk longer distances to school. What do we make the limit? Two miles? Five? And where do we start? Who tells the children that there will no longer be a hot lunch for them? Who tells the children that there will no longer be after-school activities? Who does the telling?

All right, I hear you say, we want the techers to have a living wage; we want our children to retain the services they need; but what about the new building program? Certainly that can be cut.

I remind you that neither I nor the board of education has any control over the costs of construction. The prices of materials and labor will rise whether we want them to or not.

Then, I tell you to look around at the number of developments that are under construction in our township. Go to the planning board and ask them to show you the applications and plans on file for even more building. Ask the teachers how many kids are currently in a class. Ask your children how many are in their gym class. Go into a school when children are passing in the halls. Do these things and then ask why we need a building program.

Yes, it's expensive, but the costs are not likely to go down if we wait. And, if we wait as more and more children enter our schools, ask yourself who shall suffer for it. It will mean larger classes and less attention to your child. It will mean crowded conditions and increased risks for safety. It will mean that eventually, if nothing is done, the state will step in and mandate expansion, and we will have no say in the matter.

We have nothing to do with the increases in school population, but we must deal with it for our children's sake. The building plans incorporate no swimming pools or luxuries. We are adding needed classroom space. Without it, we are all in trouble.

Shall we cut the budget there? If we do, is it not like trying to rescue a man who has fallen into a thirty-foot hole by tossing him a fifteen-foot rope?

No one wants to pay one penny of additional taxes. Of course, we all understand that. But the question that each of us must answer is can we afford NOT to pass the budget? Can we afford to wait until such time as the children are visibly suffering and construction costs have skyrocketed even further?

I believe in this budget. I believe it is the best that we could come up with for the children of this township. I believe there are no acceptable alternatives.

This I believe, and I can only hope and pray that, come election day, for the sake of your children, you will feel the same way.

Thank you for your attention.

Good evening.

SPECIAL DATA: *Time of speech six to ten minutes, depending upon the amount and nature of the material inserted.*

If this speech sounds somewhat strong and forceful, it is because it is strong and forceful. We feel that it is what would be called for under the circumstances described in the SPECIAL NOTE at the beginning.

Notice that the administrator acknowledges that there is opposition. He then appeals to the audience's sense of fair play to let him be heard. He then presents the budget and comments on it, something that could not be done effectively in a newspaper or flyer. He then proceeds to anticipate objections and answer those objections. In all, that is a good plan for a speech of this type.

Notice, also, how he identifies himself with the audience. Phrases such as "our children" and "for us" help to create an atmosphere where the speaker is looked upon as "one of us" by the audience. This feeling can help to sway the audience in their opinions toward the point of view of the speaker.

145

TOPIC: **Sex education.**

AUDIENCE: **Adults; some educators but mainly parents.**

(SPECIAL NOTE: Here it is—one of the most controversial topics of our time. It seems that everyone has an opinion about it, and those who are vehemently in favor of it are matched in their fervor by those who are vehemently opposed to it. The following speech would be given by an administrator who was under directive to begin a sex education class with the new term. Here, the administrator addresses an assembly of parents as well as some of the teachers in the school. It may be safely assumed that many people in the audience are opposed to it.)

Ladies and gentlemen...

I am told by the principal of another school that he was once faced by a boy who had been sent to the office for disciplinary reasons. Before he had a chance to read the discipline slip that came with the lad, he looked at him and said, "Well, I hope that you will learn something from all this."

"I've learned something already, sir," said the boy.

"Oh, and what is that?"

The boy sighed and said, "I just learned that you don't giggle in the sex education class!"

Now, I don't tell you that to be frivolous. I tell it to make a point. The point is that sex is a serious matter.

Let's begin by coming to an understanding. Sex is a natural and, many believe, a God-given function. Sex can be pleasurable. Sex is necessary for the continuance of humanity. Sex is one of the prerogatives of marriage that is recognized by every religion in every land on earth.

But, as we all recognize, there is another side to sex which is neither pleasurable nor wholesome. The reports we read of rape outrage any conscientious individual. We are all troubled by the seeming increase in promiscuity and the rise of the illegitimate birth rate. Venereal disease has reached epidemic proportions. Sex can be vicious.

Yes, sex is a very serious matter, indeed.

That is why we have gathered here this evening. That is why I am speaking to you now.

The board of education of our township has mandated that, beginning with the new term, sex education will be a class in our schools and part of our curriculum. Since this affects your children directly, we have called this meeting to inform you of precisely what will be taught and done, and your role in the process.

For, make no mistake about it, the board believes and I believe that sex education is the prerogative of the home.

We also believe that you don't take a teenager, teach him how to drive a car and then turn him loose on the highway with no knowledge of speed limits or what is meant by a stop sign.

Perhaps that will take a little explaining.

We look around us, and we see the results of ignorance. We see young lives ruined by moments of thoughtless pleasure. We deal with teenagers whose lives have been radically altered by pregnancy or venereal disease.

And, don't make the mistake that this doesn't happen to "good" kids. We have dealt with some of the nicest kids from caring and loving homes. They had the love of their parents. They had the care and concern that bespeaks a decent home. They had intelligence and personality and a good school career going for them. In fact, they lacked only one thing.

They lacked any knowledge of what sex was about.

I could tell you horror stories. I could tell you of the girl who was amazed when she found out that there were people in the world who went out on dates without having sex. She had heard only one side of a story told her by someone who wanted something from her. She knew no different. Her "instructor" had also told her that the only time she could get pregnant was during her menstrual period.

Having no knowledge, being a teenager anxious to belong, she went along, she believed, and she suffered.

This is the very thing we hope to avoid by the instigation of this class.

No parent would think of allowing a child to walk to school unless he was certain that the child understood traffic signals and knew how to look both ways before crossing the street. This would be unthinkable. Yet, although the child of which we speak is older, does not the analogy apply? Here is a boy or girl who is undergoing puberty and has a thousand conflicting emotions and feelings each day, sometimes each hour of the day. Yet, in the vast majority of cases, that teenager—that confused and frustrated teenager with the body of an adult and the emotions of a child—finds himself or herself exhorted into dating and social life with no knowledge of how or why his or her drives are working or what to do about these strange feelings that invade his life.

Therefore, we say to everyone: Yes, instruct your child in the home. That is your prerogative. That is your right. If he has that reinforced in school, it can only make you look better in his eyes for having told him already. If he has not learned it at home, then at least he will be receiving accurate and compassionate information that will prove some armor against the sharp blows that can be caused by ignorance.

We all realize that the mechanics of sex are but a part, a small part at that, of the total experience. There is an emotional side to it. There is a maturity that is needed to fully handle its ramifications. And, since most sex is tied up with family and family living, there is a need to investigate that as well.

All this we know, and all this we intend to incorporate into that curriculum.

Now, I know you must have questions, and we are going to try to supply the answers. But, before we invite your questions, I have a question for you.

Is there anyone here who found it pleasant to give up the child they had borne and nurtured to an institution called "school" that was filled with strangers who knew nothing abut your child? You don't have to answer. Of course there isn't anyone who enjoyed that. We love our children. We want our children with us. We also realize that they need an education, and the school is set up to handle that task.

So, we sniffled a little, although we didn't let our child see us, and we sent him off to school. We did it for his future. We did it because we loved him. We did it for his good.

So it is with this situation. We have instigated a sex education class not to usurp parental rights, but to help our children; not to teach them mechanics, but to give them the knowledge to deal effectively with a very real aspect of life; not to break down a warm and loving act, but to build up respect for that which, for most of them, will be an essential part of their adult lives. This is what we propose to do.

Because we love our children, we can do no less!

SPECIAL DATA: *Time of speech; about seven or eight minutes.*

Following the speech and the applause (hopefully) that follows, the speaker would then invite the audience to participate by asking questions.

This is another one of those "hot" topics in education with which administrators must deal. This speech presents a clear exposition of one administrator's feelings about the subject. We feel that it is a rational approach presented in the best possible manner for understanding. Of course, you will never reach everyone in the audience and sway them to your side, but if this is presented forthrightly, with conviction in the voice, then no one in the audience will be able to say you are not sincere and honest, whether they agree with you or not.

One of the main concerns of parents about sex education is the impression that it will take away from them the right to tell their children in their own way about a very personal and highly charged subject. This speech goes a long way toward alleviating this concern.

AFTERTHOUGHTS

Every time there is a special event in and around the school, the administrator is usually expected to give a "special" speech. We hope that, within the previous pages, you have found something that will be of value to you when one of these situations arises.

Although we have stressed it time and time again, it bears repeating here. The keynote of ANY speech is the honesty and sincerity of the speaker. It does not matter that the situation may be emotionally charged; it does not matter that the audience may be hostile; it does not even matter if the audience is on your side, as in a speech accepting a testimonial or at your retirement. Whatever the situation, if you honestly speak what you feel in such a manner that the audience KNOWS that what you are saying is from your heart, then the audience cannot help but be reached and respect you and your presentation.

Whether you choose one of the speeches in this section, adapt one to your particular set of circumstances, or compose your own, if you deliver it with your heart, you won't go wrong. Be sincere, and all else will follow.

SECTION TEN

Holiday Speeches
Throughout the School Year

Most people's years run from January 1 through December 31, but, as we are all aware, that is not what an educator means when he refers to a "school year." For students and parents, that "school year" begins in late August or early September and extends through late May or June of the following chronological year. While the exact dates of opening and closing school vary from district to district, this ten-month span is the rule throughout our nation.

Within those ten months there occurs a number of holidays and holiday-like situations. While these usually engender a lack of school for students, quite often there are school assemblies that precede the event. Students may be asked to present programs that comment on the holiday, and the administrator may be asked to speak. At these assemblies it is common to find many parents and community members as well as the school population.

Therefore, when an administrator is asked to speak, the "holiday speech" he delivers will be heard by many people besides the students. Moreover, administrators may be asked to deliver such speeches at civic functions and patriotic gatherings as well. Many times, an administrator will be asked to be a guest speaker for a holiday function at another school. In all, speeches about the various holidays that occur during the school year should be part of every administrator's repertoire.

From Labor Day and the beginning of the school year to the end of the school year and an injunction to the summer, holiday speeches throughout the school year are thoroughly covered in this section in the order in which they occur during that year. We have even included an Independence Day speech in the event that you should be called upon to speak during the summer recess.

We are certain that you will find something that will suit your holiday needs.

146

TOPIC: Labor Day—beginning of the school year (first Monday in September).

AUDIENCE: Suitable for all audiences.

Good afternoon ladies and gentlemen...

Labor Day is a holiday that was established in order to honor the working people of America. This is as it should be, because America has been made great by the workers of our nation. From those who built the great dams that helped supply us with needed power to those who spanned the county with railroad tracks, each has played a part in contributing to the good of society; each has made America great.

Each day that goes by would be impossible were it not for a host of Americans working at jobs to keep our country going. From the farmer who grows the crops, to the manufacturer who turns those crops into bread and food products, to the truckdrivers who deliver them to the stores, to the clerks who sell them, America depends on all sorts of workers to keep it moving. Every worker, every job that is done, is one more note in a gigantic symphony—the song of America.

It is entirely fitting that we set aside a day such as this to remember and honor the workers of our nation, the men and women who keep us going and add to our country's efficiency and greatness.

But it is also fitting and proper to remember ourselves on this day, to remember that our work is very valuable in the entire picture of a growing and vital America.

Whether as a student or a teacher or a parent or a school administrator, we are involved in work that is very valuable indeed. We are engaged in building the future of America.

These are not merely words, but a very real analysis of the situation. To you students, I say that your work as students is most important, for you are studying now in order that you may learn skills that will be put to use when you become a part of the adult work force. It is you who will build the skyscrapers and highways and computers of tomorrow. It is you who will plan and shape the world that is to come. Therefore, your work now is the most important thing that you can be doing, and on this Labor Day we honor you for it.

For the rest of us, I ask what is more difficult, more important or more rewarding than helping these young people step into that future? Our work, in a very real sense, is to prepare them for their work. We have the very arduous and demanding responsibility of seeing to it that they receive what they will need in order to assume their places in the world that they will inherit. From the teacher in the classroom who teaches them to read or to work algebraic equations, to the administrator who sees to it that they can learn in an environment conducive to study and growth, to the parents who nurture and love them, help them along their way, and support them in their work and their growth—we also work at a very important job, a job that is vital not only to their success but to the future of this land we all love so well.

So, to everyone here, I say that this Labor Day is truly our day. Let us take pride in that as well as in the dignity of work that makes us the outstanding nation that we are.

Happy Labor Day.

SPECIAL DATA: *Time of speech; about three minutes.*

Any time you can incorporate the audience into the speech you are giving, you have a winning speech. This one does just that by identifying the audience with the holiday being spoken about. As such, it would be bound to get good audience reaction.

This is the type of speech that would go well at an assembly attended by parents as well as students. It is also an injunction to keep at the work that each party must do throughout the coming school year.

147

TOPIC: **Columbus Day (October 12).**
AUDIENCE: **Suitable for any audience.**

Good afternoon, ladies and gentlemen...

Imagine, if you will, that you are standing on the edge of a very large forest. Imagine that you have just been told that in that forest there are dangerous animals just waiting to attack and destroy you. Imagine that you believe that on the other side of that forest is a city where you can find food and rest, but you are not certain; you are not sure that it exists at all. What's more, many people have told you that if you enter that forest, you may never come out again. Now, imagine that in spite of all that danger and all that uncertainty, you take a step and enter that forest anyway.

If you can imagine this, then you will have some idea of what Columbus faced when he set out on his journey to what he believed would be the Orient and what turned out to be the new world. In Columbus' day, people believed that sea serpents existed, and beyond that, they had no knowledge of what other terrors might await them.

Yes, like what I asked you to imagine, it was a very frightening situation. I am certain that they must have started out in their ships with fear as a companion. But, and here is the most remarkable thing, they went anyway. In spite of their misapprehensions, in spite of the unknown that lay ahead, in spite of the terrors that surrounded them, they took the chance, they went out into that unknown; they tried, and the rest is history.

And, if it is history, it is a history lesson worth learning.

How many times are we faced with a situation where we are not certain of the outcome; where we do not realize what will happen if we do or do not do some particular thing? At such times, there is apprehension about what lies ahead, and we pause for a moment uncertain of what to do. At such times, perhaps it would be worthwhile to remember Columbus who faced the unknown and had the courage to try.

And, if we try; if we tackle the unknown; if we have the courage to strike out at a new situation; what will we find?

We may just find, like Columbus, that we can do it; that all the fears we had were unfounded; that we are capable of taking action and taking command of the situation and our lives.

Just as Columbus had no idea of what his journey would mean for the future, so will we never be able to tell what might happen if we have the courage to face the unknown and try.

Today we honor a man of courage, and we take a lesson from his life. If we want to honor his memory, let us resolve in our own lives not to be taken in by rumors, not to be overcome by the seeming enormity of the task ahead, and not to say that something cannot be done until we have put our hands to it and tried. Let us resolve that this man of courage and determination will be honored in our lives by our determination to tackle new and unusual projects, by our willingness to listen to different ideas and concepts, and by our ability to face tomorrow with anticipation and hope.

That is a living tribute that Columbus would have liked very much, indeed.

SPECIAL DATA: *Time of speech; about three minutes.*

In this honor to Columbus, the speaker also weaves in the theme of dealing with the unknown, an injunction to courage and the acceptance of the new and different.

This holiday speech might also be effective in a school where new programs are about to be initiated, where there is a new curriculum that parents are apprehensive about, or in a brand-new school where these are the first people to use the facilities.

You get the idea. This speech has more than one effect upon an audience and can be used to enhance a situation where the speaker wishes to gain the audience's cooperation in trying something new and different.

148

TOPIC: VETERAN'S DAY (November 11).
AUDIENCE: **Suitable for all audiences.**

Ladies and gentlemen...

Freedom does not come cheaply. The first colonists to this new land learned that lesson in the hardships they faced. The lesson was reinforced on the battlefields of Yorktown and Saratoga. It was taught again at places like Gettysburg and Shiloh. It was refined on the Maginot line and sharply drilled in places like Tarawa and Monte Casino, and on Omaha Beach in a place called Normandy; on Pork Chop Hill and in Hue and Da Nang.

These are names that fill our history books and that are a part of our heritage as Americans. These places, whether on our own land or in some foreign corner of the world, have stood and continue to stand as reminders that freedom is purchased at a very high cost.

This is not unique, since we have come to realize that freedom is the most prized item on earth. There is always someone or some force that waits to take it away from us if we are not vigilant; if we stand unwilling to pay the price for it. What is unique and wondrous and marvelous is the fact that, since the founding of our great nation, America has never lacked for individuals who are willing to come forth when the need arises to pay that price with their honor, their devotion, and, when necessary, their lives.

The former English colonists who fought with flintlock and musket for the unheard of ideal of living their lives free from oppression did not ask if it was going to be easy. Rather, they saw the need, and they filled it. They went out and fought for their new land. They gave of themselves unselfishly and with the greatest devotion to the ideals of liberty. Through their efforts a new nation was forged.

Because of this, we honor their memory. Yet, their sacrifices, as wondrous as they were, share equal rank with those of the men and women who have come forth to serve their country in times of trouble. If the colonists were heroes, which, most certainly, they were, then so are those who battled on the sands of North Africa, in the mountains of Italy, across the rivers of central Europe, and in the steaming jungles of the Pacific islands. And, so were those who, in the face of derision and ridicule from some of their peers, believed enough in the concepts of liberty to trudge through the rice patties and jungles of a place called Vietnam. All were and are heroes.

These are the veterans. These are the men and women who left their homes, their safety, their comfort to place themselves in the front lines and on the battlefields in order that freedom, a concept bigger than any individual, would continue to thrive and flourish.

These are the veterans. These are the men and women who, to paraphrase the words of John F. Kennedy, asked not what their country could do for them, but asked what they could do for their country.

These are the veterans. These are the men and women who, when they were called, answered with enthusiasm, and, like their brothers and sisters at Lexington and Concord, did not ask if it was going to be easy. They came; they sacrificed; they gave of themselves in the belief that they were defending liberty; a liberty which, if they did not live to see it, would stand as a shining beacon for the children who would come after them.

These are the veterans. These are the men and women whom we honor on this special day.

As they have honored us through their service and devotion, let us honor them in our thoughts, our prayers and our hearts—today and throughout all of our free tomorrows.

SPECIAL DATA: *Time of speech; about three minutes.*

This speech would be suitable for presentation in a school, before a civic group, or before a specific organization such as the VFW. It says some very basic things that we all feel but don't think of often enough.

149

TOPIC: **AMERICAN EDUCATION WEEK (third week of November).**
AUDIENCE: **Suitable for all audiences.**

We are all students; we are all teachers.

If you are wondering how I can make such a statement, I will tell you that it is no problem at all, because it is so true.

Think back for a moment to the time when you were very small. Do you remember how you stood in awe of those "big people" who could do so many things that you couldn't? Your father could drive a car; your mother could count money and tell you how much you had; your brother could play the piano; your sister could ride a bike. All of these things were mysteries to you; incomprehensible.

But you grew and you learned. Perhaps your sister taught you how to ride that bike; perhaps your mother told you what those coins meant. In any case, you learned as you grew. You went to school, and there you began to learn other things as well. You ran home with all this new knowledge, bursting with the news of what you had learned.

Gradually, the world became less of a mystery and more of a wonder to be explored. At the store, you counted the change with ease; you got on your bike and rode home effortlessly; perhaps you picked out a tune on the piano, and, when Dad came home, you sat behind the wheel of the car and realized that the wheel made the car move where you wanted it to move and this pedal made it go and that one made it stop.

But that wasn't the end of it. Nothing stopped there. As the years passed you learned more and more, to the point where you all but forgot that there ever was a time when an automobile was an incomprehensible monster or when two plus two didn't make four.

Now, for many of us, there are little ones of our own, and we sit them on our laps behind the wheel of our car; we guide them on their first wobbly bicycle ride; we sit and listen to the first recognizable song that floats out of the piano under their fingers; we give them an allowance and teach them how to count the money.

As we were taught, so now we teach, as, one day, those we teach will teach others who will, in turn, teach still others and on and on to the point where the future fades in the mists of time.

There is a word for this. That word is EDUCATION. It is a lifelong process in which we are all students; we are all teachers. It is the basis of life.

At this time of the year, we are celebrating American Education Week, which is the reason that we have all gathered here today. It is altogether right and proper that we should set aside a time in our lives to honor education, which is such a vital part of our lives. But, let us not forget that education is not something that can be reserved for a single day or a single week of the year. Let us remember that it is a process that begins the day we are born and does not end until the day we leave this world to those who will come after us.

Let us honor eduation in our hearts each and every day of the year. We are a part of the learning process that is life, and, as we learned from others, so we pass on that learning to others, some of us in a classroom in a school but all of us in the classroom called life.

And, when this week ends, there will still be things to learn; things to teach.

So, let us honor education during this special week and throughout all the weeks of our lives. Let us go forth and educate—students and teachers all.

SPECIAL DATA: *Time of speech; approximately four minutes. While this is a speech about education and the educative process that is well-suited to a special time such as American Education Week, it could easily be adapted to fit any occasion where the topic is the value of education.*

150

TOPIC: **THANKSGIVING (fourth Thursday in November).**
AUDIENCE: **Suitable for all audiences.**

Ladies and gentlemen...

It is only right, at this special time of the year, that we pause for a moment and ask ourselves just what it is that we have to be thankful for. If there is a special day for giving thanks, let us know, at least, what it is for which we give that thanks.

The answer is not always at our fingertips; is not always clear. We read the headlines of newspapers; we listen to the voice from the radio; we watch the TV screen, and what do we see? We see crime so horrible that it sickens every decent man and woman. We see the results of war and pestilence mirrored in the horror-stricken faces of its victims. We see tragedy upon tragedy: hunger, poverty, degradation. This is what we see, and, certainly, the doubt must come that we have little to be thankful for in this far-from-perfect world.

Yes, we can understand how this feeling could arise, for certainly there is much in this life which causes us pain and frustration; there is much which we regret and condemn.

Yet, as Abraham Lincoln once wrote, "I can see how a man can keep his eyes on the mud and conclude that there was no God, but I cannot see how anyone could turn his eyes to the heavens on a starry night and deny the existence of a Supreme Being." Perhaps that is our problem here; a problem of point of view. We realize that we have a choice in our personal perceptions of the world. We can concentrate on what is wrong, or we can appreciate what is right.

And, make no mistake about it, there is much that is good and worthwhile in this world.

If we look for it, we can find individuals who give of themselves in every way. We find people who risk their own lives to save others who are the victims of unexpected tragedy. We find people who, when tragedy strikes, are there to provide relief and comfort to those who suffer. We find people who, time and time again, have been there when they were needed and have asked nothing in return except the chance to serve again. This we can find if we choose to look.

If we look for it, we can find love conquering hate every day. We find homeless children in the world, it is true, but we also find men and women with hearts full of love, a love so large that it incorporates those children so that they are adopted and raised in families that are thankful for the chance to share that love with a child. For every mugging or robbery or act of terrorism, we can find an act of kindness, an act of giving, an act of love. It is there if we look for it.

Let us ask ourselves what it is for which we may be thankful. And, let us answer our own question. We can be thankful for each other. We can be thankful that, in this world filled with tragedy, we have people whose lives are a triumph, a triumph of love. We can be thankful that, for every individual who takes from society in terms of crime and terror, we have ten, twenty, a hundred, a thousand who give each and every day of their lives in terms of love and care and selflessness and concern for others.

Therefore, let us all rejoice in these wonderful things and be thankful, on this very special day and throughout the entire year, that we are here to appreciate them and each other.

A Happy Thanksgiving to everyone!

SPECIAL DATA: *Time of speech; about three and one-half minutes.*

Perhaps it is just a matter of perception, but we have always found much to be thankful for. We think that you probably feel the same way. Therefore, this Thanksgiving Day speech can be delivered with conviction and will be very effective.

Of course, there is no reason why this speech could not be given at any other time of the year, since it incorporates some very basic values.

151

TOPIC: **WINTER, including Christmas and Chanukah (December).**
AUDIENCE: **Suitable for all audiences.**

Ladies and gentlemen...

We are at a very special time of the year. In schools throughout the land, children grow excited at the prospect of what is to come. Stores are jammed with shoppers, streets explode with light, and messages of good will abound. Even when people say hello to each other, there is a special feeling in it; a bright and warm feeling that pervades our days.

Yes, we are at a very special time, indeed.

What is it that takes the dark and cold days of winter and fills them with light and warmth? It is the anticipation of some special holidays which we will soon be celebrating.

For some of us it is Christmas, and for some of us it is Chanukah. Whatever the holiday, the feeling it engenders transcends any boundaries of religion and unites us all in a common feeling of affection for each other.

This is as it should be. The Jewish holiday of Chanukah is called the Festival of Lights. A candle is lit each night for seven nights to commemorate a miracle of light. The Christian holiday of Christmas has been called a Feast of Love. It commemorates the birth of Jesus, who has been called the Prince of Love.

So, what do we have? We have a combination of the feasts of Light and Love. Light and Love. Love and Light. Here are two qualities that fill the world at this special time, and the world becomes a better place for it.

What a need there is for each of them. The world is filled with corners of darkness where lurk the demons of ignorance and prejudice and hate. These are corners where the light of knowledge and truth has not yet reached. If only we could reach every crevice with the light of learning, what a bright and happy world this would become for us all.

And, what a need there is for love. Each day we read in the papers or see on our television sets the tragedies that hate and fear bring about. We hear of horror upon horror perpetrated in hate which destroys and tears down and mutilates. If only we could reach each mind so twisted by hate and replace that hate with love, what a change there would be and how much better the world would finally become.

Love and Light; Light and Love—in combination, what wonders could they not produce? Together they could build a world where kindness would be the rule, where concern for each other would be a part of daily life, where each individual would grow and thrive and contribute and find happiness and compassion.

What a world THAT would be!

At this special season of Light and at this special season of Love, let us have the courage to believe that this is not a dream; not a fantasy. Let us believe that it is a possibility within our grasp.

If, for this one season of the year, our lives can be filled with happiness and warmth and a spirit of giving—a spirit of light and love—then surely we can work at making that feeling last throughout the rest of the year as well. Yes, it would take work and cooperation and compassion, but wouldn't it be worth it if the warmth that came from within lasted the whole year through?

Let us resolve to honor these special holidays in our lives the whole year through. Let us cherish them and hold them dear, and then let us spread that feeling, that light, that love, to all we meet.

Then the world would truly be illuminated and warmed by light and love.

Whether you will celebrate Chanukah or Christmas, let me leave you with the same wish: May Light and Love be yours forever.

Merry Christmas, Happy Chanukah, and thank you.

SPECIAL DATA: *Time of speech; three to four minutes.*

Our schools have long realized that in a pluralistic democracy, the beliefs and traditions of all people make up a rich legacy for everyone. December brings with it the holidays of Christmas and Chanukah, and, as mentioned in the speech, there is a special holiday feeling that is evident. Therefore, this speech is a good one for an assembly program. It incorporates both beliefs into a positive statement highly appropriate to the time.

152

TOPIC: **MARTIN LUTHER KING DAY (January 15).**
AUDIENCE: **Suitable for all audiences.**

Ladies and gentlemen...

Let me set a situation for you. Suppose you were given the task of swimming from one side of a pool to the other. Let's assume that you knew how to swim and, under normal circumstances, it would present no problem to you. You see the task before you, and you are willing and anxious to try.

So, you slip into the water and are about to start when someone comes by and tells you that you had not understood; you had to swim the pool wearing a special pack that contained a hundred pounds of lead weights.

If you can picture this in your mind and if you can imagine how you would feel, then you begin to see what something called prejudice can do. It can take a person of normal abilities, who has a chance to contribute to life and live that life with dignity, and weigh him down with such penalties that "making it" becomes a Herculean task.

Therein lies the inherent danger of prejudice. It keeps people from becoming all that they can be. If, because of prejudice, a potential doctor never graduates from medical school, the world has lost. If, because of prejudice, a potential engineer does not go to school, the bridges of the future may never be built. If, because of prejudice, a teacher or a scholar or an artist remains only a potential, the world is less. We all lose out. We all suffer.

That was the truth that became evident to a man of peace and vision named Martin Luther King. Here was a man who had firsthand knowledge of the horrors that could be wrought by prejudice. He saw the suffering and limitations placed upon a people by virtue of nothing more than the color of their skin.

If anyone had reason to hate, it was he. He was, however, a man of God and a man of peace, who chose to fight prejudice and hate with the most devastating weapon of all—love. With love as his guide, he fought for justice with a fervor and conviction that comes from the knowledge that your cause is just and that, with perseverance, hate can be overcome.

Although his life ended in an act of hate, crushed by an assassin's bullet, the love he taught by the example of his life continued after him and continues even today. It is a love for all mankind, unhindered by race or creed. It is a love that realizes that every man's freedom is a part of our individual freedoms and that an injustice done to my brother is an injustice done to me and to all of mankind.

His was a love for freedom that places him in the ranks of the greatest of Americans. His was a love that teaches us to care for the members of our family, the family of mankind. His was a love that inspires us to be the best of which we are capable of becoming in every way.

Therefore, let us honor this special man by keeping the precepts of love and brotherhood foremost in our lives both on this special day and throughout the days of our lives.

SPECIAL DATA: *Time of speech; slightly over three minutes.*

This speech honors one of the foremost men of our generation in a manner that gets across the basic tragedy of prejudice. It is a fitting speech for this day, which is a legal holiday in many states. It is well-suited to any school assembly.

153

TOPIC: **LINCOLN AND WASHINGTON'S BIRTHDAYS (February 12 and 22).**

AUDIENCE: **Suitable for all audiences.**

Ladies and gentlemen...

The names of George Washington and Abraham Lincoln are a part of the history of our nation. They are instantly recognizable not only throughout America, but in lands throughout the civilized world. They bespeak the best in honor and devotion to the cause of democracy.

What is sometimes difficult for us to imagine when we think of them is the fact that they were real people who once walked this land. People who ate and slept and suffered and laughed like every human being. Because of their greatness and what they achieved and the years that have passed, they have achieved the status of legend. Stories abound about them, some of which are true and many of which are myth.

When you take away the myth, you are left with the man. In both cases, that man is more than enough to assure their places in the honored archives of our nation's past.

What were they like, these men who achieved so much? What were they?

They were men. One came from a fairly well-to-do family while the other was born into a poor family. One was formally educated while the other largely taught himself. One inherited lands and was a successful farmer, the other worked at many jobs including manual labor.

Yes, there were differences in their lives, pronounced differences, but that does not matter as much as the similarities.

They were alike in many, many ways, but the foremost similarity they shared was a love of freedom and a willingness to work and devote themselves to seeing to it that that freedom flourished for all.

George Washington helped to forge a new nation that was dedicated to liberty. Abraham Lincoln saw a nation about to be divided by hate and helped to forge a single unit, a single nation dedicated to a single ideal of equality for all.

These were not easy tasks. Washington paid the price in harsh, physical suffering at Valley Forge and in the battles that won us freedom. Lincoln paid the price in agony as he saw brother fight brother in the Civil War and paid the final price at the hands of an assassin.

Yet, they paid that price willingly, for they knew in their hearts that what they were working for, what they were sacrificing for, what they were suffering for was a concept much bigger than themselves. They were working for a concept called America. They were working for liberty, which they loved.

Because they worked not for their own advancement, but for the good of others, they achieved a work that stands as a wonder of the world—they built and united a nation. They did not do this singlehandedly, and they would be the first to tell you that. Rather, they supplied the leadership, the drive and the direction that people devoted to truth and honor could follow in the greatest of all endeavors, the building of a land where people of all nationalities and beliefs could work and live and worship and rear their children in that most cherished of all states—in freedom; in liberty.

For that leadership, for that devotion, for that struggle and triumph, we honor their names and recognize them as true models of those who made our country great.

And, as we honor them, let us resolve that their efforts will never be wasted on us; that we shall cherish and defend the liberty for which they strove; that we will practice it in our day-to-day lives and in our dealings with all of mankind.

THAT is a memorial they would really appreciate.

SPECIAL DATA: *Time of speech; a little over three minutes.*

This is another speech that is relatively short but to the point and well-suited to an assembly program, over a public address system, or even as part of a civic holiday celebration that might be held in a town hall. Such celebrations usually incorporate both holidays since they are so close together. Therefore, it is ideal for such an occasion.

154

TOPIC: **SPRING, including Easter and Passover (April).**
AUDIENCE: **Suitable for all audiences.**

Ladies and gentlemen...

If we took all of the poems and songs that had been written about spring, I doubt there would be enough room in this whole place to hold them.

Spring inspires poems and songs. It's as if, after the cold grayness of winter, the entire world is bursting with song and with life. We look at trees and see the buds which are the promise of the leaves and flowers that will come. We look at the earth and see the ground thawed out and lying rich with the promise of the life that is to come. We see these things, and, after the winter, they fill our hearts with hope and our throats with the songs of life.

The poet Tennyson wrote that "in the spring a young man's fancy lightly turns to thoughts of love." I would add that not only young men, but men and women of all ages cannot help but be affected by the spring and be filled by the love of life as life grows all about them.

At this time also, Judaism and Christianity celebrate two holidays that are important parts of their beliefs and which, incidentally, remind us of life as well. I speak, of course, of Passover and Easter.

Passover celebrates the time when the Angel of Death, sent by God as a punishment to Pharaoh, passed over the houses of the children of Israel. It is celebrated today as it has been celebrated for centuries. It speaks of the gift of life given by God.

Easter celebrates the rising of Christ from the grave, following his crucifixion and death. It is a celebration of the conquering of death and the triumph of life. It is a joyous reaffirmation of life.

Both holidays in both religions take place in the spring and are celebrations of life.

It is time to turn our thoughts from the darkness of winter to the brightness of spring. It is time for all of us to start thinking about life.

A life lies before each and every one of us. It is a life of promise; a life rich with rewards. We know that there will be struggles and hardship and pain, but we also know that there will be laughter and love and growth, and those are qualities well worth working for.

What our lives will be depends almost entirely upon us, for they will be what we make of them. Each of us has the opportunity to make our lives something special, for each of us is something special.

In this season of life; in this season of renewal; in this season of growth; let each of us resolve to be the best that we are capable of becoming; to strive for the best in everything we do; to live our lives in a positive manner that, like spring, will lead to growth and happiness and improve the quality of life for everyone. Let us live for life.

We will all be the better for that.

SPECIAL DATA: *Time of speech; three or four minutes.*

> *This would be a very acceptable speech for a school prior to the "spring break" as it is called in many districts. Many systems try to arrange that break at such a time that it covers both Passover and Easter.*
>
> *This speech, therefore, would be ideal in such a district since it incorporates both religions and religious observances and finds a similarity.*
>
> *This speech might also be well-received at a PTA function.*

155

TOPIC: **Arbor Day (fourth Friday in April).**
AUDIENCE: **Suitable for all audiences.**

Ladies and gentlemen...

It was in Nebraska, in the year 1872, that Arbor Day was first celebrated. It was proposed by a man named J. Sterling Morton who would later become a United States Secretary of Agriculture.

In 1885, Nebraska made Arbor Day a legal holiday, and other states soon followed suit. At first, this holiday was chiefly promoted by farmer's groups and agricultural associations, but the idea of an annual day set aside for the planting of trees so captivated school authorities, that it was soon made an annual school function, much like the one we are now attending, and the popularity of Arbor Day spread throughout the United States and even over the border to Canada.

As its popularity spread, its purpose also changed. At first, Arbor Day was intended for the planting of single trees to beautify public grounds. Now, it has become an occasion for all of us to stop and remember the importance of our environment.

Therefore, we are gathered together today to have these trees planted on our school's grounds. I know I speak for everyone in the school when I thank the board of education and Mr. James Tynan for their contributions. These trees are beautiful, and we know that they will continue to beautify our school in the years to come.

A tree is a marvel of nature. It provides us with shade in the summer. It is a wind break in the winter. It is a sight of spectacular beauty as its leaves change color in the fall. Its roots help to keep the spring rains from eroding the soil. It provides us with fuel to heat us when it is cold. It provides the lumber to build our houses. Its sap contains materials that are made into many products to help us in our day-to-day living. All this a tree does.

Moreover, if it were not for trees, we would have difficulty even breathing. Trees, through marvelous internal processes, take the wastes called carbon monoxide and convert them to oxygen, which all living creatures need to live.

Yes, without trees we would have a difficult time living on this planet.

Therefore, it is important that we have days like this, and it is important that we plant trees. If we take trees from the land and leave that land bare and scarred, we will be doing more than destroying the natural beauty of our country; we will be destroying a natural asset that cannot be replaced by mechanical means. It is only by planting new trees, as we are doing today, that we can assure that future generations will have their beauty and their benefits.

These tiny saplings that we plant today will take a long time to grow, but grow they will. Eventually, they will reach over thirty feet in height, much taller than our school. You will be out of school, be married and have a family of your own before that happens. That's how long it will take, but it will happen, and one day in the future, groups of students that may contain your sons and daughters or even your grandsons and granddaughters will stand beneath their leafy shade and appreciate their beauty.

Therefore, as we begin this ceremony, and, as these trees are planted, let us dedicate them to the future. Let us plant them now with the knowledge that they will give us pleasure and comfort today and will remain to provide the same services to students yet to come.

We do this today for all our tomorrows.

SPECIAL DATA: *Time of speech; about three minutes.*

> *This is a somewhat different speech from those that have preceded it. The others concentrated on a larger philosophy associated with the holiday. This one is strictly expository. It details the history of the holiday (which could be easily found in an encyclopedia), and some fairly well-known facts about trees. Nonetheless, it is an effective, if not dramatic, speech that would fit in well with any Arbor Day activity.*

156

TOPIC: **MEMORIAL DAY (May 30).**
AUDIENCE: **Suitable for all audiences.**

Ladies and gentlemen...

It was in the year 1868 that John A. Logan, Commander in Chief of the Grand Army of the Republic, issued a general order that designated May 30, 1868 as a day "for the purpose of strewing with flowers or otherwise decorating the graves of comrades who died in defense of their country in the late rebellion." This was done, according to Logan, "with the hope that it will be kept up from year to year."

The "conflict" to which Logan referred was, of course, the Civil War. The original purpose of this "Memorial Day," or "Decoration Day" as it was also known, was to honor those soldiers who were killed in that war. Subsequently, it came to honor all those who gave their lives in wars.

It is altogether fitting that we pause in our labors on this special day to remember, each of us in his own way, those who have given the ultimate sacrifice in the service of their country.

There are few of us who have been untouched by the scourge of war in some way. We all have had someone who lost his life in a conflict or was injured or maimed in wars. Perhaps it was a father or an uncle or a brother; perhaps there are those in this audience who bear the personal scars of war. Whatever the case, we are all touched by it in some way.

In these cases which are so personal that they are held within the secret places of the heart, it is often difficult to gain perspective, since the loss is so close, so costly. It remains for the rest of us, therefore, to put into words on occasions such as this exactly what we feel for those who have given so much in order that the rest of us may breathe free air and live on a free land.

We are told that there is no greater love than to lay down one's life for one's friend. If that is true, then we are faced with an abundance of love today. We speak of men and women who were not anxious to die; who loved life; who wanted homes and families and the good and wholesome things that life has to offer. As much as they loved life, however, they loved an idea more—the idea that their children should live free, in a free land, under the blessings of democracy.

They realized that the price of freedom is a vigilance and that freedom must be defended from those forces of oppression that would take it from us. Because of that belief and dedication, they went when they were called; they went to defend this land and protect their families and the families of those who would come after them; they fought in defense of what they held dear; and they gave their lives in order that others might live.

As they gave us that gift of love, let us return that love today. In our thoughts, in our hearts, and in our prayers, let us remember them and honor their sacrifice.

Let us also resolve that this honor shall not be on a single day of the year, not only in the light of ceremony, but on each and every day of the year; let us remember their love, remember their devotion to the ideals of democracy, remember their hopes for our future, remember the sacrifice they made for us—let us remember and be proud.

SPECIAL DATA: *Time of speech; slightly over three minutes.*

Here is a combination of exposition and commentary that works well. The speech starts out with historical data about the holiday and then branches into a commentary about those for whom the holiday was established in the first place.

The thrust of the speech ends up as a memorial to those who have died. This would be suited to an assembly in school or any civic ceremony in a town.

157

TOPIC: Summer, **including the end of the school year (June).**
AUDIENCE: **Suitable for all audiences.**

Ladies and gentlemen...

It was the great lyricist Oscar Hammerstein who wrote, "June is bustin' out all over." All we have to do is to look around us to realize how appropriate that line is. Trees have broken out in leaves, flowers abound, and the entire world seems to be bursting with life.

Nor is the earth the only thing that is "bustin' out." There is a spirit within each and every one of us that longs to be free to walk out under those trees, to smell those flowers, and to be a part of summer. That spirit bursts from within us now, and we are anxious to be out of school and into the life under the summer sun.

This is as it should be. We are meant to enjoy life, and the summer offers us opportunities we have at no other time of the year.

Yet, it is also a time when we must pause for a moment to remember that we are completing another school year. And, while summer brings a momentary end to school, it does not bring an end to your education.

Over these past ten months you have worked at your studies and learned many things which you did not know when school began. What you learned was the result of many factors, not the least of which was your efforts; your individual efforts. It has been said that we get out of life what we put into it. Your efforts in studying, in writing, in practice, and in the hours you have put into your classes have been rewarded by the new knowledge you have gained; knowledge that no one can ever take away from you.

Now this school year draws to an end as summer approaches, but your learning continues, for all of life is a school, and we learn by everything we do. This year in school has continued your education for life, but it is life itself that will complete that education; it is life itself that will temper what you learn in school and prepare you for the living of it.

Therefore, with the start of summer and the end of the school year, I tell you to go out and live life and learn from it as surely as you have learned from us over this past year.

It is my sincere wish for each and every one of you that the coming summer may hold only pleasant experiences for you. May you live life to its fullest; may you enjoy it; and—may you learn.

Have a good summer.

SPECIAL DATA: *Time of speech; about two minutes.*

This is a rather short speech that would go well at an end-of-the-year assembly program or at an "awards night" for parents and students held toward the end of the year. It is not a graduation speech in any way (you will find those elsewhere in this book), but is an injunction to lifelong learning on the part of the students of the school.

158

TOPIC: **INDEPENDENCE DAY (the Fourth of July).**
AUDIENCE: **Suitable for all audiences.**

Ladies and gentlemen...

Not that it matters one bit, but we are here on the wrong day. You see, the resolution of independence, the fact that we had finally severed the last ties with Great Britain, was actually approved on July the second. It was the Declaration of Independence, which was drafted to justify this momentous decision, that was sanctioned on the fourth of July, and it was not until July 8, 1776 that it was publically read in the yard of the Pennsylvania Statehouse in Philadelphia.

All other dates were quickly forgotten, however, and one year later, on July 4, 1977, the signing of the Declaration of Independence was celebrated in Philadelphia by an adjournment of Congress, a ceremonial dinner, bonfires, the ringing of bells, and, of course, fireworks. This custom so caught on that the day is almost universally marked by parades, military displays, picnics, patriotic pageants and community fireworks displays.

With all that goes on every July Fourth, with all the good food and color and bands, it is easy for us to forget the real purpose of this day. We are here to celebrate and remember the birth of an idea, a concept so bold that it shook the entire world. We are here to celebrate and remember the birth of democracy.

We celebrate the fact that a group of people believed that they and their children should be able to live free from tryanny and oppression. We celebrate the fact that a group of people believed that democracy was worth fighting for; was worth having for themselves and for all people who loved and cherished freedom. We celebrate the fact that a group of people so longed to live free that they had the courage to proclaim to all the world that freedom was a God-given right which no dictator could take away; that from that date onward they were free men and women; that they and future generations would defend that right against all threats.

This is what we celebrate on this special day.

And, in a very real sense, it is ourselves that we celebrate today. We are America. We are her people. We are her spirit. We come from many backgrounds. We are black and brown and white. We are Catholic and Protestant and Jew. We are Polish and German and African and Italian and a host of other nationalities. We are Democrats and Republicans and liberals and conservatives. We are all these things and one thing more.

We are Americans, and we love freedom.

We may argue and fight among ourselves, but we are one body and one mind against anyone who would take our freedom from us. We realize that we are not perfect; that we still have faults that need correcting, but, to our credit, we recognize this fact and we have made of our democracy a vital and ever-changing process where laws can change and wrongs can be righted, and we work for justice and for the ideal of freedom for all. We try, we fail, but we pick ourselves up and try again, and we succeed. We do all of this in a never-ending quest for the perfection that freedom inspires. We love freedom. We are Americans.

Therefore, let us enjoy this day, for it is truly our day. Let us celebrate the joy of freedom that we hold so dearly. Let us remember the men and women who have made this country great. And, let us celebrate ourselves and resolve that, by the love of freedom that we hold in our hearts, this country, this shining example of the blessings of democracy, this America shall continue to be the hope of all mankind, today and throughout all July fourths for our lifetimes and the lifetimes of all who shall come after us.

SPECIAL DATA: *Time of speech; about three minutes.*

> *While the Fourth of July does not fall during the normal school year, we felt we must include this Independence Day address, because administrators are quite often called upon by their districts to speak at civic celebrations such as may be inspired by this most celebrated of all secular holidays in America. This may certainly be categorized as a patriotic speech and would be well-received as is. It might also be adapted with a few changes to suit any situation where a speech of patriotic nature was called for.*

AFTERTHOUGHTS

You will notice that the dates we have given for all holidays are the traditional dates that apply in most states. Some of the holidays mentioned are not celebrated in some states or are celebrated on dates other than indicated. Moreover, with the advent of the Monday holiday laws, many of these holidays are relegated to certain Mondays. Memorial Day, for example, is not celebrated in every state and in some states it is known as Confederate Memorial Day. It is now celebrated, where it is honored, on the fourth Monday in May, whatever that date may be. We thought that it would be best to give the traditional dates for those holidays most widely celebrated in most places across America.

If the majority of speeches in this section sound patriotic, it is because the majority of holidays are patriotic in nature.

We think you will find something here that will enhance every holiday occasion throughout the school year.

part two

an administrator's blueprint for preparing and delivering a speech

INTRODUCTION

We could write a book ten times the size of this one and place in it every speech ever given in a school or school-related situation, and there would still occur that inevitable time when the educational speaker would have to compose an individual speech on his own.

Invariably, special circumstances or special events will dictate that a particular speech, perhaps containing specialized information, be composed by the administrator. At such a time, preparing a speech can be a very trying occasion, unless some special rules are followed in its composition; rules that have been developed to make the composition of that speech a painless and efficient process.

Even if, to save your valuable time, you can adapt or deliver one of the speeches in the first part of this book, you are still faced with delivering that speech. Most of the time, everything goes well, but if you speak frequently enough, you are aware that there are some pitfalls that await speakers which can disrupt any speech, unless the speaker is prepared to deal effectively with them.

Presented here is a step-by-step guide that has proven effective for us in the preparation and delivering of a speech. You will find practical advice for avoiding the pitfalls of public speaking, which has been gleaned from years and years of practical experience; a guide that will serve you well in every speaking situation.

With these two guides to serve you, you will find it a relatively easy procedure to compose and deliver, free from any drawbacks, an exciting, appropriate, and memorable speech.

We know that these guides will continue to serve you, as they have served us, for a long time to come.

SECTION ELEVEN

A Step-By-Step Guide
for Preparing and Delivering
a Dynamic Speech

When presenting an effective, stimulating and memorable speech or presentation, we have found a proven and dependable success formula that has served us well under all conditions. We call it the P R E P A R E formula. Each letter stands for one building block in the foundation of a good speech.

P—PREPARING AND PINPOINTING YOUR TOPIC

If you were asked to speak on "education," your first question would be, "What phase or aspect of education?" Giving a loose, rambling speech makes an audience restless. Make every effort to limit your topic and pinpoint a specific area that you can cover in depth within your allotted speaking time.

Whenever asked to speak, you should ask certain questions:

What is the composition of the audience?

How many people will you be addressing?

Where will your speech fit into the total program for that afternoon or evening?

What event, activity, speech, etc. is to proceed or follow you?

What speaking facilities (microphone, podium, dais, head table/audience, stage/audience, etc.) will be available?

How much will the audience know (or think they know) about the topic before you speak?

How does the program coordinator perceive your speech? (Entertaining? Persuasive? Informative?)

What is the maximum and minimum time you will have to speak?

In short, ask any question that you feel might have a bearing on the physical environment and/or content of your speech. This attention to detail will help you prepare the right speech for the right audience at the right time. For example, would you give a forty-five minute speech if you were speaking just BEFORE dinner was to be served? Would you give a serious speech at a parent-child dinner where Santa Claus' appearance was to follow yours? Pinpointing your topic and preparing for the physical surroundings of your speech is your first step on the road to success.

R—RESEARCHING FOR SUCCESS

Obviously, you need to KNOW what you are talking about. Few speakers deliberately try to mislead or misinform the audience, but trusting to memory is risky at best and disastrous at worst. It is at this point that you begin to prepare yourself to meet your audience. Consequently, you will need some information:

What will your audience want to know?

What kinds of questions will they ask?

What kind of humor would they find best?

What would antagonize them?

What would please them?

Once you have determined the answers to these questions, you can begin your research.

Compile the information you need. If you are going to speak about a person, find out about him. If it is a current issue, review the local newspapers. Use Part I of this book and other speech books to select appropriate anecdotes, stories and humor. Remember that the QUALITY of your research will pave the way to a successful speech.

E—EXAMPLES AND THEIR USE

Good speakers use examples to prove or clarify their points throughout a speech. To get the most out of the examples you use, follow these rules:

1. The example should be appropriate. It must make the point you want it to make. To use an anecdote, however clever or delightful, that has no bearing on what you are saying will only confuse your audience.

2. The example should be understood by everyone. To describe two fellow educators as "the Castor and Pollux of the educational world" is fine—providing that everyone in the audience knows who Castor and Pollux were. Otherwise, the analogy is lost.

3. Avoid "inside" jokes. Every profession has its "inside" humor—those anecdotes and stories that are amusing only to those persons in that

particular profession. To use such material before a "mixed" audience could lead to confusion and antagonism. Therefore, they are better left untold.

P—PRESENTATION AND POISE

Once you have written your speech, you will eventually have to give it before an audience. This phase of preparation is vital. Whether this is your first speech or your hundred and first, you should rehearse it thoroughly before you set foot before an audience. Sequester yourself, if need be, and stand in front of a mirror. See yourself as others will see you. Pay attention to your gestures, your eye contact, how you use your notes, your posture. Record your speech and listen to it with an open mind. Are you speaking too slowly? Too fast? In a monotone? Are your words distinct? Finally, decide what you will wear that day. You already know what type of function you are attending, so you won't be wearing a leisure outfit to a black-tie dinner. Make an effort to select clothes in which you look best and feel best. If you feel good about your appearance, you will project confidence to your audience.

A—ANALYZING YOUR AUDIENCE

When you have arrived at the place where you are to speak, you will have an opportunity to analyze your audience. Look at them, listen to them, and particularly pay attention to their reactions. Is the atmosphere formal or informal? Are they quiet and respectful or noisy and restless? If there were other speakers before you, how were they received? Your analysis of the audience will tell you what approach to take when it is your time to speak. Even a prepared speech may be delivered in several ways. It can be formal, conversational, or even intimate, as friend to friend. Your approach will be determined by your perception of the audience.

Finally, once you begin speaking, you will FEEL your audience. There is no way to describe this; it must be experienced. Through this rapport—this psychological bond—the audience will tell you what they think of your speech. You must take your cues from them and adjust accordingly.

R—RELAXING AND ENJOYING YOUR SELF

In most cases, your audience WANTS you to succeed. They are on your side. If you have done everything in your power to make your speech entertaining, informative, clear and concise, then you need do only one more thing to ensure your speech's success—relax and enjoy yourself. If you are nervous, your audience will be nervous. If you are uncomfortable, your audience will be uncomfortable. But, if you are enjoying yourself—SO WILL YOUR AUDIENCE.

Speaking before people can be a truly enjoyable experience. If you really believe that and learn to enjoy speaking, then you will be a good speaker. If you don't believe that, if speaking is nothing more than a task, and an arduous one at that, then don't worry about it—you won't be asked to do it often. Be at ease, enjoy your audience, and you WILL be in demand.

E—ENTHUSIASM AND EMPATHY: KEYS TO SUCCESS

Be enthusiastic—believe in what you are saying. If you are, then even if your audience does not agree with what you are saying, they will still respect you as a person of knowledge and conviction. Your enthusiasm can build a lasting positive impression in the minds of your audience. If your speech is to be followed by a question and answer session, you will find that enthusiasm is your greatest ally.

When dealing with those questions from the audience, EMPATHY is the keynote. Put yourself in the position of the questioner. If you do this, you will never slough off a question or make light of it or the person who asked it. There will be no need to become defensive, and, because you have done your research, you can answer the question straightforwardly and comprehensively.

This, then, is the P R E P A R E formula. As we said, it has served us well for many years in the preparation and delivery of numerous speeches. May it bring you similar success.

SECTION TWELVE

An Administrator's Survival Guide for Avoiding the Pitfalls of Public Speaking

Public speaking can be an enjoyable experience, but it can also have its pitfalls. What, for example, is the best way to answer a question from the audience so that everyone understands the answer? What if you are faced with a hostile audience? How can you ensure that your charts or graphs will be seen by everybody? What happens if you are asked an obviously hostile question?

These are some common pitfalls of the public speaker, but they can be handled to the speaker's advantage. This section offers proven suggestions that will help you to overcome them and deliver a memorable and enjoyable address.

HOW TO USE VISUAL AIDS TO ADVANTAGE

You can have the best, most thoughtful, most interesting presentation in the world, but it will count for nothing if it remains unseen.

Consider it from the audience's point of view. How frustrating it is to have your attention called to a map, chart or diagram only to find that visual aid blocked, either wholly or partially, by the speaker's body. What makes it worse is that frequently the speaker is unaware of the problem.

Obviously, this is no problem when you are addressing a small, intimate group where everyone is afforded an unobstructed view of everything, or where they may move themselves or their chairs in order to obtain that view. It is when you are appearing on a stage or dais, before a larger audience, that this may prove a difficulty. Surprisingly enough, it is within the physical layout of the stage that your solution to the problem lies.

Most halls or auditoriums are set up so that the chairs for the audience are placed in rows, from just before the foot of the stage backward to the far wall of the room. The chairs on either ends of these rows are usually set up in line with the proscenium arch on either side of the stage.

Therefore, if you will conceive of your shoulders as pointers, it will become obvious that your audience will always be able to see you and your display if, when you are facing to your left, you keep your right shoulder pointed at the right proscenium arch and, when you are facing to your right, you keep your left shoulder pointed at the left proscenium arch. This affords every member of the audience, in every seat, a clear line of sight to what is happening on the stage.

You will also find it useful if, when gesturing, you gesture with your UPSTAGE hand, the hand closest to the back wall and furthest from the audience. If you will keep this in mind, you will never "reach across yourself" when gesturing, which is very unattractive from the audience's point of view, and can also block your speech and your display.

Certainly, everything you do to make your presentation as pleasant, clear, and intelligible as possible will aid in establishing rapport with your audience and leaving them in a receptive mood. You will find that the gratification your audience displays will make any effort on your part well worthwhile.

HOW TO ANSWER QUESTIONS EFFECTIVELY FROM THE AUDIENCE

One of the severest tests of a good speaker is the ability to answer questions from the floor in a tight, efficient and effective manner. If a question from the floor is handled in a halting, stammering, erratic manner, the audience may begin to suppose that the speaker is either unsure of his material or trying to mislead them in some way.

Fortunately, there is a tested and proven way of answering questions that not only conveys to the audience exactly the information which their questions require, but does so in such a precise and effective manner that both the answer and the answerer are remembered.

The method involves two steps. When a question is asked, you:

1. Repeat the question.
2. Use the A R E A formula of response.

Let's examine each of these steps.

When you are asked a question from the floor, the first thing you ought to do is to repeat the question. This serves two purposes. First, it ensures that everyone has heard the question and heard it exactly as the questioner intended. Second, it gives you time to think.

Quite often, the only one to hear the question is the speaker and a few people in the immediate vicinity of the questioner. This may be due to the acoustics of the hall or the soft-spoken manner of the questioner, but it happens more often than not. Therefore, your repetition of the question gives the rest of the audience the chance to hear what has been said. It also ensures that what you have heard is what the questioner indeed asked, so there will be no confusion later or claims that the question was not answered.

Repeating the question also provides you with time to think and organize your answer. You will be surprised at how even a few seconds provides you with time to get your material in order for presentation.

When it comes to actually answering the question that has been asked, there is no better or effective way of presenting your viewpoint than the use of the A R E A formula. Each letter stands for one step in an effective answer. They are:

A—Answer

R—Reason

E—Example

A—Answer

First, give your ANSWER. Make the point you wish to make. Tell the questioner the answer that his question engenders.

Next, tell the REASON for your answer. Tell clearly and concisely why you gave the answer you did.

Third, give an EXAMPLE that shows why you gave the answer you did. There is nothing like a concrete example to get across a salient point. Almost anything can be put into the form of an anecdote or story to which the audience can relate, no matter how intelligent you may think them to be. Everyone profits from a solid example.

Finally, repeat your ANSWER. This time it should be a natural outgrowth of your reason and example. Also, leaving the questioner and, by projection, the audience with an answer gives them something to think about, and something which they will remember for some time.

Let's look at how the whole method would be used in an actual situation. Suppose you were speaking, and it came time for questions. The person you call upon asks, "Which do you feel are better: heterogeneously or homogeneously grouped classes?"

"The question has been asked," you state to the audience, "which I feel are beter: heterogeneously or homogeneously grouped classes. Is that correct? It is. I assume you mean 'better for the students involved,' is that correct? It is. Thank you."

You have been addressing the questioner. You now turn and give your answer to the audience as a whole.

"I personally feel that heterogeneously grouped classes are better for students than homogeneously grouped classes, because they allow for more flexibility in teaching methods and greater student-initiated help. When a teacher uses a variety of methods, as he or she must in a heterogeneously grouped classroom, *all* childaren benefit, because the material is covered from several different angles. Furthermore, the students who get the material more slowly can benefit from the aid of those children who get it more quickly, while at the same time reinforcing the knowledge in the quicker-learning child.

"For example, let's take a math problem—five times three equals fifteen. For some, just the explanation of the mechanics and techniques of multiplication is enough, but in a heterogeneously grouped classroom, the teacher might also use three sets of five children walking to the front of the room. He might also let students come up with their own examples which they would 'share' with others, thereby ensuring their learning and others learning as well. Everyone participates and grows from the interaction. Therefore, I believe that heterogeneously grouped classes are much more beneficial in education."

Notice how, in the example, the question was not only repeated, but a potential area of misunderstanding was clarified before it caused any concern. Then notice how the question was answered in strict accord with the A R E A formula. Notice, too, that the entire answer was concise and did not ramble.

The next time you watch a televised press conference with any politician, pay attention to how he or she handles the questions asked by reporters. You will see them repeating quetions, and, if you pay particular attention, you just might see the A R E A formula staring back at you from your TV screen.

While a huge factor in an audience's acceptance of an answer is the personality of the speaker, still, a decided factor is the way in which the answer has been presented to them. Repeat that question, give your answer, state the reason for your answer, use a solid example, and then repeat your answer, and you will have answered that question with effectiveness and dispatch.

HOW TO DEAL WITH THE HOSTILE AUDIENCE

That you may one day be faced by a hostile audience is not a far-fetched assumption, particularly for the educator who may find himself addressing groups of citizens suspicious of "new" programs and wary of tax increases. There may, indeed, come a time when you must face an audience that is not willing or eager to accept what you have to say; that may, indeed, be hostile.

It will not be easy, but it can be made bearable and antagonism can be kept to a minimum if you keep a few rules in mind:

1. Acknowledge in the beginning that there are differences of opinion: "You might not agree with what I have to say tonight...."

2. Do not apologize for yourself. Say: "... but I believe in what I am about to tell you, and all I ask is that you hear me out...."

3. Base what you say on hard, cold FACTS: "... As I see it, THESE are the facts of the matter...."

4. NEVER get personal: To attack an audience's personal beliefs or opinions is the surest road to complete alienation. Let the weight of your argument win them to your side.

5. Be aware of the possibility of hostile questions. Handle these questions with tact and by stating provable facts, never opinions.

Under any circumstances, facing a hostile audience is a far from pleasant experience. Fortunately, 99 percent of your public speaking will be before receptive audiences, but it is well to be prepared for an unpleasant possibility. In such cases, you will survive it if you follow the rules above and make every effort to project an image of confidence, assuredness, and calmness.

EFFECTIVELY OVERCOMING THE HOSTILE QUESTION

Does the term "hostile question" really need a definition? It is any question so stated that it is designed to put you on the spot. Please understand, we are not talking about a difficult or intricate question that is honestly asked. We mean the "When did you stop beating your wife?" variety that begs the question and whose sole intent is to put you in an unfavorable light.

You can deal effectively with a hostile question if you:

1. Remain calm and treat the questioner with respect and courtesy.

2. Break a question into its simplest parts, both stated and unstated, and then answer each part separately.

Now, let's examine both steps.

First, it is essential that you remain calm. You can think more clearly and you will gain the respect of your audience if you stay rational in the face of hostility. Treating the hostile questioner with courtesy and civility will further aid in swinging the audience's support to your side.

Next, make certain that everyone knows exactly what is being asked. Let's assume that someone has asked this question: "What makes you so superior that you have all the answers?" (We think you'll agree that that's a hostile question.) Here is a response that exemplifies Step Two: "I'd like to answer that qustion, but, as I see it, you have asked several questions. I think you're asking IF I feel superior; IF I do, then what makes me feel so; and DO I have all the answers? The answers are 'no,' 'it doesn't follow,' and 'most certainly not.' Now, let's examine each one of them in turn...."

By handling the hostile question in this manner, you have turned a potentially embarrassing situation into one that will be advantageous to you by gaining the respect of the audience and perhaps the hostile questioner as well.

HOW TO LEARN TO LOVE IT

Finally, let's deal with the single biggest drawback faced by the beginning speaker—nervousness.

Actors call it "stage fright"; radio announcers call it "mike fright." You may call it what you will, but it is that feeling, just before you are introduced, that your knees have turned to jelly, your spine is made of water, your voice has just departed for parts unknown, and you would rather be anywhere—from an arctic iceberg to the middle of a desert sandstorm—than where you are. It is something that happens, and it is something you must deal with. If it is any comfort to you, Helen Hayes, that marvelous veteran actress of thousands of public appearances, once reported that before every public appearance she made, she would get so nervous she would become physically ill. Yet, anyone who has ever had the honor of watching her perform will know that never once was that anxiety communicated to the audience.

What is the solution to this problem? Many have been suggested. We were once told to picture the audience sitting there in their underwear. The picture becomes so ludicrous that you can't possibly be nervous. Another speaker told us that he never looks at the audience, but focuses on the hairline of audience members. This gives the impression of looking directly at them without having eye contact.

Each of these solutions worked for the person who used them. We have never had to. Yes, we have been nervous, but, here, a matter of philosophy has always been our salvation. You see, we have always expected to love every audience to whom we spoke, and we have expected them to love us. We have not been disappointed. Nervous? Certainly, but the minute the first words come forth, we get interested in THEM—the audience—and we forget OURselves, OUR problems, and, most importantly of all, OUR nervousness.

Try it; it works!

APPENDIX

The School Administrator's
Locatomatic Index
of Speech Topics and Occasions

HOW TO USE THIS INDEX

The following index will allow you to automatically locate the correct speech or anecdote for the topic YOU have in mind, hence its name. It is thoroughly and vigorously cross-indexed, and can direct you to exactly the material you require in a matter of seconds.

The numbers following the topics in the index indicate the NUMBER OF THE SPEECH OR ANECDOTE in which the topic is covered. THEY ARE NOT PAGE NUMBERS. Look up your topic, and you will immediately be directed to the speech or anecdote that contains information on it.

Look for the larger topic first, and see what you can find. Then, you may wish to look up some of the topics which you could consider as subheadings of your major topic.

For example, suppose you are giving a speech on the retirement of a fellow administrator. First, look up RETIREMENT, and you will be given two speeches that apply. But, you might also want to look up ADMINISTRATOR, where you might want to incorporate some of the material under the various subheadings such as "Difficulty of the Job," "Career as," or "Testimonial for." You might wish to add some of this material to your speech.

Whatever your intent, this LOCATOMATIC INDEX will prove invaluable.

Locatomatic Index

NOTE: The numbers following the entries in the Locatomatic Index indicate the numbers of speech topics.

Index